Moralities of Everyday Life

Moralities of Everyday Life

JOHN SABINI

MAURY SILVER

OXFORD UNIVERSITY PRESS
Oxford New York Toronto Melbourne
1982

Oxford University Press
Oxford London Glasgow
New York Toronto Melbourne
Nairobi Dar es Salaam Cape Town
Kuala Lumpur Singapore Hong Kong Tokyo
Delhi Bombay Calcutta Madras Karachi

and associate companies in
Beirut Berlin Ibadan Mexico City

First published by Oxford University Press, New York, 1982
First issued as an Oxford University Press paperback, 1982

Library of Congress Cataloging in Publication Data

Sabini, John, 1947–
Moralities of everyday life.

Bibliography: p.
Includes index.
1. United States—Moral conditions—Addresses, essays, lectures. 2. Social psychology—Addresses, essays, lectures. I. Silver, Maury, 1944– II. Title.

HN90.M6S2 302 81-11004
ISBN 0-19-503016-8 AACR2
ISBN 0-19-503017-6 (pbk.)

Chapters 2, 3 and 7 have appeared in slightly altered form in the *Journal for the Theory of Social Behavior,* and are reprinted here with the kind permission of Basil Blackwell.

Chapter 4 appeared in J. Dimsdale (ed.), *Survivors, Victims and Perpetrators: Essays on the Nazi Holocaust,* and is reprinted here by the kind permission of Hemisphere Press.

The quotation from Seymour Epstein in Chapter 8 is drawn from D. Magnusson and N. Endler (eds.), *Personality at the Crossroads,* and appears with the permission of Lawrence Erlbaum Associates and the author.

Chapter 10 was a paper delivered at the *Houston Conference of the Philosophy of Psychology,* 1979, and will appear in its proceedings published by Sage Publications, Inc.

Parts of Chapter 11 have also appeared in the *Journal for the Theory of Social Behavior.*

Printing (last digit): 9 8 7 6 5 4 3 2 1

Printed in the United States of America

To Stanley Milgram
Mentor and friend

Contents

Preface

One day, several years ago, at Hunter College in New York City, after hours of drinking coffee, eating bagels and cream cheese, and, of course, arguing, we sketched on a blackboard, in a classroom lifted for our office, the themes for two doctoral theses and, we dared to hope, one book. The themes were "embarrassment" and "moral reproach." If we did not then add "arrogance" as a theme among the moralities of everyday life, and if we have not added it since, still we feel it was present at the conception.

The themes changed as our theses and this book developed. "Embarrassment" was abandoned, not through lack of interest but simple exhaustion. Exhaustion caused one of the authors to feel acutely envious of a friend with an unwithered topic; envy became a theme and eventually a chapter. Procrastination, for one of us a calling and for the other a burden, was added after six years of intermittent work. Gossip and flirtation were first indulged in and then eventually embraced as subjects of our study. Remnants of the abandoned "embarrassment" were salvaged and added to "reproach." And so on. Still, through all our fits and starts, across several states and two countries, despite divorce, one civil war, several depressions, the rulings of various committees, and the words of various critics, our focus and this project—the moralities of everyday life—have remained clear.

How did the moral and the mundane come to be our focus? We took with us an interest in morality when we entered graduate school—one after serving as a conscientious objector cum mental hospital orderly, the other after a few years as a merchant seaman cum ship orderly. We found there the psychologist most sensitive in probing moral questions—Stanley Milgram. After a year or two under his guidance we came to comprehend the importance of understanding "everyday life" for understanding morality. Stanley taught us by his wit, his playful example, his delight in argument, his breadth of interest, his appreciation of style, and, of course, his haunting obedience experiments. Further, he guided us in the ideal setting, New York City. For all of this we are grateful.

We would like to thank the Metropolitan Museum of Art for supplying the space for the many drafts of our chapters written by the Saint-Gaudens fountains. We thank the City of New York for its parks—Fort Tryon, Central, and vest pocket particularly; its universities—CUNY Graduate Center and Hunter; and its restaurants—especially the Szechuan, Hunanese, Cantonese, Thai, Japanese, Arabic, Hungarian, and Jewish dairy for both their tables and their fare; and, of course, Madison and Fifth Avenues and the subway system, to say nothing of the bookstores and several coffeehouses, in SoHo, Little Italy, and farther north, especially the Continental Café and Sacco's.

In exile we salute the Department of Psychology of the University of Pennsylvania and all of its transplanted New Yorkers (in fact or spirit), especially its quondam shark trainer, Paul Rozin, for his excessive, unfailing, exuberant, teasing support. The Johns Hopkins University Department of Psychology has also facilitated this endeavor. We also thank La Universidad Centroamericana, El Salvador (UCA), for its support of this work in the midst of its (literally) everyday life-and-death moral struggle; our contacts with the Jesuit community remind us of the importance of moral and political concerns in everyday life.

Paul Secord, friend and guide, and Marc Boggs, editor, lunch companion, and friend, have given us constant, even reckless, encouragement.

A congeries of acknowledgments for helping us appreciate the aesthetics of baseball, art movies, flirtation, surgical and grammatical dissection, hospitality, Arkansan, Bessarabian, and Neapolitan ethnography, and New York in concrete are due to Jack Silver, Eva Paulus Sabini, Esther Riff Silver, Mario Sabini, Judith Stivelband, and Janet Norton. For their typing with wit we thank Jeanette Brack, Dianne Rothman, Joan Krech, and Eileen Velmartin.

New York City J.S.
October 1981 M.S.

Moralities of Everyday Life

CHAPTER ONE

Introduction

Morality is central to the social life—as it is lived and understood. This view unifies the diverse considerations of this book. Our view, it is true, is not the prevailing one; most professional social psychologists will find, we suspect, our concerns hard to identify as their own. For those familiar with the field we want to trace our differences; readers lacking this background or concern may wish to pass on to the next chapter. Our other essays don't presuppose a familiarity with the field.

SOCIAL PSYCHOLOGY AND THE MORALITIES OF EVERYDAY LIFE

To place this work in the social psychological tradition requires that we have some picture of that enterprise. Yet any sketch we might offer will be a caricature. This is so in part because sketches leave out details, and professionals are concerned with details. But this sketch will be inadequate for a second reason—we don't think social psychology, as it is currently practiced, is unified. In our opinion, no textbook since Asch (1952) has been able to present a coherent portrait; even a text as thoughtful as Brown's (1965) treats the field as a collection of isolated topics. Our social life is rendered in modern texts, and in modern research, as a collection of incidents rather than as a coherent biography. It is hard to sketch such a portrait. Still, there is something that does hold the field together: a commitment to an approach.

Most social psychologists start by considering something someone might do, say, help someone, or something that might happen to someone, say, being attracted, and they then ask: what causes individuals to do this sort of thing, or what makes this happen to people? Some have left behaviorism and start at a higher conceptual level with "attributions," "attitudes," "affect," "attraction," or "aggression" and then ask: what are the underlying causal factors? Typically, the endeavor then proceeds by constructing some causal theory, or at least a serviceable causal hypothesis, and then by arranging some circumstance or other in which this putative cause is shown to have just the effect it is said to have. Quite a number of causal factors have been found in this way in the last thirty years or so. And more loom on the horizon.

Harré and Secord (1972), Harré (1980), Gergen (1973), Pepitone (1976), Buss (1979), and Ginsburg (1979), among others, have offered reasons to change this approach. Our sympathies, we must confess, lie with the critics and their reasons. Still, there are always critics, even sensitive, incisive ones. Yet the arguments against a scientific endeavor are blunted when used against a record of cumulative, deepening understanding which the old approach, however flawed, has achieved. In the face of this accomplishment, critics become underemployed. However, in our view, it is just this record of accomplishment that social psychology lacks. There have been brilliant experiments in social psychology—we rely on several of them throughout our essays—but not a record of cumulative and deepening theory. For this reason, we have turned away from the tradition, though not, we hope, from particular, important discoveries social psychologists have made. As Bertrand Russell points out, there is an infinitude of ways to go wrong, so our turning has no guarantee. But then, as Sartre insists, this provides no exit from choosing. Our approach will be different in three ways.

Approach

Causal questions are not the first we raise. We first describe, or define, or analyze phenomena such as envy, gossip, and procrastination. We want to know precisely how these phenomena differ from their relatives, e.g., jealousy, rumor, and laziness. Much of our effort is devoted to this. Of course the experimental literature is also concerned with definition, but defining and getting on with it, as we shall see shortly, has a different point from conceptual analysis. Admittedly, causal questions are important, and we address them, but we think it both important and interesting to know *what* phenomena one is explaining first.

Second, despite our appreciation of causes, we have a different attitude toward them. We don't expect to find a simple, elegant theory of most important human behaviors, or even of less-touted ones, such as gossip. We expect a list of the causes (or reasons) for gossip, say, to be diverse. Further, we think such a list must be open: people can always find a new reason to gossip.

Third, we approach the issues we consider at a different level of abstraction. Instead of studying, for example, envy, moral reproach, anger, and gossip, each in its own regard, theorists often subsume them under the traditional term *aggression*. (There is a large body of social-psychological literature on aggression.) And in this tradition, understanding the particular was to come from understanding the general. At one time it was hoped that a theory of aggression was to be had, i.e., a simple, elegant causal explanation of aggression in general. The theory has not been forthcoming. We prefer, on the other hand, to think that there is little to be gained from dealing in such broad terms. We think there is a good bit to be gained from untangling the complexities of phenomena that might be subsumed under, if not absorbed by, the traditional categories. Skinner (1938) represents the traditional view of the appropriate level of generality well: "The vernacular is clumsy and obese; its terms overlap each other, draw unnecessary or unreal distinctions, and are far from being the most convenient in dealing with the data" (p. 7). In the main, social psychologists have shared this sentiment, i.e., that we should concentrate on only a few very general notions both for the targets of our explanations and for the terms within which to explain them. We, like Heider (1958), in some of his moods, and surely Austin, have a different attitude toward the vernacular. We suspect that, as Austin says:

> Our common stock of words embodies all the distinctions men have found worth drawing, and the connexions they have found worth making, in the lifetimes of many generations: these surely are likely to be more numerous, more sound, since they have stood up to the long test of the survival of the fittest, and more subtle, at least in all ordinary and reasonably practical matters, than any that you or I are likely to think up in our arm-chairs of an afternoon—the most favoured alternative method.
>
> (1970, p. 182)

Of course, both Skinner's and Austin's claims about ordinary language must be put to the test—which should we start with, theoretical constructions or the terms of our language? If one believes that the vernacular makes unreal or unnecessary distinctions, then one begins with a few broad, theoretical terms. But if one believes that the language makes, by and large, the necessary distinctions, then a small, abstract vocabulary obfuscates the necessary. Skinner's ploy has been tried; we think it has failed.[1]

1. Of course, theorists had a way to tie abstract terms, like aggression, to something concrete—particular behaviors; they had the doctrine of operationalism. This doctrine holds that the meaning of a concept *is* the operations used to measure it. But this is too permissive. It allows a researcher interested in aggression to study it by focusing on *any* behavior he wishes, e.g., filling out a questionnaire; the question of whether this behavior is *really* aggression cannot, under this doctrine, be raised, since so long as the researcher calls his questionnaire behavior 'aggression' it is aggression. The absurdity this leads to (intelligence is what intelligence tests measure) was simply embraced as a virtue of the method. But scientists were more responsible than their doctrine; no one, to our knowledge, used the length of a forearm as an operationalization, i.e., expression of the meaning, of political preference; though that they shouldn't was nothing operationalism could acknowledge. Obviously, researchers had some criteria in picking their operational measures. They had to use common sense; they had to use the criteria implicit in ordinary language. But the details of the criteria implicit in ordinary language terms were uninteresting to them—so long as their operations had some plausible relation to broad, commonsense terms, they could get on with their empirical work. Perhaps this was the right strategy; perhaps there was no need to be concerned with details—good science is often intuitive. Well, did it work? Did it provide deepening understanding? Did it work for the study of attitudes, for example?

While there may be interesting discoveries in the attitude change literature, we don't believe this research has been revolutionary. Perhaps, we are being unfair to this literature. We refer the interested reader to a standard text, Middlebrook, 1980, and the eighteen general conclusions she draws from the literature as a test of the depth of this work. We quote a few just to give the flavor of the results: "In general, high-credibility sources are more effective in changing attitudes than low credibility sources" (p. 200), i.e., all other things equal, we are persuaded more by people we believe than by those we don't. "In general, liked sources are more persuasive" (p. 202). "Variations in style sometimes influence communications persuasiveness" (p. 208), and sometimes they don't. "Whether distracting the audience increases attitude change depends on other variables" (p. 220). We defy anyone to find these findings an improvement on Aristotle's *Rhetoric,* Book 1, chapter 2, lines 1356 and following.

Methods

What may surprise a social psychologist most about our calling these essays social psychology is not their content, but their method; they may seem to be speculation about matters better left to experimentation.

We use two principal methods uncommon in the experimental tradition: (1) we arrive at the nature of phenomena through linguistic analysis, and (2) we use "ideal type" explanations. We owe an account of how these methods are disciplined.

Linguistic Analysis

Often in these essays we describe behavior (and the situation in which it occurs) and ask whether people would call it envious, procrastination, or gossip, etc. But (1) why should psychologists care what ordinary speakers call something, and (2) how can someone know our answer is correct?

As we have said, we agree with Austin that the proper starting point of analysis is ordinary language, and that ordinary language is likely to provide the important distinctions that are necessary to understand the social life. (Perhaps one day science will give us a better set of distinctions. We doubt it; in any event, it hasn't yet.) Now as to the second.

Suppose you find you disagree with us about our use of a word. What might this mean? Either you or we might be wrong—one of us might have idiosyncratic usage. To check up on us, we recommend looking up a sensitive and literate native speaker—or, if handy, several. You might find that we—or you—are isolates. If so we retract our claim, just as we would for a set of disconfirming experiments. Our method is corrigible. (You should be especially suspicious of us when we need a particular usage as part of a theory; our findings need replication—your sensitive and literate friend will be very helpful for this.) Of course if you ask a few people about our use of, say, 'procrastination', you may find that some people agree with us while others agree with you. There seems to be little point in calling the majority right here; rather, there are two different linguistic communities. And in that case our essays are directly relevant only to ours. A translation would be needed for the other. But we shouldn't jump to "different communities." As Austin says:

> Well, people's usages do vary, and we do talk loosely, and we do say different things apparently indifferently. But first, not nearly as much as one would think. When we come down to cases, it transpires in the very great majority that what we had thought was our wanting to say different things of and in *the same* situation was really not so—we had simply imagined the situation *slightly* differently: which is all too easy to do, because of course no situation (and we are dealing with *imagined* situations) is ever "completely" described. The more we imagine the situation in detail, with a background of story—and it is worth employing the most idiosyncratic or, sometimes, boring means to stimulate and to discipline our wretched imaginations—the less we find we disagree about what we should say.
>
> (1970, pp. 183–84)

We leave the rest of the story to Austin.

Of course you might find current usage of a particular word inchoate, promiscuous, all too flexible. If this is so, then, the word should be avoided, at least for social psychological work. We trust that the concepts we use, given their place in ordinary language, are robust. That's why we picked them (and not, say, 'attitudes').

Another possibility is that a particular term has a variety of senses, though each sense is shared within the linguistic community. In "subjectivity," (ch. 10) for example, we encounter such a word. In this case it is senseless to ask: which is the correct sense? It has various uses, and we try to show their relations.

We have in these essays tried to use concepts in ways shared by a linguistic community. We have no surveys; we cannot prove that they are used this way, except in the way that a linguist "proves," but we know of no method that proves with certainty, save, perhaps, mathematics. (But see Kline, 1980, for a chastening view even of mathematics.) So our method does not yield certainty; it is just corrigible—like science.

In uncovering people's use of a term we are never interested in definitions people offer; we are only concerned with ways people use a term to talk about concrete situations. We are interested in the distinctions embodied in people's capacities to use their language.

As odd as the method of linguistic analysis may seem to social psychology, it is after all traditional in one important way: it is a method of analysis, just as the experimental method is.

Another Method

There is a second method we use, akin to the method of ideal types. This method is addressed in part to causal questions. In chapter 7, for example, we suggest some ways people may come to procrastinate. Our analysis is designed to show that if people take certain paths, we can understand how they end up procrastinating. And here, no doubt, is where we look most like we are speculating—and we do, a bit.

We claim, for example, that sometimes when people procrastinate they do so by becoming entrapped in a particular sort of activity, like playing pinball. Now we don't know how often this is the case. That's why the "sometimes." Claims based on experiments are like this too.

In an experiment a cause is shown to have some effect on a behavior in a particular situation—on average. If a mean effect on the dependent variable arising from an independent variable is found, the independent variable is established as a causal factor. But the experiment cannot tell us how commonly this independent variable has effects outside the laboratory, or how potent it is in the world. All we know from the experiment is that something is, in one circumstance, causally efficacious. Now this is just the result we have; we have tried to show that some cause is relevant, but we don't know how common or potent. In the experimental literature, this is called the problem of "ecological validity." We, or an experimentalist, might take steps to fill out our information.

One thing we, or they, might do is look for a situation in the "real world" and then show that in that situation the putative cause works too. But note that this still doesn't tell us how common or potent the cause is—except that it has a frequency of 1. But a further extension of this line of work can be carried out.

Someone might, in the laboratory or the world, carry out a

study in which several putative causes are included, and then find out how much of the variance each accounts for. Then we would know, in one situation, how potent the cause is though we would still not know how common or commonly potent. But we would be able to say factor x accounts for y percent of the variance, while z accounts for w—in this (or these) situation(s). A vigorous researcher might, then, take the last step.

To do this, to answer the frequency and potency questions, such a researcher would have to sample randomly all possible situations relevant to his claim, count the number of situations in which the cause has an effect—to discern frequency—and average the percent of variance information to answer potency. We don't know of any social psychological research like this. It would be tedious.

And, even if there were such a heroic effort, it would still have a problem—generativity. Suppose someone invented a new situation relevant to procrastination. This would, of course, affect the frequency and potency findings. So even such a heroic effort would just tell us about the momentary values. And history has surprises.

But there is a more important reason not to recommend this heroism: the numbers one got in the end would be rather uninteresting for another reason. We believe that pinball, as a cause of procrastination, accounts for some of the variance; we are quite sure it doesn't account for all. We speculate that it has a non-zero frequency, but we don't believe that it reaches 100 percent. We can't get too excited about finding out just which number between 0 and 100 is correct for the moment. Now if someone had a theory that predicts frequency or average potency, *then* it might be worth finding out. But we don't have such a theory; nor do we know of a single instance in the social psychological literature of a theory that predicts precise (or intervals of frequency) results of this sort. Of course, one might have extra-theoretical reasons for caring about this.

A dean, student counselor, or concerned parent might want to know just how serious the threat of pinball is. Or a pinball distributor might want to know how much she could get away with charging. But we don't have these concerns, and we aren't writing a treatise on how to help others counsel or merchandise. So we are content, as are most experimentalists, to stop where we stop with "at least sometimes." We don't mean this as a critique of the experimental method; we all suffer the same ignorance.

We also should point out that on rare occasions numbers, even in experiments, do matter. The numbers in the Milgram experiment do (see chs. 3 & 4). And this isn't because they confirm or refute a theory. But because so many ordinary people obeyed orders contra their conscience, we believe the results speak to human nature rather than idiosyncratic pathology. Yet our conception of human nature is upset by what they did. Notice that "ecological validity" isn't relevant here in the way it is in other experiments. Even if, contra our analysis in chapters 3 and 4, no one acted like that anywhere else, still, because what people did is so important, morally important, our conception of human nature is advanced by being forced to accommodate this fact. The Milgram experiment is important not just because it is a model of something else, as experiments try to be, but because what people did in the experiment itself is important by any commonsense standard.

It might be objected that our method will lead in the end to an incoherent collection of particular insights, not an integrated theory. Unfortunately, descriptions, ideal types, and linguistic analysis may be the best we can do at the moment. Or there may be a harder truth for us to face. There may never be an elegant, enlightening, nontrivial, general theory at the social psychological level of explanation. Perhaps, we shall in the end find nothing both true and of a sufficiently general nature to be said by our field. This would be a pity for those who see such theories as the sine qua non of science. But those of us who, like Austin, are content with less sweeping contributions, are prepared to be patient. In any event, Vermeer has charms Rubens lacks.

Lacking a general theory, we have made do with a modest surrogate. We use the commonsense notion that people typically act intentionally, i.e., to reach goals, they adjust means to ends. Harré and Secord (1972) have elevated this notion to a model of human action, the "anthropomorphic" one. To a generation of behaviorist psychologists, the notion of "intentionality" was suspected of concealing ghosts. (There were always exceptions to the regnant intention phobia, e.g., Tolman, 1932,

Irwin, 1971, and the gestaltists more generally.) The challenge to behaviorist psychology was to explain "so-called intentional action" in other terms. But times have changed. Ryle's (1949) exorcism has had its effects on philosophers, and Miller et al. (1960) have shown psychologists that to talk of plans and purposes, it is not necessary to converse with spirits. Now that intentionality has returned from exile, the challenge is reversed: the challenge is to show the place of *un*intentional behavior in an intentional frame. Each of these essays is concerned with some problematic application of the intentional model.

One further theme that appears repeatedly is the objectivity of the moral order, i.e., the taken-for-granted assumption by commonsense actors that the moral standards, achievements, and defects they perceive are facts about the world that people know and are constrained by. This sense in which moral matters are objective is articulated most comprehensively in chapter 10, and put to work in chapter 11. In the essays on moral reproach and the Holocaust we argue that the very objectivity of the moral order leaves moral perception vulnerable to distortion by the actions of others. In the chapter on gossip we discuss one of the ways that the objectivity of the moral order is given flesh by actors in the course of their everyday conversations. In the chapter on envy we point out that the perception that someone is envious involves seeing them as transgressing moral standards. Anger (ch. 9), in our account derived from Aristotle, assumes an objective moral order, and we argue, contra traditional drive theories, that to understand another's anger one must appreciate the moral order of which the angry person is a part. In chapter 8 on character we take people's characters to be something they earn by living up to, surpassing, or failing various standards. To know another's character is to know, in part, where she stands vis-à-vis the shared moral order.

In the chapters on procrastination and flirtation we address problems of intentionality and, in particular, ambiguities that infect intentions. Since our moral understandings are affected by what people aim at, as well as by what they bring to pass, ambiguities of intention affect, obscure, and add subtlety and charm to our perception of character. In chapter 6 on flirtation we treat ambiguity not only as a fact—that intentions are often ambiguous—but as a resource that people sometimes use.

A final, related theme recalled in our chapters is "the evil that good people do." We develop this explicitly in our chapters on the Holocaust and moral reproach, but it appears in other guises in other chapters.

Now, on to envy.

CHAPTER TWO

Envy

I am envy, begotten of a chimney-sweeper and an oyster-wife. I cannot read, and therefore wish all books were burned. I am lean with seeing others eat . . . But must thou sit and I stand? Come down, with a vengeance!

CHRISTOPHER MARLOWE, *The Tragical History of Doctor Faustus*

ENVY AND THE SEVEN DEADLY SINS

Traditionally, envy has an important place in the account of human misbehavior. Cain slays Abel because Abel's sacrifice is more pleasing to the Lord. A Greek is cautioned to avoid the envy[1] of the gods as well as that of his fellows (see the Athenian justification for the institution of ostracism, Ranulf, 1974). St. Thomas Aquinas excoriated envy as one of the seven deadly sins, which not only are evil in themselves but spawn other transgressions. Recently, Helmut Schoeck (1969), a sociologist, hypothesized that deep-seated envy and the fear of the envious are primary energizers of society's ills—both of revolution and

1. This is also sometimes translated as jealousy of the gods. Envy and jealousy have overlapping uses and also areas in which their meanings are clearly distinguishable. If my lover runs away with another man, I might be jealous of him, but not envious. I might be envious of him also if his *savoir faire* in seducing my lover highlights my lack of it (see Kingsley Davis, 1936, for a provocative analysis of jealousy; also Simmel, 1899/1955). One entry for "jealousy" in the Random House *American College Dictionary* is "envious resentment against the successful rival or the possessor of any coveted advantage." Hence in talking about reactions to a success, envy and jealousy may be interchangeable.

social stagnation. Heider (1958), in a less-sweeping analysis, proposed that envy is one of a group of negative affects caused by the positive state of another: a person is envious when he wants what someone else has just because that person has it. According to Heider, this feeling, in part, derives from an "ought force"—people who are similar should have similar outcomes.

Although much has been written about the sources and deleterious effects of envy, to our knowledge no one save Heider has given sustained attention to a linguistic or phenomenological analysis of envy itself. This may be because we usually think of envy as a feeling, in the sense of an immediate unitary experience. Although questions are often asked about the causes of this experience, the experience itself is treated as a given, not susceptible to dissection. Yet 'envy' is often used in ways that do not manifestly involve experiences, i.e., to characterize an individual or supply a motive for action. We shall analyze the ways the concept of envy is used;[2] perhaps we shall then discover something about envy as an experience.

Depending on the context, 'envy' may refer to an emotion ("He was overcome by envy"), a reason for action ("He acted out of envy"), or a characterization of an action as a transgression of a moral order, i.e., a sin. 'Sin' suggests that envy is part of a system of norms treated by a community as objective, i.e., having an existence independent of particular purposes at hand (see Berger & Luckman, 1967; Schutz, 1973). This objective aspect of envy, open to commonsense discussion, clarification, and debate, can be captured by the analysis of commonsense talk. We shall first examine envy as a sin and then turn to the subjective facets of the phenomenon—envy as a motive and as an emotion.

Envy is a curious sin. It is felt to be a nastier, more demeaning, less natural sin than the others. It is also puzzling—why

2. Our theory treats a central, moral use of the term envy; the way 'envy' is used when a person complains that he is bothered by his own envy or that he has been maligned because of the envy of others. Another common use of 'envy' is as a compliment: "That's wonderful, I envy you." Here presumably the speaker is not confessing a delict but doing something else, i.e., saying that "that" is so wonderful it is the sort of thing which could tempt a person into sin. Compare this with "your kid is so cute I'm going to kidnap him" or "that Cezanne is so marvelous I could just steal it." As Heider suggests these confessions as compliments are most likely to be used just where they don't literally apply (kidnappers are usually more disciplined).

people are envious is less obvious than why they are greedy or lustful. Merely look at 'envy's' entry in a dictionary of thoughts (Edwards, 1936): "Every other sin hath some pleasure annexed to it, or will admit of some excuse, but envy wants both"—Burton. "Other passions have objects to flatter them and which seem to content and satisfy them for a while, but envy can gain nothing but vexation"—Montaigne. As Rochefoucauld has pointed out, "We are often vain of even the most criminal of our passions; but envy is so shameful a passion that we can never dare to acknowledge it."

To articulate the odd qualities of envy, we need other sins to compare it with. The seven deadly sins provide us with a list of some of the more common, serious flaws in human nature—greed, sloth, wrath, lust, gluttony, pride and envy. Moreover, as it is a traditional collection, and since envy is already a member, we can be sure that our frame of comparison is not solely determined by its convenience for our analysis.

What do the seven deadly sins have in common? Most generally these words characterize a "self" as demeaned, lowered, or spoiled (see Goffman, 1971, for the notion of a spoiled identity). These sins typify a person as greedy, lustful, arrogant, lazy, etc.; yet the typification is not supported by other evidence about the self,[3] but by the particulars of the person's misbehavior. This is also true of other sins: if we say that a person is a murderer, then the behavior to which our charge points is killing.

However, the misbehaviors to which the seven deadly sins point have a distinctive feature. Consider the accusation that a person is greedy. The behavior to which we point is that of acquiring goods. Killing another person is held to be wrong in itself in a way that acquiring a possession is not. Each of the seven deadly sins, apparently excepting envy, implicates behavior that is not in itself evil. When I call someone greedy, I point to his acquisitiveness, but I do not call acquiring goods,

3. 'Self-worth' or 'self-esteem' would be more commonly used here. However, these phrases suggest subjective feeling rather than an objective social fact. In our usage, the self is an object that can be known by the actor and others and has value as determined by socially grounded standards of comparison (see Goffman, 1959; Blumer, 1964). We would reserve 'self-esteem' and 'self-worth' for the particular impression that an actor has of the value of his self. This impression may only loosely fit the facts of his accomplishments. A person may be in error about his own value.

in itself, evil. *Sloth* is a sin, but rest, a commandment. Although *lust* is considered evil, enthusiastic conjugal sex meets with clerical approval. Righteous indignation is a mark of virtue; *anger* is a sin. A priest denounces our *gluttony*, but may wish us a hearty appetite without being a hypocrite. *Arrogance* is evil, but self-assurance is said to be the seal of maturity. The six deadly sins other than envy *involve acts having goals which are not in themselves evil but which have been done inappropriately or to excess.* Moreover, not to pursue the very goals which are the ends of the proscribed sins is held to be pathological. Frigidity, anorexia, and cowardice require explanation; sexuality, appetite, and self-assertion do not. It is easy to understand why these sins are, to quote Nietzsche, "human, all too human." To convince someone that we are incapable of lust or gluttony is to convince them that we are more or less than human. The deadly sins, then, point to characteristic flaws of our common nature. Envy is out of place on this list, as it does not appear to point to a natural goal. This is the paradox of envy.

Envy as Reason and Cause

Envy is also advanced as an *explanation* of action (see Schoeck, 1969); yet if we consider the other sins, we shall see that they are rarely used with explanatory force. One way to explain an action is to point to its goal, but in most cases the other sin words are applied to behaviors where the goal is patent. To accuse an adulterer of lust does not report a goal for his acts, as if what he hoped to achieve by his adultery were mysterious.[4]

Perhaps sin words are used as causal explanations as opposed to explanations in terms of reasons and goals. In everyday talk we often give a causal account of an action when it appears to have no sensible goal (see Peters, 1958). (For present purposes we are bracketing the question of the ultimate compatibility of cause and reason explanations, see Melden, 1961; Alston, 1967.) A causal explanation of general paresis is sought precisely because shaking, stumbling, losing one's memory, and dying are

4. In certain exceptional cases, sin terms can furnish a goal for action, and thus have explanatory force. For instance, we might explain that a prostitute's sin is one of greed, rather than lust. The explanatory power of 'greed' in this example derives from its pointing to a deviation from the obvious goal of a sexual act.

not the sorts of behavior for which sensible goals can be found. Given that the goal of a sinner's misbehavior is only too transparent, what aspect of it remains to be accounted for by a causal explanation? The only aspect of behavior that sin words might explain is what caused a person's *transgression* in the pursuit of a normal goal. Although these sin words imply a lack of restraint, they do not, in themselves, supply its cause; at most they are stand-ins for a causal explanation. For instance, in Catholic theology original sin is held to be the real cause of the failure of restraint to which the sin of lust points. Similarly, a hypothalamic disorder is held by physiologists to be, in some cases, the cause of overeating—gluttony. Envy seems to have more explanatory force than the other sins; it appears to give a real causal account and not to be merely a stand-in for one. "He overate out of gluttony" seems otiose; "he maligned her out of envy" seems explanatory. We hold in abeyance how envy functions as an explanation. We shall be particularly interested in whether envy has more explanatory force than the other sins, and if so, in what way. But we first turn to envy as an emotion.

Envy as an Emotion

Envy can be a feeling that possesses a person, takes hold of him, often to his dismay. Envious thoughts may come to us unbidden—even when we wish we could join in the celebration of a friend's success. Envy is often a conscious feeling, i.e., it is episodic, as in "I had a pang of envy" or "I felt envious for a moment." Yet we must be careful when we speak of envy in this manner. Using a phrase like "the experience of envy" may mislead us into assuming that answers have been given before we have explored which questions are to be raised. For instance, do we experience one mental content when we report an experience of envy, or is envy a way to characterize a class of contents? Are there particular experiences which in themselves constitute envy, or is it necessary that we have these experiences in a particular context? How does the presence or absence of the feeling of envy qualify our judgment of whether a person is envious? As is our wont, we shall explore these questions in regard to some of the other deadly sins, and then, having created a framework, we will turn to envy.

What might be passing through the mind of someone who is guilty of the sin of lust: fantasizing a sexual tryst, focusing on chest or crotch bulge, perhaps experiencing a genital tingle? But having these experiences is not equivalent to being guilty of lustful thoughts. We doubt that this description would currently be taken as evidence of lust, even by a conservative clergyman, if it were to refer to the thoughts of newlyweds on their wedding night. A Victorian, on the other hand, might hold that these thoughts would be lust if entertained by a woman, though not by a man. (St. Paul might damn them both.) Lustful thoughts are not just thoughts with sexual content, but rather are thoughts of sex which are held by a particular community *to be inappropriate to their context.* Although the other sins can be shown to fit this mold, the sin of envy is again problematic. Although all thoughts about sex are not necessarily lustful, all lustful thoughts are about sex. What are envious thoughts about? Are they all inherently envious, or does context separate the sinful from the moral?

Often, people argue that they could not have acted out of envy, as they didn't feel envious. Is this a compelling argument with the other sins, or does it appear credible because of some odd quality of envy? Consider lust—suppose a friend says he was not guilty of lust, because he was not horny that day—he just happened to find himself in bed with a woman. Does this modify our judgment of lust? No. If his partner were married and not to him, then our judgment of lust will depend upon our sexual ethic and not upon knowing his prior mental state. Is the prior experience sufficient, even though not necessary, to determine that someone has acted lustfully? No. There are many chaste horny people, either through extraordinary effort of will or, more typically, through lack of opportunity. Hence, pointing to a prior feeling can neither support nor defeat a charge of lustfulness.

Although a prior feeling is irrelevant to the moral characterization of an action, it may be a part of a causal explanation, for example, "I woke up that morning and couldn't think of anything but sex. If I hadn't been so horny, I would not have accepted her invitation and . . ." Here a heightened sensitivity is given as one part of a causal account of why something happened. So for the other sins, a prior mental experience does not enter into moral characterization of acts, although it may furnish evidence of an unusual sensitivity, which could enter into a causal account. But envy, perhaps because it lacks an obvious goal, seems to require the *experience* of envy in a way greed or lust does not. If someone denies that he acted enviously because he did not feel envious, is he denying that a certain experience entered causally into his action?

Summary

We have thus far argued that the other deadly sins involve a person's transgressing in the pursuit of a typical human goal which is not, in itself, evil. We have also pointed out that sin terms rarely have explanatory value but are merely stand-ins for a causal account. We have touched on the relation between experience and behavior for these sins. At first glance, envy does not fit the pattern of the other sins; we have pinpointed sources of this peculiarity. In the next section we hope to show how envy, like the other sins, may be analyzed as a characterization of a person that is grounded in particulars of his behavior and experience. In doing this we will see the manner in which envy does parallel the other sin terms, and we will attempt to show how the paradoxes of envy arise and how they may be resolved. Our approach will be to focus first on presentations of self in interactions affected by the issue of success. We will then see how the characterization 'envy' emerges from the problematics of such situations.

ENVY AND SELF-PRESENTATION

There are many ways to lose standing in "the local scheme of social types" (Garfinkel, 1956) and wind up with a depreciated self. There are depreciations that we are fully responsible for and those that we merely fall into: crimes, faults, failures, gaffes, and missteps. We may be depreciated through another person's malice: be falsely accused, snubbed, ridiculed, taunted, or spat upon. Most curiously, a loss of esteem may just happen to us, not through our fault or another's spite, but merely because selves are linked in the social world. A person may be diminished inadvertently, as a by-product of someone else's success. It is often held that if an individual feels diminished by another person's accomplishments, then it must be due to his own idiosyncratic sensitivities, perhaps a "low self-esteem."[5] But when particular cases of success and failure are considered, what others have or have not achieved is a background to our assessment. It is not only, as social comparison theory holds (Festinger, 1954), that a person evaluates his assessment of his own status by comparing his assessment with that of others, but also that his status, as evaluated by himself or others, is inherently comparative. Is there a question as to which of the two following events is a greater loss: being rejected for a position that all of one's friends have attained or being rejected when they too have failed?

How can a person defend an eroding position? If this erosion is caused by something she has done or has been accused of doing, then she has many options for remedial action. She may deny the charge and even return one, calling her accusers malicious or rude. She can give a justification (showing how her apparently inappropriate behavior was, in fact, appropriate) or an excuse; or she can accept the charge while pointing to mitigating circumstances. She can belittle the import of the charge by admitting that it describes her behavior but also claim that, although it constitutes a major flaw in someone else, because of her particular position it is not a major flaw in her (e.g., an inability to add is a major failing in an accountant but a peccadillo in a poet). Barring all else, she might apologize, stating that her action was unfortunate. If these accounts are not tenable, then she could acknowledge that the act was typical of her behavior in the past, but that she has reformed (Goffman, 1971). As a last resort, if she cannot lessen the loss of face, then she can at least avoid those who know of it.[6]

The remedial actions we have discussed can be used only

5. We might even say that a person who feels demeaned by another's accomplishments is prone to envy. It is tempting to immediately treat the concept of envy in this connection. Yet to do so at this moment would confuse the issue. Only when the full complexity of this social situation is presented will we be able to elucidate the connection between this sort of depreciation and envy.

6. The extent of a person's objective loss is analytically distinct from the extent of his reaction to that objective loss, e.g., he may perceive that his social self is being lowered yet do nothing to prevent it. Perhaps status in the particular group doing the lowering is irrelevant to him; he isn't a member of the community. At the other extreme, the awareness of a minor loss may possess him, and he may find himself preoccupied with his lowered status.

when the individual and her audience are aware that there is something that must be answered for. This occurs when a moral charge has been made, or when the act is of the sort that typically calls for an explanation, apology, or excuse. Consider, however, the predicament of someone indirectly demeaned by the accomplishment of another. The defense of her lowered status must be made in the absence of an accuser or an overt charge. She has done nothing, hence she has nothing to retract or justify. Nor can she point to the other person's deliberate harm-doing, for there hasn't been any.[7] The options open to her to prevent or minimize diminution of self are severely restricted and hedged with difficulty.

This situation can also be uncomfortable for the individual announcing his success and even for witnesses. Consider a social occasion in which a success demeaning one participant is announced. The person demeaned has a problem in preventing an erosion of his esteem. Yet he also, as a party to the interaction, is expected to participate unreservedly in the acclaim undermining his position. The person who has succeeded is also in a difficult spot. He understandably wants his success known. Moreover, if he does not announce his success during the encounter, he may insult those present, his reticence being taken as evidence that their approval is irrelevant to him. On the other hand, any excess or poor timing in his announcement may leave him open to the charge of being a braggart. If he attempts to underplay his accomplishment, he must do so skillfully. Otherwise, he will be guilty of false modesty, or even worse, he may be seen as implying that his attainment is so easy the others should have achieved it also. Even a third party who cannot be demeaned by this particular success faces a problem: he must celebrate the success of one without tactlessly underscoring the lack of accomplishment of the other. Examining how a skillful third party can carry off this delicate maneuver will exhibit tactical possibilities without bringing up additional complexities of personal gain or loss.

7. There are other instances of this predicament in the social life, e.g., it underlies the stickiness of dealing with being ignored. The difference between being ignored and being snubbed hinges on the fact that the ignored cannot point to any special dereliction in the distribution of attention; being ignored is cumulative, not involving any overt violation of constitutive rules of social interaction. Hence, it is extremely difficult to deal with (Geller et al., 1974).

How can he carry it off? He may take the fortunate person aside and congratulate her privately; he is then free to ignore or play down the matter in front of the person who might be hurt. If such an opportunity does not present itself, he must make his congratulations in the presence of the person whose position may be undermined; he will have to moderate his use of superlatives. Better yet, he might link the success to the other person's support, if this is at all plausible. He will also have to attend to the temporal limits of the celebration by changing the topic at the appropriate moment. He might, if he can find a suitable context, pick a topic that will allow for the failure to display his accomplishments.[8]

What if a person whose status is threatened were to use these strategies? It is doubtful we would call him tactful. Using such techniques for selfish rather than altruistic ends seems wrong, further demeaning their user. Yet it can be misleading to identify a characterization of an action with its presumptive motive. Judgment of an action, as we have found in our analysis of the deadly sins, depends more on the appropriateness of the action to its context than on the goal of the actor.

Suppose someone who is speaking has gone on too long. Changing the topic would be merely an appropriate response to a tedious monologue. Consider a braggart for whom you supply the missing modesty by taking him down a peg. If this were done with finesse, in an amusing manner at the right moment, your response would be an entertaining repartee, not a transgression. Everyday conversations involve a measure of self-presentation; they also involve changes of topic, turns at display, affirming team aspects of individual accomplishment, etc. If each of these parts is played without mishap, the propriety of the interactions is not called into question, even in the case where one or more of the participants could be seen as demeaned by the success of another. But what if one of them blows his lines, for example, changes the topic too quickly or brings up his own success in a forced, clumsy manner? It is in this case that the question of ulterior motive arises—not be-

8. This strategy is delicate. You must choose a topic that will not in any way undercut the success of the person who is celebrating. Typically, the further this area of accomplishment is from the celebrant's, the better. In addition, you must be careful to pick an area of commensurate worth, or you will heighten the contrast and humiliate exactly the person you are trying to protect.

cause we had not realized that the parties in the interaction were displaying themselves or attempting to limit the display of others, but because until this moment, these aims were part of the natural fabric of the conversation.

As Peters (1958) points out, in commonsense talk the question of motivation arises when a transgression of social norms is believed to have occurred. In such contexts, talking about motives, in part, supplies the goal that the person was pursuing when he transgressed. Of course, should they be pressed, participants in almost any interaction could supply such goals for perfectly blameless behavior (self-enhancement, for instance, is one common goal of ordinary conversation). However, supplying a motive in commonsense talk both points to a goal and characterizes its pursuit: saying that a person acts out of envy both describes the person's goal and has the force of characterizing that goal as inappropriately pursued. When someone inappropriately pursues a goal of self-protection, common sense is likely to use the epithet 'envy'.[9] This is especially true if he has done so by limiting the import of another's success or in some other way devaluing that person.

Let us closely consider this analysis of the commonsense use of 'envy'. It assumes the truism that people wish to have worthy selves. The transgressions, or sins, that occur in pursuit of this end are broadly of two sorts—those of pride and those of envy. The charge of pride (arrogance, boastfulness, being a braggart) arises when the transgression is in the service of self-enhancement; the charge of envy arises when the transgression is an attempt to prevent self-diminution. Since an attribution of envy presupposes that the actor's self has been diminished, or at least that he perceives this to be the case, to be seen as envious is doubly damaging. Not only has he committed a transgression, but he has tacitly acknowledged his lessened worth.

9. Sometimes even an expression of admiration may be seen as a sign of envy if it is stuttered, stammered, delayed, or otherwise misplayed. In these cases we would say that the congratulations were insincere. Insincerity is a difficult concept. It is often taken to involve a mismatch between what a person says or does and what he "really feels," i.e., a disconsonance between expression and internal state. Yet one can sincerely avow love while experiencing a gas pain. Can one sincerely congratulate another while *regretting* his success? This appears to be a difficult feat. It may be, but it is possible since it is what is meant by good sportsmanship. In fact, one can congratulate the winner of a race for his superb skill even while telling him you wished that the race had come out otherwise because you had bet on his opponent.

Not every situation of inappropriate *self*-protection is proper grounds for a charge of envy. A student who, after failing an exam, calls its fairness into question in a patently self-serving manner is a whiner and complainer, but not necessarily envious. However, if he remarked on the unfairness of the test only after being informed that acquaintances had gotten A's, his behavior might warrant a charge of envy.

Only those situations in which the advantages, attainments, etc., of other people demean an individual provide a context for the charge of envy. "We also envy those whose possession of or success in a thing is a reproach to us" (Aristotle, *Rhetoric*, Book 2, chapter 10).[10] But for a person's behavior to warrant this charge, it must not merely be an inappropriate response to being demeaned, it must be an attempt to protect against being lowered—or at least must be interpretable as an abortive or blocked attempt to do so. One might burst out weeping or commit suicide because of another's success. These actions, though inappropriate, need not be envious. They may be signs of a painful recognition of, or perhaps incorrect belief in, the diminution of one's status, rather than an attempt to cope with a diminution.

There is one other element in our analysis of envy: the method of self-protection is by undercutting the other person. If we redouble our own efforts because we are shamed by a rival's attainments, we are not envious. In fact, if our efforts are honorable, we are exemplifying the competitive spirit, indulging in virtuous emulation.[11] A coach, in the movies if not in

10. We have so far stressed that the linkage among the statuses of individuals is an *objective* phenomenon. Any social actor can understand that a person may be demeaned by certain successes of other people or that someone may attempt to protect himself from being demeaned. This objective aspect of the phenomenon provides us with a necessary background for our understanding of personal differences in reactions to other people's attributes or accomplishments. Using this socially shared knowledge allows someone to recognize that another person is feeling intensely envious even if he himself has never experienced a pang of envy. Some people appear to be much more prone to feelings of envy than do others. It is likely that this is related to idiosyncrasies in the way an individual perceives himself, i.e., he is susceptible to accomplishments of others that would not even be noticed or would be considered irrelevant by the rest of us.

11. Focusing on another's accomplishment and our lack is *likely* to lead to envy but need not. It might result in simple admiration, even though tinged by sadness or depression. Consider two examples both involving depression caused by another's success, but only one announcing envy. In a letter (*New York Review*, 1977) Edmund Wilson described how reading a draft of *The Great Gatsby* saddened him by showing how far he was from mastering a style shown in its polished form by Fitzgerald: "I was re-reading *The Great Gatsby* last night, after I had been going through my page proofs, and thinking with depression

life, may stimulate the waning spirit of his team by dwelling on how the other side's superior performance is making fools of them. Although being put down by the other side's performance is here a goad to competition, we wouldn't call this extra effort envious, even if it were to involve poking, gouging, and other unfair play. The team might be guilty of poor sportsmanship, but insofar as they are attempting to prevent themselves from being demeaned *by trying to win the game,* they are not acting enviously.

We have thus far examined the question of when an action gives rise to a *charge* of envy. But when we call a person envious, we are typically not judging a single action, but a character, or self. The fact that envy refers to both actions and selves adds further complexity to our analysis. 'Envy', to borrow and extend the use of Ryle's phrase (1949), is a "mongrel categorical" term, one that both characterizes a single act and makes a claim about the actor. Because of this duality, commonsense actors may introduce evidence to support or refute a charge of envy in a specific case by mentioning facts that are not about the action under discussion and might hence seem to be irrelevant. These facts are about the person's typical ways of perceiving and reacting to situations involving his esteem (see ch. 8). An action by someone who often brags is more easily seen as envious than the same act by someone else known for modesty. An individual who is obviously sensitive to slights, snubs, and other signs of lowered status will similarly be more liable to be seen as envious. An evidence of fragility in a person's feelings

---

how much better Scott Fitzgerald's prose and dramatic sense were than mine. If I'd only been able to give my book the vividness and excitement, and the technical accuracy, of his! Have you ever read Gatsby? I think it's one of the best novels that any American of his age has done." Wilson admits depression and even makes clear how it is Fitzgerald's particular accomplishment that perfectly brings out his own failings; yet he does not come across as envious. Why not? In this passage Wilson is clearly admiring Fitzgerald, there is no trace of backbiting, begrudging, demeaning. In contrast, let us consider a passage from a novel by John Powers (1975):

> His family was extremely wealthy. He was good looking and smart, he was a great athlete and he could play seventeen different musical instruments, all at the same time. Worst of all, Earl Benninger had such a pleasant personality that it was impossible for anyone, including myself, to dislike him. Earl Benninger was a very depressing person to be around.

The narrator of this passage appeared to be envious, albeit in a minor key. The force of the passage is not that the protagonist was depressed, but that Earl was depressing; the narrator can be seen as demeaning Earl by making, or at least hinting at, a moral reproach. Since he said that Earl's behavior is blameless, the reproach is inappropriate and hence, evidence that he is envious.

of self-worth may feed into the assessment of whether or not he is envious. The judgment that a person is envious is not reached simply by counting the number of times that he has committed envious actions. Judgments about selves are not collapsible in any simple way to judgments about actions.

Envy as Sin, Motive, and Emotion: A Question of Fit

We now return to the question raised earlier: whether envy fits into the pattern of the deadly sins. We noted that the other sins have goals which are not evil in themselves. Their pursuit is considered normal, natural, obvious, not requiring special explanation; it would be the failure to pursue these goals which would require a special explanation. What made these behaviors sinful was not their end but the inappropriate manner of their pursuit. The sin of envy, on the other hand, seemed less human as it did not appear to involve a natural goal. We have attempted to demonstrate that there is a natural goal of envious behavior and that, as with the other sins, it is its inappropriate pursuit which constitutes the sin. When we say that a person is envious, we are, in part, implying that a goal of her behavior is to prevent herself from being demeaned. We have detailed a number of ways, both appropriate and inappropriate, that she may attempt to do this. When we say that a person, in pursuing this goal, is envious, we ground our statement by pointing to a particular class of inappropriate behaviors—behaviors that directly or indirectly attempt to belittle another person.

Our analysis has, in a sense, debunked the mystique of envy by removing its mysterious quality. We have argued that the goal of the envious person is no more perverse than that of the miser or lecher. But if his goal is so obvious and natural, why do thoughtful commonsense actors find envy so perverse?

Let us look again at our comparison of envy with the other deadly sins. Adultery is obviously a member of the class of sexual acts; whether it is evidence of lust depends only on our sexual ethic—our evaluation of its appropriateness. Inappropriately belittling someone, on the other hand, may be an aggressive act, an envious act, a thoughtless act, or an arrogant act. It is only when we can connect someone's act of belittling to a goal of self-protection that we see it to be a token of envy. To be greedy a person need attempt nothing more than to acquire a good; an envious individual is attempting to belittle another person in order to do something else, i.e., to protect his self-worth. Envy's perversity derives from the fact that demeaning somebody is an end—something that the envious individual is trying to bring about—but not the ultimate goal. What makes envy natural—self-protection—is not what betrays the act as envious—undercutting another person. What is immediately perceived is not the ultimate goal—self-restoration—but the indirect manner of achieving this goal—demeaning another person. The sexuality in a sin of lust is patent and unavoidable; *the self-protection in the sin of envy is obscured by envy's secondary but more overt end, the demeaning of another.*

ENVY AS AN EXPERIENCE

We have treated envy in the perspective of sin. This vantage makes salient the active, goal-pursuing nature of the phenomenon and slights its passive, afflicting, involuntary quality. Thus, it naturally places envy in the context of talk about motives, but obscures perhaps the most prominent aspect of envy, that it is an emotion that comes on a person, torments her, and preoccupies her against her will. Although the perspective puts to one side what is most prominent to first reflection, it does so in order to fix on what is distinctive about envy.

Consider a relationship stricken by envy. A friend joyfully shares the news of her fine achievement. The less successful friend wishes to, wants to, intends to, and indeed tries to create a sincere congratulation fitting with the excellence of her accomplishment and the warmth of their friendship. But he botches it. The congratulations come out forced, choked, diminished, and cool. What is more *prominent,* compelling, about this unfortunate mishap is its unwilled, afflicting character: that it is an *emotion.* But what makes it *distinctively* envy is his failure to come forth with his friend's due. The failure takes on meaning as envy because it is what he would do if in this context he were trying to undercut her accomplishment, i.e., if he were moved by envy. The emotion takes its meaning from the motive. Reversing this perspective and treating the most prominent aspect of envy—that it can be an emotion—as if it were the key to understanding the *motive* envy (as has been done most recently in a rather extreme and diffuse form by Schoeck, 1969, in his treatise on the effects of envy) obscures our understanding of envy by treating it as a mysterious homogeneous entity, an essence, whose contingent effects can be collected but whose nature remains untouched. Working on this assumption produces the paradox that each new fact can only increase envy's oddness, e.g., envy is: the sin against the brother (i.e., to those whom we owe the best, we do the worst—Aristotle, *Rhetoric*, Book 2); a torment to the envious; more likely to be provoked by small than large differences in lot, etc. Until we use a conceptual analysis of envy these facts perplex us rather than help us understand.

Starting from the view of envy as an emotion fixes us on envy's aspect as an experience—a content of consciousness—since this is such a prominent part of emotion. Yet, as shown in our previous analysis of the deadly sins, this approach is misleading. For example, when we say that a person is feeling lustful, we do not imply that lust is the content of his consciousness but, rather, that sex is. Sometimes recognition of a reduced position due to another person's accomplishment leads to thoughts that undermine the moral worth of that other person. One may merely notice the other person's unworthiness or be obsessed by it. On occasion the actor may recognize that his criticism or feeling of outrage is inappropriate. He may realize that his criticism is ungrounded or overblown, that the other's moral failings are none of his business, that his concentration on these failings betrays an obsessive preoccupation. He may also recognize that it is his own diminution by the other's accomplishment that has occasioned such moral charges. If an actor comes to believe that he has reacted in such an inappropriate way as a defense of his reduced self, then he would be said to realize that he has experienced envy. The fact that he has characterized this reaction as envious does not mean that it ceases to occur. It may keep popping into his mind, along with an awareness of tight muscles and pounding heart, even though he realizes that the reaction is inappropriate. Such a recognition may lead to a further reduction in his self-esteem. This realization of the flimsiness of "self" shown to him by his unwilled and uncalled-for defensive reaction is one of the torments of envy—knowing that he is envious. On the other hand, it is possible to feel demeaned by another person's accomplishments, also feel critical of him, and yet not believe that there is any connection between these two attitudes. Or it is possible to recognize the connection but not believe the critical attitude is inappropriate; rather it may be perceived as a justified response to his arrogant behavior. In this case we might be right, but at another time, even though we did not believe that we were envious, someone else, if she could show that our feelings were overblown or overpersistent, would be warranted in asserting that we were possessed by envious thoughts. She might even convince us that we were envious.

We have argued that some form of criticism, undercutting, or demeaning—either overt, implicit, or experienced—is necessary for envy. Yet people sometimes firmly believe that someone is envious and may even offer evidence for their assertion, though they cannot point to any belittling. We would argue in such cases that some of the criteria for a person's being envious are manifestly fulfilled, for example, his being shown up by the other person's success. And this leads to the inference that the person is envious, i.e., that the other criteria are also fulfilled. The force of this inference, that the person is envious, is that the person would like to or has some tendency to begrudge or belittle the other person's success. If it could be shown that this was not the case, then the inference that the person was envious would be wrong.

As Kenny (1963) would point out, our position is somewhat overdrawn in that commonsense actors do accept "partial cases" as instances of emotion, even though they deviate from the standard case of the emotion. For instance, the paradigm case of fear involves an assessment of threat, a typical symptomology (shaking or trembling) and *qua motive* an attempt to avoid this threat. Yet we meaningfully talk of objectless fear. Consider the case of someone who cowers under a bed and says that he feels afraid. Even though he has not mentioned perceiving a threat, one would infer that he must be. Yet what if he were to deny perceiving any threat? Must he be lying? To characterize this case *without being misleading* one would have to call it fear and point out that it is an odd case of fear. Insofar as one can grasp, talk about, this odd case it is because of the features it shares with the standard one (see ch. 9 for a more detailed account using anger).

IMPLICATIONS FOR THE EMPIRICAL STUDY OF ENVY

We have treated envy as a word in a language, a concept people treat as objective. A virtue of this approach is that it restrains the tendency to view envy (or emotions and motives generally) as an entity causally and, hence, contingently related to its consequents: envious actions. Following the logic of this "realist" view, we might assess the strength of an envy motive, perhaps by a TAT-based procedure, and then discover the relations between "high envy" and such hypothesized consequents as belittling another. Yet if we did not discover such a relation, wouldn't we say that we were not, in fact, studying envy? Belittling another person is part of what we mean when we say that someone is envious. Treating this as an empirical discovery and not a conceptual clarification is misleading and leads to studies whose persuasiveness actually trades on our understanding of the meaning of the terms we use—a practice all too common in "empirical" social psychology (Peters, 1965). Our "nominalist" approach does not preclude empirical investigations on "the effects of envy," but it refocuses this research and is a necessary prolegomenon to it.

Instead of searching for the causes of envy, for instance, we might look at the way that selves are linked in our objective moral universe, how people commonly and idiosyncratically interpret or react to this linkage, and the moral failings attendant on these reactions. Envy as a feeling is subjective in that some people suffer greatly from it and others are not touched. As an example, Scheler, in 1910 (tr. 1961), pointed out that women were considered to be the envious sex. Imagine this were true. Instead of looking for the biological or biographical antecedents of women's susceptibility to this particular emotion, we would first look at the determinants of objective comparability in a particular social structure at a particular moment. At the turn of the century, given the restriction on women's entry into careers, politics, etc., the dimensions on which middle-class women, at least, were comparable to each other, e.g., attractiveness, domestic ability, clothes, or husband's earnings, were fewer and *more widely shared* than those in which middle-class men were comparable. This is not a fact about feminine personality per se, but about women's position in life. There are further questions to be asked about the idiosyncratic, personal reactions of individual women; understanding this social, structural aspect of comparability gives us a background against which to study its personal expression. Note that the focus of investigation has now shifted from the study of the determinants of envy to how individuals interpret and react to social comparability.

The lability of self-worth is common to depression as well as envy. There are many ways a person may react to a belief that his worth has been lowered. He can try harder, show how the other's accomplishments are really in a different area than his, show how selves are linked such that the other person's success enhances his own, or he may perceive a diminution and do nothing. In the empirical study of envy, we would look for the determinants of why an individual put down another as opposed to emulated the other, competed against the other, dwelt on his demeaning, did nothing, and so forth. *The determinants of the selection of any of these responses are different from the determinants of why the person was sensitive to or imagined a particular self-diminution.* Of course, which response is made is related to opportunity as well as personality. We are not denying that some people are more prone to envy than others (Farber, 1961; Daniels, 1964). We believe that this is a most important issue and one we have not addressed. We have attempted to clear the ground for such an analysis.

CHAPTER THREE

Moral Reproach

Consider a situation in which you observe someone doing something heinous, e.g., beating a child repeatedly with a spiked rod. How might you react? You might sit back and enjoy it, applaud the passing of the age of permissiveness, notice that something improper is occurring without feeling the slightest twinge of outrage or tug to intervene. Or you might boil with outrage but still not act because: you believe that it is morally improper to intervene between parent and child, you are afraid of spiked rods, the person doing the beating is your boss or the president of the United States, no one else is doing anything, you have a deep and abiding relationship with the assailant which you are loath to upset, or although you find you have none of these *reasons* (or any others), and you *do* want to rebuke him, you "just can't." If you can somehow bring yourself to act, there are many forms your action might take. You might: offer him fifty dollars to desist, or wait until he pauses and then administer the fifty dollars as reinforcement for pausing behavior, ask him to stop as a personal favor, threaten to use your revolver (which you just happen to be carrying), threaten to fire him if you are his boss, or arrest him if you are a cop (or find one if not), attempt to convince him that it is not in his long-range best interest to continue (at least in public), distract him so the tot can run away, or you might *morally reproach* him to his face—telling him that he is doing something wrong, and exactly what it is that is wrong about what he is doing, and what it is that his wrongdoing makes him—a cad, creep, or moral leper—or more simply just call him a creep for short; or, failing to tell him off to his face, you might find it easier to do so to a fellow onlooker, or to your spouse later that night—evoking and sharing your outrage. The conditions under which any or several of these strategies will be employed have received some attention in the social psychological literature. The further question of which, if any, of these strategies will succeed has also been investigated (see Tedeschi, 1972, for an overview).

MORAL REPROACH AND MORAL ACTION

The focus of this paper is on a particular subset of these reactions, which has not as yet received its share of attention (Sabini, 1976; Sabini & Silver, 1978). The subset consists of cases in which an actor feels outraged, "wants to tell the wrongdoer off," i.e., make a moral reproach, but "just can't."[1] That an actor would refrain from telling off a villain who has a gun, badge, or other sign of "fate control" is not surprising, and is what we'd expect from rational calculation. On the other hand,

1. What exactly is a moral reproach? The notion of a reproach seems straightforward: a reproach is, at least, an unfavorable criticism. The question "What is a moral matter?" is quite problematic.

Hart articulates "4 cardinal features" of rules and standards, most commonly called moral (1961). He argues that moral standards are always: (1) seen as something of great importance to maintain, (2) seen as immune from deliberate change, (3) concerned with voluntary (vs. involuntary) action, and (4) enforced by appeal to the violator to respect rules that he presumably shares (pp. 164–80). Hart's second criterion is closely related to the notion of objectivity of the moral order as discussed in Berger and Luckmann (1967) and Shutz (1973). The central point of these notions is: actors treat moral standards as external, in-the-world objects, not subject to individual whim, mood, state, or interest, as things others can, and ought to, perceive as they do. Features 3 and 4 taken together come close to a definition of a moral reproach. They imply that a moral reproach calls upon an actor to do as he *can* and *ought*. A fully developed moral reproach would, then, articulate some rule and assert that the other ought to follow it.

What this outline omits is the fact that characterizations of an actor or his action in socially undesirable terms often serve as a moral reproach. Thus any comment that, in Garfinkel's phrase, "transforms [someone's identity] into something looked on as lowered in the local scheme of social types," is a moral reproach. This definition is fuzzy at the edges. All sorts of attributes that we would not call moral matters can lead to another's being lowered in the local scheme of social types. Race, sex, physical grace, and inherited wealth are all attributes by which one is raised or lowered in social status; yet, since they are not voluntary actions, they would not seem to be in the moral domain. Still commonsense actors treat such characterizations as reproaches. Goffman, in *Stigma* (1963a), develops the many ways in which being called ugly is like being called a thief both for a person's self-concept and for others' assessment of his worth.

the actions we shall focus on are surprising in that they do not appear to be the outcome of a rational calculation. Those actions that are not rational, although regular, require explanation in other terms (see ch. 7).

Still, our concern with making a moral reproach seems prissy, as if a by-stander's most pressing concern should be to assess the moral worth of a child beater, or to make a safe affirmation of her own character, rather than to save the child. Reproaching someone as he is beating a child seems far from the most natural, reasonable, or effective thing to do. Hence, it would seem that our attention ought to be on the failure of action not utterance. And it is.

Sometimes people do not take effective action in circumstances that clearly call for it, not only out of rational self-interest, but because of a feature of such action that is less apparent: *action may imply reproach*. What makes direct action legitimate is exactly what makes a reproach called for; intervention forces the attention of the malefactor, the person who intervenes, and the audience to the moral interpretation of the circumstances that justify such extraordinary action. Intervening becomes a reproach. For instance, wrestling a child from his mother who is "disciplining" him makes the implicit claim that the "discipline" is in fact battery.[2] Thus, the inhibition of direct action can be seen as derived from the inhibition of making a moral reproach.

THE INHIBITION OF MORAL REPROACH AND ACTION

In our analysis we shall try to bring out why the moral nature of a reproach inhibits. We shall develop this, in part, by an analysis of some social psychological experiments that are designed to explore action in contexts of moral import but do not address the question of when an actor will make a moral reproach. A careful consideration of these situations can shed light on the inhibitions actors feel in making a reproach, and how these inhibitions shed light on the failure of action.

Milgram's (1974) studies of obedience to destructive authority

2. This hypothetical case appears hyperbolic; after all, no one would really be inhibited from intervening if a child were being publicly beaten with a spiked stick. Yet, consider the elaborate advertisement campaign found necessary to get people to report child abuse.

compellingly portray the nonrational quality of the inhibition of moral action. The subject finds himself in a situation in which he wants to prevent harm to an innocent victim, yet he is unable to bring himself to do so, even though he is the agent of that harm and can prevent it without cost. Subjects are ordered by an experimenter to give increasingly painful shocks to a vehemently protesting confederate posing as another subject. In violation of the a priori estimates of psychiatrists and laymen that less than .1 percent (psychopaths) would continue to the most extreme shock levels, over 60 percent of the subjects continued to deliver dangerous shocks until told to stop by the experimenter. Many subjects, while continuing to obey orders, gave evidence of extreme emotional distress. Perhaps one difficulty that subjects had in attempting to withdraw is a consequence of the face-to-face relationship between the subject and the experimenter: invoking a moral norm important enough to justify disobedience implies that the experimenter *ought* not order them to continue. Thus, any justification they might have offered for refusing to continue would have involved an explicit or implicit condemnation of the authority. Faced with the evidence that the experimenter, also aware of the protesting of the victim, continued to order them to go on, subjects were forced to act as if either the moral principle were not so important after all, or the experimenter was evil in not recognizing and acting on it. It was difficult for subjects to act in accordance with the latter conclusion, especially to the face of the experimenter. In fact, when the experimenter was physically absent, interacting with the subject by telephone, the rate of obedience was considerably reduced (from 65 percent to 20.5 percent). The experimenter's absence, of course, did not alter the *moral* nature of the subject's predicament. It should be noted that subjects believed the victim was being exposed to dangerous, indeed possibly fatal, shocks, and that there were no grounds for the subjects to see themselves as threatened by the experimenter.

Not only did a majority of the subjects continue until told to stop, *but even the minority who did stop failed to reproach the experimenter for his evil instructions* (Milgram, personal communication). Yet this is surely a situation in which a moral reproach would be expected: it was one of utmost gravity, without danger to the one who ought to make the reproach and with no other cost to the subject. The absence of a reproach in a situation so clearly requiring it is the sort of failure which a commonsense actor explains by the notion of an inhibition—some sort of counterforce restraining the most natural response.

Many subjects attempted to have the experimenter stop the proceedings by asking, pleading, or pointing to the difficult situation of the victim; one revealing attempt is portrayed in the Milgram (1965a) film report of the experiment. This subject said, "I don't mean to be rude, but I think you should look in on him." This formulation is far from a preemptive injunction such as, "You have to see if he's alright before we continue," or, "You have no right to tell me to continue." The subject himself explains why he did not use these stronger, more forceful forms; he points out that such reproaches are rude. We treat the subject's explanation seriously: the making of a moral reproach *is* rude. We follow Milgram (1965a, p. 209) in arguing that this rudeness is a source of the inhibition against reproaching another. Yet this explanation is unsatisfying, not because it is wrong, but because it is absurd to be concerned with courtesy when another's life is at stake.[3] Further, this explanation would mean that people would never reproach each other, even in situations of grave import; yet people sometimes do. To relieve this paradox, consider some situations in which people are *not* inhibited about reproaching another.

REQUIREMENTS OF MAKING A REPROACH

We propose that situations in which it is easy to reproach another fulfill two conditions: (1) the actor stands in a proper re-

3. Goffman (1959, p. 13) amplifies this point: "In consequence, when an individual projects a definition of the situation and thereby makes an explicit or implicit claim to be a person of a particular kind, he automatically exerts a *moral* demand upon the others, obligating them to value and treat him in a manner that persons of his kind have a right to expect." [emphasis added]

Making a moral reproach, denouncing another, would be a violation of this claim. Goffman's use of moral in this context is both curious and suggestive. This sort of requirement, that we not call into question the value of others, might seem to be merely a requirement of courtesy rather than morality; a commonsense actor might well call someone who violated this rule rude or discourteous, but we doubt she would call him immoral. Goffman seems to use this stronger term to emphasize: (1) the interpenetration of morality and the construction of identities (a point we shall discuss later); (2) that demands of courtesy sometimes compete with patently moral demands (a point well illustrated in the Milgram experiment); and (3) that the violation of these rules leads to an emotional state—embarrassment—distinct from shame or guilt, which are closely tied to moral precepts.

lationship to the wrongdoer; and (2) she perceives that the action is in the proper relation to the norm invoked in the reproach.

Relationship to the Wrongdoer

What relationship does a person making a moral reproach typically have to have to the wrongdoer? She typically occupies a position of authority over the person she reproaches.[4] Parents, for example, have little difficulty bringing themselves to reproach their children, at least until the children are old enough to call into question whether the parents remain in positions of authority. Priests, ministers, and rabbis, at least from their pulpits, easily address moral reproach.

A person not in authority over another can still be in a proper relationship to the transgressor to make a moral reproach if the transgression involves her directly in that her interests are affected by the transgression. For example, if a thief steals *your* radio, holding fear aside, you will not be inhibited about making a reproach. There are two differences between having your radio stolen and seeing someone else's radio stolen: (1) you have more to lose, since it is your radio, and (2) you see yourself, and know that others see you, as having the *right* to involve yourself in the matter. That you have more to lose may mean that you are more eager to make a reproach, but it does not, of itself, remove the inhibition against doing so. Your knowing that others know that you have a right reduces the inhibition against reproach: objectifiable *rights* ease the way to action.

4. In Garfinkel's language a moral reproach is a transformation of an actor's self into something looked upon as "lowered in the local scheme of social types." That this sort of "transformation" is typically reserved for authorities acting in the name of the collectivity seems to be an instance of the general rule that all transformations of objective identity, the characteristics that an actor is known to have by others of that collectivity, are the prerogative of the community and are performed by its representatives. Thus marriage, the awarding of degrees, divorce, and even birth and death are ratified by representatives of the state. Members of groups that would convince others of the value of membership in that group typically petition the state to license that membership (clinical psychologists and chiropractors fall into this class). Even less-enduring transformations of one's social worth are forbidden; attempting to elevate one's own worth is condemned as bragging and has the reverse effect.

Standing

This principle parallels the principle of "standing" in common law: to sue another one must show that one's interests *in particular* are obstructed by his misbehavior. Third-party suits are forbidden; correcting a third party's behavior is "not done" in everyday life lest one be seen as a meddler.[5]

The notion of 'in particular' further develops a parallel between law and life. It is not merely that one suffers a loss, is a victim, that gives her the right to intervene—standing either in common law or in common life—but that violations of a community norm may entail costs for all members (shoplifters cause increased retail prices for all). Yet Gelfand et al. (1973) found that 72 percent of those who witnessed a particularly flagrant case (staged) of shoplifting did not report the crime. Polluters, whether industrial or cigarette smokers, also produce costs for each member of the community—they lessen everyone's life span.

The common-law principle of standing prevents any, and hence every, member of a community from suing air polluters for damages since no *one* member of the community in particular is injured by the pollution. Specific legislation is often enacted just to deal with this paradox. Legislation that solves the problem by allowing class action suits is seen as an exception to common law to be used to cover only limited, specified purposes. Similarly in common life, on a bus trip we may fervently hope that the person down the aisle would stop smoking, but we recognize that it is not just us but everybody on the bus who is assaulted by the smoke and that we do not, thus, have standing. So we look to the bus driver to exercise his real, though limited, authority.

There are laws, of course, against smoking on a bus, and the bus driver is charged with enforcing them. But there are no specific laws against, for example, delivering a political harangue in a loud voice on the way to Duluth; yet, since all riders lack

5. Arendt (1958) points out that the classical Greek term for meddler and tyrant were the same; the two sorts of behavior are similar in that each is an inappropriate invocation of a community's moral norms. Both the tyrant and the meddler attempt to control the behavior of others in an unauthorized way; they usurp powers drived from, and the property of, the community as a whole.

standing, they would expect the driver to prohibit the harangue as his is the only *authority* that can be squeezed out of the situation. Of course, standing too can be strained out of situations: the person closest to a smoker can be seen to be harmed to a greater degree than those further away. We would expect that his failure to act would thus further inhibit others farther away from acting. (Mann, 1969, has carried out a similar analysis of the problematics of enforcing rules in queues.) Note that we predict that those closer to a nuisance will, and will be expected to, act first, independent of the question of who is most bothered by it. According to a rational calculus of pleasure and pain, it should be irrelevant whether others are bothered or not; what should determine action is one's own discomfort.

Indirect Standing

In some cases, one's right to act may be indirect: one may be a parent, spouse, friend, relative, or agent (by virtue of enduring relationship or temporary covenant) of someone who is the particular victim of another and, therefore, has standing. Insofar as one can show that he is acting on behalf of another who does have standing, he has the right to act, i.e., he has "indirect standing."

Consider in this light Moriarty's finding (1975) that a stranger's simple request to "Watch my things?" tremendously increases the likelihood that people will intervene against an apparent thief. The tacit acceptance "commits" subjects in that they become the temporary fiduciaries of the stranger with both a responsibility to him and standing with regard to the theft of his belongings. They know that they are in an unassailable position to give a perfectly acceptable answer to the question "What business is it of yours?"

Latanè and Darley (1970) introduce a notion similar to standing to express the fact that in an emergency with several people present each may fail to respond since each may think: "Why should I be the one to get involved? Maybe someone else will help." They argue that with many others present there is a "diffusion of responsibility." We suggest that the concept of diffusion, the dispersion of a preexisting substance through space, provides a poor metaphor because it misses the important fact that responsibility or standing is *generated* in immediate interaction out of relationships. More specifically, one has a responsibility and standing to intervene on another's behalf as a consequence of the *contrast* between the relationship that an actor has to the party in distress and the relationships that others have to him. These relationships may be spatial (the closest person to another should help), temporal (old friends are called upon to help before new friends), or familial (family members have particular rights and responsibilities to become involved).

Relation of the Act to a Norm: Crystallization and Objectivity

We have proposed that an individual's difficulty in reproaching another depends not only on the relationship between her and the wrongdoer, a relationship we have just considered, but also on the relation between the wrongdoer's action and the norms against which it is to be judged. In particular, she must perceive that the action is in the proper relation to the norm to be invoked. Let us now consider this second relation. In condemning another, one asserts that the other's behavior is in violation of what is taken to be a preexisting mutually binding rule. The difficulty in this is that, as the labeling theorists (Becker, 1963; Schur, 1971; Erikson, 1964) suggest, *such rules crystallize in the process of their application to particular people in particular circumstances.*

Although this way of putting it is a handy gloss of the difficulty, it conceals a family of related problems—a family with relatives in the disciplines of sociology, philosophy, jurisprudence, and even psychology. These problems can be seen through a close examination of a superficially simple notion: people apply general rules to specific cases. Wittgenstein (1953), Garfinkel (1967), and J. Austin (1832/1954), among others, have recognized that there is always a logical gap between a rule and its application to a particular instance; specifying a rule still

6. Garfinkel treats this issue in his discussion of the *"etcetera"* clause; Circourel (1970) under the rubric of meta-rules; the symbolic interactionists, in part, in terms of the "definition of the situation"; legal scholars in the long-standing debate between the positivists and legal realists (see Hart, 1961); and Wittgenstein in his treatment of the gap between rules and their application. Labeling theorists and some social psychologists (e.g., Sherif, 1958), have treated the problem as one concerning the emergence or crystallization of group

leaves to be specified how that rule is to be applied.[6] But any attempt to cast the specification of how to apply a rule in the form of another rule, a rule of application, develops to an infinite regress. Thus, while it is true and important that actors act as if they were applying general rules to specific cases, it is also necessary to recognize that at the heart of the matter of applying rules lies something problematic, the problem of how it is that actors come to know that a particular application of a rule is correct. (We shall follow the formulation of this problem in terms of the crystallization of group norms, as developed in labeling theory and social psychology.) The problem of knowing how to apply a rule arises not only for theorists, but for commonsense actors. The theorist needs a general solution for her aims; the commonsense actor needs a specific but reliable one in order to make a moral reproach. He must know that the moral rule on which the reproach is based is the right rule applied in the right way, and that he is seeing what anyone would see, and thus, doing what anyone should do in this situation.

Agreement at a general level about moral rules is often deceptively complete. Much less agreement exists about whether a particular instance is a case covered by a particular rule or whether some exemption justifies behavior proscribed by a rule, or whether a particular situation is one in which the proper application of the rule is preemptive. For one example we return to our consideration of the Milgram experiment. Everyone agrees that people should not inflict pain on others; most would agree that the pursuit of scientific knowledge confers *some* degree of exemption, but in the concrete reality of the Milgram experiment, at exactly what shock level does this exemption fail to justify the continued shock?[7] In a prison or a mental hospital how much force is justifiable in maintaining or-

---

norms. It should be pointed out that Sherif (1958), Mac Neil and Sherif (1976), and Jacobs and Campbell (1961) in their discussion of the convergence of group judgments in the autokinetic effect, see their demonstrations in terms of the closely related problem of how norms or rules are constructed. In our view, however, these demonstrations are most profitably viewed as illustrations of the way actors reach an agreement about how to apply preexisting concepts to ambiguous instances.

7. The subjects' difficulty here is exacerbated by the fact that the only justification they have for shocking their fellow subjects is that they were told to do so by the experimenter. As the shock levels increase from the trivial to the deadly, subjects are less and less comfortable about following his instructions; but, at the same time, the inviolability of these instructions becomes more and more necessary as a justification for their behavior.

der? Where is the boundary between reasonable force and torture? The argument of the labeling theorists is that moral norms, considered to be the boundaries between the reasonable and the wanton, *crystallize* around the act of condemning others.

Preference versus Principle

Conflict between norms and the problematics of seeing that a norm covers a particular case are not the only sources of ambiguity facing those who would apply moral principles. They must also distinguish between personal preferences and objective moral requirements. Language and practice distinguish between those actions an actor doesn't like and those he knows to be wrong. Likes and dislikes, tastes and distastes, are individual preferences not to be forced on others. Moral requirements, on the other hand, are taken to be "what everyone would see," or at least they are so treated. They are objective phenomena, things that are taken to be (following Berger & Luckmann, 1967) real, shared, and independent of our wants, inclinations, and purposes at hand. They cannot be wished away or altered by an act of will. They are known rather than just felt or experienced, i.e., potentially they can be perceived by any other member of the community. Although two individuals may at any given moment have a different perception of a reality they both assume to be objective, they will treat this disagreement as due to differences in their perspective, not differences in reality (see chs. 10 & 11; Schutz, 1973). Sherif (1958) has illustrated the consequences of actors treating a phenomenon, although not a moral one, as an object to be known rather than as a mere element of subjectivity. He asked people to give their judgment about the extent of motion of a point of light in a thoroughly darkened room. He found that these individual judgments converged, even though the source did not move and the motion was an illusion. That this convergence resulted from actors treating the phenomenon as objective and from the fact that they knew that neither they nor their fellow subjects happened to have a certifiably correct answer (they knew that they were estimating not measuring) is nicely illustrated by Alexander et al. (1970). They informed subjects that the apparent motion was an illusion and found no convergence.

We would argue that morally reproaching another places one in a position parallel to that of the subjects in Sherif's study. In that study subjects treated the extent of motion of the light as a problem for which a correct answer could be found: as an objective problem. Similarly, in reproaching another, people assume that such action can be done correctly or incorrectly as judged against some objective standard for the proper application of moral principles. It is just that actors naively treat moral standards as "things" in the world that can be known in much the same sense as the extent of motion of a light can be known, which allows for the possibility of distinguishing between personal preference and correct judgment (see Berger & Luckmann, 1967, for a treatment of morality as "real"). Just as in the Sherif experiment, where subjects could only reach agreement in the process of their judging the extent of motion, in everyday life the correctness of people's application of moral principles to wrongdoers is confirmed by their offering judgments focused on particular others. Paradoxically, in making a moral reproach one must first act as if the other's behavior were objectively a violation; yet the proof of the correctness of the particular application of the norm is social consensus, which can occur only *after* the moral charge has been made. Latanè and Darley make a similar argument with regard to emergencies. They argue that actors will only treat a situation as an emergency if others in their presence do so also—by reacting to it as an emergency. Since an emergency is fully defined as such only *after* it has been treated as one by at least one other person, they find that similar inhibitions about intervention in emergencies arise.

Inhibition and Doubt: When Objectivity Fails

That actors treat judgments of the moral character of an act as objective makes it possible to *doubt* that the assessment they have reached is correct. This doubt, we have argued, can lead to the inhibition of the expression of one's position. So far we have shown how this doubt is possible in novel circumstances where a settled judgment has not been reached. But doubt about the correctness of what should be an obvious, settled judgment about the objective world can also arise. And doubt in such circumstances can be more powerful and paralyzing than doubt about what one knows to be unclear. A series of experiments by Asch (1952), although not about a moral matter, clearly shows the paralyzing, emotionally intense reaction that can result from finding oneself in disagreement about "that about which there can be no dispute."

Subjects were asked to select one of three lines that was the same length as a standard line. The judgment was deliberately constructed to be as easy as possible (when tested alone subjects were correct over 90 percent of the time). In the experimental condition confederates gave a patently incorrect response before the naive subject had an opportunity to express his judgment. When confronted with a group of confederates giving an identical incorrect answer, approximately three-quarters of the subjects gave the same incorrect answer. What is even more important for our analysis is that all subjects, including those who remained independent of the confederates' influence, exhibited anxiety, doubt, and confusion. This powerful emotion develops about a judgment the content of which is trivial—the length of a line—showing that the emotion is not generated by the intrinsic gravity of the task, but by finding one's perceptions in conflict with what seems to be objective, i.e., "what everyone else seems to see." The very obviousness of the correct response contributed to the doubt and confusion the subjects felt. The correct response was obvious in a double sense: not only was it obvious in that subjects experienced little difficulty in selecting the correct option when left alone, but it was also obvious in that they expected there to be no disagreement about the correct answer.

Asch produced doubt by having confederates give patently wrong judgments. How can this sort of doubt infect judgments about an obviously immoral act? Unless many confederates have set upon him, can a person in ordinary circumstances be thrown into such ontological doubt? Yes, in a very simple way: he need only be in the presence of someone who brazenly violates that which "everyone knows" ought not to be done. (Garfinkel's studies, 1964, of the background expectancies of everyday life show, in a similar way, that calling into question "what everyone knows" throws interactants into doubt and confusion.) An actor faced with a blatant violation of what hitherto appeared to be a shared, objective, moral norm by someone who ought equally well to know it, can similarly be placed in doubt and confusion, and hence be inhibited from reproaching him. Of course, the more people who violate the norm, especially if they appear to be independent of one another, the more powerful the effect.

Not every disagreement about an objective standard forces people to doubt the correctness of their judgments; if this were so, it would never be possible to morally reproach another. It is not disagreement per se but the characteristics of both the person disagreeing and the disagreement that produce the doubt and confusion which infects those faced with a challenge to their view of the objective social world. We understand that some people, for example, are blind and hence do not respond to light as we do. We have no doubt about the objective superiority of our visual perception to theirs. Similarly, we know that there are people with flawed moral perceptions, "evil" people, who may differ with us about a moral point; their moral perceptions are to be discounted. (If only they could be compelled to carry a yellow cane.) Thus, it is disagreement only with those who "ought to know better" which causes doubt.

Children with their undeveloped equipment for perceiving the social world are known not to "know better," are easily identified, and are hence not taken seriously as moral witnesses. And they are fair game for the reproach of any passing adult. Sometimes in adults moral blindness is a temporary state; those under the influence of drugs are assumed to perceive both the physical and moral world in a distorted way, and thus their opinions are discounted. The insane are assumed to perceive the world either more or less clearly than other people do (depending on the attitude of one's culture) and correspondingly are treated as either moral arbiters or fools. Strangers to the local scene, recently emerged from the cave, are temporarily blinded to obvious truths; their doubts are to be resolved, not copied.

It is even possible to violate a moral norm while participating in its maintenance. As may have become clear to recent American political figures, the very act of concealing a transgression insures that, if discovered, it will be unreservedly condemned, since it is thus made clear that even the wrongdoer knew it was wrong to do. The likelihood that someone will condemn another, then, depends not only on the degree to which unambiguous moral standards have emerged before the offense, but also on whether the qualities of both the transgressor and the transgression cast doubt on, or substantiate, those standards.

CONSEQUENCES OF NOT MAKING A MORAL REPROACH: MORAL DRIFT

Now that we have examined some sources of inhibition in making a moral reproach, and attempted to show how they arise from defects in certain relationships, we shall turn to a consideration of the *effects* of making or failing to make a moral reproach. One possible effect of making a reproach is that it may deter the wrongdoer from continuing or repeating his transgression. The focus of our discussion will *not* be on this direct effect, but will be instead on its less obvious consequences: for the person making the reproach and for observers of the reproach. In making a moral reproach an individual's subjective, personal, inarticulate, and vague moral impressions become externalized for himself and others, and thus become a part of the social process. It is an important first step in the crystallization of the consensual wrongness of a particular act in a particular context. The previously discussed Sherif experiment is a model of how group norms concerning objective reality emerge. This model, however, fails to consider when people in everyday life will proffer their moral positions. In the experiment subjects gave their impressions of how far the spot of light moved in response to questions from the experimenter; hence the problem of whether it was appropriate to offer an opinion did not arise. In everyday life there is rarely an experimenter present to solicit moral positions; hence the possibility exists that norms will not emerge via the process Sherif suggests. If the making of a reproach clarifies and concretizes moral precepts, the failure to do so allows them to remain unclear both for others and for oneself.

Because the Sherif model does not consider the prior problem of the conditions under which people will take a moral stand, it may mislead us into assuming that actors' individual judgments will converge and norms inevitably emerge. If one makes this assumption, and finds groups of people doing something patently evil, one is lead to believe that either the group members are intentionally disregarding the moral aspect of their action or they have reached a consensus that the action we see as evil *is* appropriate. Matza (1968) discusses a case in which neither of these views is accurate. His subjects were members of delinquent gangs. In analyzing their antisocial behavior, he stresses that the individual members of the gangs actually lacked a firm commitment to their deviant behavior. He reports that each of the boys in the gang was privately disturbed by his own behavior, but each was unwilling to express his reservations publicly. Each appeared to the others, therefore, to be fully committed to the group's delinquency. Although gang members appear to disdain conventional morality, this disdain may be a facade; a facade, however, that is strong enough to produce destructiveness, which no individual member fully intends.

Traditional moral categories treat misbehavior as being either a product of ignorance, i.e., "he didn't know any better," or as sin, a transgression occurring in the pursuit of some typically understood satisfaction; i.e., lust, greed, gluttony, or pride are readily understood since their goals are assumed to be satisfying. (See ch. 2 for an analysis of sin as a category of social psychological analysis.) The misbehavior that Matza discusses does not fit either category since the gang members gave evidence of recognizing the incorrectness of their ways, and their vandalism led to no obvious satisfaction. Of course, one might hold that a less-obvious satisfaction was involved, remaining a member of the group, and thus assimilate this case into the second category. The difficulty with this is it implies that members participate in the group's wrongdoing because they realize that if they were to take a moral stand they would be ridiculed or rejected. We hold that, at least in some cases, if individuals were to realize that this were the only cost and that their private reservations were reflections of the objective immorality of the delinquent actions, they would be willing to incur the cost of leaving the group.

Let us bring our analysis to bear on an instance in which immoral behavior not only occurred, but escalated: Zimbardo's (1973) study of prison dynamics. Subjects in this study were arbitrarily assigned the roles of guards and prisoners. They were all college students of the same age, social class, race, and sex who, on the basis of psychological tests, had shown themselves to be well adjusted. The study was conducted in a realistic model of a prison. According to Zimbardo, subjects quickly lost their sense of themselves as "actors" and became their roles; to their shock, the relationship between prisoners and guards became emotionally charged, antagonistic, and brutal. Because the study so well reflected offensive aspects of prison life and produced extreme emotional upset, the simulation, which was to go on for two weeks, had to be ended after only six days. Zimbardo reports that many of his mock guards were "good" guards who did not themselves brutalize prisoners. Their attempts to treat prisoners well reflects a moral sensitivity; yet none of them ever reproached one of his associates for the behavior he found reprehensible. Notice that here, as well as in Matza's example of delinquent groups, moral drift occurred, even though most of the individuals did not want this. On our account this escalation occurred because none of the good guards ever expressed his moral sensitivity publicly—about some concrete behavior.

Our analysis suggests that they did not reproach their evil colleagues for two reasons: (1) no guard had authority over other guards—nor did any have standing in a direct, fiduciary, or other indirect sense with regard to the harm done to the prisoners, and (2) the situation of a guard makes it difficult to distinguish wanton brutality from legitimate control. Thus the paradox: it is precisely the observing of a guard reproaching another or otherwise articulating the moral norm, which would have made it possible for other guards to reproach another.

We believe that had such a condemnation occurred, moral norms would have crystallized around the condemnation.[8] The knowledge that a moral consensus proscribes certain actions can be expected to inhibit at least some actors from violations of those norms. At the very least, the failure to condemn allows those who ignore simple moral requirements to do so more easily.

8. Although an actor delivering a moral reproach might crystallize a norm, this crystallization has its costs. Reproaching another without obvious standing or being unable to make the objectivity of the offense fully patent may be very embarrassing—cause one to look like a fool—even if one is acting on the most virtuous of motives and is successful in stopping the offense (see Sabini, 1976). Morally reproaching one's group, although it may prevent "moral drift," may make a person look like a prig, a whimp, or a do-gooder.

Arendt writes, "As Eichmann told it, the most potent factor in the soothing of his own conscience was the simple fact that he could see no one, no one at all, who actually was against the Final Solution" (1965, p. 116).

GOSSIP AND MORAL REPROACH

Our discussion of moral reproach has focused on face-to-face condemnation, which is both rare and inhibited. Another form of moral reproach, however, is common: the condemnation of another *in absentia*. Moral characterization of another behind his back, the sort of talk we might roughly identify as gossip, is an everyday constituent of social life.[9] (In chapter 5 we shall take up more about the character of gossip and show its place in the moral life as a substitute for direct reproach.)

Although people are not inhibited about gossiping in the way they are about making a direct reproach, they do face a certain danger in gossiping; for instance, they may find that the person they are gossiping about is an uninvited, unannounced party to their conversation. This discovery is likely to produce an intense, immediate unpleasantness we call embarrassment. Hence, gossip, like the making of a direct reproach, suffers from a social disability. The embarrassment occurs, in this case, at precisely the moment at which the gossip is converted into a direct reproach. This suggests the possibility that the sort of inhibition we have been discussing is related to the sort of action that is embarrassing. This intuition is supported by the fact that the inhibition we have discussed seems best under-

9. A consideration of what is or is not a popular topic of gossip is also informative. Consider that Sutcliffe and Hoberman found in 1956 that their subjects considered adultery to be a serious moral failing. We would propose that at that time adultery was also the juiciest topic of gossip among these subjects. We further propose that the attractiveness of this topic results from the combined effect of its being a violation of an important moral principle and, at the same time, an offense for which only the trespassed partner has either direct or indirect standing; outsiders certainly have no standing in the sexual behavior of consenting adults. Gossip seems to allow condemnations that cannot be done directly. Any violation of a community's important principles can become a hot topic of gossip; one can imagine that the news that a famous scientist has altered her data would become a topic quite as popular in scientific circles as the news that she was enjoying the favors of her secretary.

The relationship between appropriate topics of gossip and the values of a community is highlighted by the difficulty that newcomers have in determining what the appropriate topics of gossip are. In a community that licenses nonexclusive sexual behavior one may find that the news that someone is sleeping with someone else will be greeted with a "so what" rather than the heightening of interest associated with good gossip.

stood by considering it in relation to the immediate structure of interaction, i.e., the relationships that actors have to one another and the relation of their actions to external, objective standards. This is exactly the sort of analysis we believe will be most likely to make embarrassment sensible.

SUMMARY

In this paper we have argued that the determinants of the inhibition of moral reproach—lack of direct or indirect standing and the inability to make the objectivity of the offense patent—determine the nonrational failure of moral action. In addition, we argued that this inhibition is a cause of "moral drift," the slippage of group anchoring for individual moral judgments, which creates the 'need' for an indirect form of moral reproach. As we shall see, gossip tenuously inhabits this niche: reinforcing moral boundaries, preventing moral drift, and establishing affective ties.

CHAPTER FOUR

On Destroying the Innocent with a Clear Conscience: A Sociopsychology of the Holocaust

In Paris on November 7, 1938, Herschel Grynszpan, a seventeen-year-old Polish Jew, shot and killed Ernst von Rath, third secretary of the German Embassy. In Germany the response was *Kristallnacht*.

During the days of *Kristallnacht*, synagogues were razed, shop windows shattered, thousands of Jewish businesses destroyed; tens of thousands of Jews were attacked, tortured, and humiliated. Nearly one hundred Jews were killed. As an outpouring of hatred, vicious anti-Semitism, and unrestrained sadism, *Kristallnacht* appears to display the essence of the Holocaust. To develop an analysis centering on *Kristallnacht* we would have to explore such traditional social psychological issues as the psychology of the mob (see Milgram & Toch, 1969), techniques of propaganda (see McGuire, W. J., 1969), and the character structure of the anti-Semite and fascist (see Adorno et al., 1950).

But *Kristallnacht* cannot be our focus: A pogrom, an instrument of terror, is typical of the long-standing tradition of European anti-Semitism, not the new Nazi order, not the systematic extermination of European Jewry. Mob violence is a primitive, ineffective technique of extermination. It *is* an effective method of terrorizing a population, keeping people in their place, perhaps even of forcing some to abandon their religious or political convictions. But these were never Hitler's aims with regard to the Jews; he meant to destroy them.

Consider the numbers. The German state annihilated approximately six million Jews. At the rate of one hundred per day this would have required nearly two hundred years. Mob violence rests on the wrong psychological basis, on violent emotion. People can be manipulated into fury, but fury cannot be maintained for two hundred years. Emotions have a natural time course; lust, even blood lust, is eventually sated. Further, emotions are fickle, can be turned. A lynch mob is unreliable; it can sometimes be moved to sympathy, say, by a child's suffering. To eradicate a "race" it is essential to kill the children.

Comprehensive, exhaustive murder required the replacement of the mob with a bureaucracy, the replacement of shared rage with obedience to authority. The requisite bureaucracy would be effective whether staffed by extreme or tepid anti-Semites, considerably broadening the pool of recruits; it would govern the actions of its members not by arousing passions, but by organizing routines; it would make only distinctions it was designed to make, not those its members might be moved to make, say, between children and adults, scholar and thief, innocent and guilty; it would be responsive to the will of the ultimate authority through a hierarchy of responsibility—whatever that will might be. It was this bureaucratization of evil, the institutionalization of murder, that marked the Third Reich. Our focus will be, then, on the social psychology of individual action within the context of hierarchical institutions. Hence, with Eichmann the bureaucrat and not *Kristallnacht*, the answer to the question "how could it have happened?" will be sought.

As Arendt (1965) tells it, Eichmann was a disappointment. Those who expected some passionate, deep-seated evil in the character of an organizer of the German death machine were frustrated, not because Eichmann revealed some nobility of character incompatible with a passion to destroy, but because the utter shallowness of the man was inconsistent with any deep principle. It is not the angry rioter we must understand, but Eichmann, the colorless bureaucrat, replicated two million times in those who assembled the trains, dispatched the supplies, manufactured the poison gas, filed the paper work, sent out the death notices, guarded the prisoners, pointed left and right, supervised the loading-unloading of the vans, disposed of the ashes, and performed the countless other tasks that constituted the Holocaust. An excerpt from the Auschwitz diary of S.S. Professor Dr. Hans Hermann Kremer (as reproduced in Cohen, 1953, p. 238) illustrates the quality of murder as bureaucratized in the Third Reich—its place in the life of its operatives, how distant this murder is from passionate impulse, and the distance between the rioter and functionary.

> *September 6, 1942.* Today, Sunday, excellent lunch: tomato soup, half a hen with potatoes and red cabbage (20g. fat), sweets and marvelous vanilla ice . . . in the evening at 8.00 hours outside for a Sonderaktion.[1]
>
> *September 9, 1942.* This morning I got the most pleasant news from my lawyer, Prof. Dr. Hallermann in Münster, that I got divorced from my wife on the first of this month (Note: I see colors again, a black curtain is drawn back from my life!). Later on, present as doctor at a corporal punishment of eight prisoners and an execution by shooting with small-calibre rifles. Got soap flakes and two pieces of soap. . . . In the evening present at a Sonderaktion, fourth time.

OBEDIENCE TO AUTHORITY

How could a *Sonderaktion* and soap flakes possibly be mentioned in the same breath? How could someone participate in mass murder without showing some emotion—distress, anger, or even glee? Our account, then, attempts to explain not mass murder, but mass murder of this special sort. Brutality, torture, rage, and even sadism in its restricted sexual sense were not missing from the Holocaust, but they were not its special features. They were neither necessary nor sufficient: what was needed was a machine not a beast. What needs explanation is not so much how the sadist could murder, but how murder could come to have the same importance as soap flakes.

Eichmann has offered an account of this kind of murder; he has explained that he (and by extension, the two million others) were merely doing their jobs (see Hilberg, 1961). This was a bizarre attempt to *justify* genocide, but could it be part of a correct *explanation?* Is it possible for someone not a sadist or a psy-

1. "The most spectacular of the mass atrocities were called Sonderaktionen [special actions]. One of these, which was practiced particularly in Auschwitz, was the burning of live prisoners, especially children, in pits measuring 20 by 40 to 50 meters, on piles of gasoline-soaked wood." (Alexander, 1949, writing about Sonderaktion reported in Cohen, 1953.)

chopath to kill innocent individuals just because he was ordered to do so? Milgram (1974) in a brilliant series of social psychological experiments addressed this question.

The method of his study, already mentioned in chapter 3, will be reviewed here in detail. In the experiment, the subject is faced with a dramatic choice, one apparently involving extreme pain and perhaps injury to another human being. When he arrives at the laboratory, the experimenter tells him and another subject, a pleasant, avuncular, middle-aged gentleman—actually an actor—that the study concerns the effects of punishment on learning. After a rigged drawing, the lucky subject wins the role of teacher and the experimenter's confederate becomes the "learner." The teacher and learner are taken to an adjacent room, then the learner is strapped into a chair and electrodes are attached to his arms, supposedly to prevent excessive movement. The effect is that it appears impossible to escape. While strapped in the chair the "learner" diffidently mentions that he has a heart condition. The experimenter replies that while the shocks may be painful, they cause no permanent tissue damage. The teacher is instructed to read to the learner a list of word pairs, to test him on the list, and to administer punishment, an electric shock, whenever the learner errs. The teacher is given a sample shock of 45 volts (the only real shock ever administered). The experimenter instructs the teacher to increase the intensity of the shock one step on the shock generator for each error. The generator has thirty switches labeled from 15 to 450 volts (ten times the sample shock). Beneath these voltage readings are labels ranging from SLIGHT SHOCK to DANGER: SEVERE SHOCK, and finally XX.

The experiment starts routinely. By the fifth shock level, however, the confederate grunts in annoyance, and by the eighth shock level he shouts that the shocks are becoming painful. By the tenth level, 150 volts, he cries out, "Experimenter, get me out of here! I won't be in the experiment any more! I refuse to go on!" This response makes plain the intensity of the pain and underscores the learner's *right* to be released. By 270 volts the learner's response becomes an agonized scream, and at 300 volts the learner refuses to answer further. From 300 volts to 330 volts he shrieks in pain at each shock and gives no answer (the teacher is told to treat the failure to answer as an erroneous answer and to continue to shock). From 330 volts on the learner is not heard from, and the teacher has no way to know whether the learner is still conscious or, for that matter, alive (the teacher also knows that the experimenter cannot tell about the condition of the victim since the experimenter is in the same room as the teacher).

Typically the teacher attempts to break off the experiment many times during the session. When he tries to do so, the experimenter instructs him to continue. If he refuses, the experimenter insists, finally telling him, "You must continue. You have no other choice." If the subject still refuses the experimenter ends the experiment.

The situation is realistic and tension-provoking. An observer has related:

> I observed a mature and initially poised businessman enter the laboratory smiling and confident. Within 20 minutes he was reduced to a twitching, stuttering wreck, who was rapidly approaching a point of nervous collapse. He constantly pulled on his earlobe, and twisted his hands. At one point he pushed his fist into his forehead and muttered: "Oh God, let's stop it." And yet he continued to respond to every word of the experimenter, and obeyed to the end.
>
> (MILGRAM, 1963b, p. 377)

We would expect that at most only a small minority of the subjects, a cross-section of New Haven residents, would continue to shock beyond the point where the victim screamed in pain and demanded to be released. We certainly would expect that very, very few people would continue to the point of 450 volts. Indeed, Milgram asked a sample of undergraduates, a sample of psychiatrists, and a sample of adults of various occupations to predict whether they would obey the orders of the experimenter. Each of the 110 people claimed that he would disobey at some point. Milgram, aware that people would be unwilling to admit that they themselves would obey such an unreasonable and unconscionable order, asked another sample of middle-class adults to predict how far *other people* would go in such a procedure. The average prediction was that perhaps one person in a thousand would continue to the end. This prediction was wrong. In fact 65 percent (26/40) of the subjects obeyed to the end.

Of course Milgram's subjects were not Eichmann. Typically they protested, complained, and frequently showed signs of tension while carrying out their task. Arendt's report of Eichmann's prison interviews in Jerusalem shows no corresponding difficulty on Eichmann's part in carrying out his orders—the Final Solution. But this difference must not obscure the central point: subjects in the experiment *did* continue to shock even though the person they were shocking demanded to be released and withdrew his consent, even after the person they were shocking had ceased responding and might have been unconscious or even dead. Subjects in the experiment acted in ways we would not expect people of no obvious deficit of conscience to act.

In two other variants of the experiment there was a reduction in the subject's protests and emotional displays and an increase in obedience. In one variation the subject himself was not ordered to pull the switch delivering the shock, rather he performed a different, also essential task, while another person (in reality a confederate) pulled the switch. In this case roughly 90 percent (37/40) of the subjects continued to perform the subsidiary task through 450 volts. The vast majority of the millions implicated in the Holocaust were involved in analogous, subsidiary but essential functions. Further, they performed them at a distance from the actual gassings, burnings, and shootings. Distance from the victim, Milgram found, also has a profound effect on the level of obedience and on the stress experienced in obeying—from 20 percent obedience and great stress in a condition in which the subject had to physically press the victim's hand to the shock plate, to virtually complete obedience and little stress in a condition in which the subject's information about the victim's suffering was dependent almost entirely on the verbal designations on the shock machine.

The central problem remains: how could the subjects in the Milgram experiments bring themselves to continue shocking the victim? This problem is exacerbated, not relieved, by the fact that some experienced great tension. If they were that upset by what they were doing, why didn't they stop?

Subjects in the Milgram experiment sometimes turned to the experimenter and asked who was responsible for (their) shocking the learner. The experimenter replied that *he* accepted full responsibility; subjects seemed to accept this and continued shocking. Yet how *could* the experimenter take upon himself their responsibility? Responsibility is not property that can be borrowed, shared, loaned, or repossessed. Responsibility is related to the *proper* allocation of moral praise and blame. Assessing a person's responsibility involves considerations of: what he intended to do, what he realized or should have realized, what he could or could not have done, as well as considerations relating to the gravity of the rule transgressed and the priority of competing claims. How could the experimenter's offer to assume responsibility alter any of these considerations? Hence, how could his offer alter whether the subjects were or were not responsible? We do not doubt that the subjects' *feeling* of responsibility did affect how they acted; however, pointing to this feeling does not in itself explain the behavior.

Consider this trivial but common example. Imagine that a person bends down and loosens his shoe because he feels that there is a rock in it, and he, in fact, discovers a rock. In this case his feeling about a rock fully explains his loosening his shoe. But what if when he bends down he finds no rock? Although he bent down to untie his shoe because he *felt* that there was a rock in it, his behavior is not fully explained—the question of why he felt that there was a rock in his shoe when there wasn't is left hanging. When we explain someone's behavior by pointing out that he felt that *X* was the case, we use a shorthand which takes for granted that the source of the person's *feeling* "*X* is the case" is the *fact* that *X* is the case. When the feelings and facts do not match, saying that a person did what he did because of the way he felt gives a promissory note to explain why the person felt what he felt even though it was not the case. When this promissory note is in default, i.e., when the feeling is not explained, reference to feeling in explaining behavior is not helpful.

As for the behavior of Milgram's subjects, while it is correct to point out that they continued to obey because they (incorrectly) *felt* that they were not responsible, we must explain how they could feel not responsible when they in fact were.[2] This

2. The support that the "rock-in-the-shoe" example lends to our claims about the feelings and the facts of responsibility rests on the assumption that the statements that "John has a rock in his shoe" and "John is responsible for Bill's death" both are statements about

need is acute since we, hearing of the experiment, see the responsibility clearly (as did jurists considering the crimes of members of the S.S.). Responsibility is not something that an experimenter or even a Führer can give or take away. How then could these subjects be guilty of this misinterpretation? Understanding how responsibility works in a bureaucracy provides a clue.

Within an organization a section head, for example, is responsible for planning a job, assigning responsibilities among his workers, and even relieving some workers of responsibilities. A subordinate is only responsible for carrying out the plan. If the subordinate executes the plan according to specifications, then it is not his fault if the larger project fails because the plan was misconceived. His boss was responsible for the plan; the subordinate was responsible for only part of the execution. We could say that responsibility has been partitioned, taken over, or shared. However, if the organization were indicted, it would be queer indeed for the subordinate to offer to the judge (as Eichmann did and Milgram's subjects might have, had it come to that), the excuse that he was not responsible, that his boss had relieved him of responsibility, and further, that he had not constructed the plan but had merely carried it out. To offer such an excuse would be to ludicrously confuse the issues of technical and moral (or legal) responsibility.

The question of *technical* responsibility, the question of who is accountable for which part of a larger plan, arises within an institution and is decided by that institution. Questions of *moral* responsibility *cannot* be confined within institutions and

---

objective facts not subjective reactions. Of course, statements about rocks and statements about responsibility are different in many ways, but one of these ways is *not* that the former is objective and the latter subjective. We mean by this claim that commonsense actors share, and assume that they share, criteria, which they can call upon to tell whether a given person is or is not responsible for his actions. (Of course they also have and know they have a shared notion of rocks in shoes—that is why it is also objective.) We are not claiming that there are not difficult cases or even ambiguous cases for the proper application of the notion of responsibility, and we hasten to affirm that "responsibility" is rather more difficult to apply than claims about rocks in shoes. In addition, we do not claim (nor do we deny) that the concept of responsibility is a cross-cultural universal or invariant. We do hold, however, that *within a culture* it is sensible to talk of responsibility because there are shared criteria for when it is correct to say of a person that he is responsible. Our argument, although contrary to the subjectivist, individualistic biases of American psychology, is rooted in both the interpretive sociology of Berger and Luckmann and the analytic philosophy of Wittgenstein (1958) and Austin (1970b). We cannot further develop this argument here but refer the reader to Kovesi's (1967) illuminating discussion (see also chs. 10 & 11).

resist resolution by institutional superiors. Obedient subjects in the Milgram experiment who felt reassured by the experimenter's acceptance of responsibility apparently succumbed to a confusion between these two sorts of responsibility. The obedient Eichmann, at least in some of his moods, refused to the death to concede that such a distinction between technical and moral responsibility *can* be drawn. So long as our institutions are legitimate and act within the limits of our shared morality, we are, as moral actors, free to ignore the broader question of moral responsibility—as a matter of convenience. Ordinarily, assuming the benevolence of the organizations of which we are a part, we do not trouble ourselves with questions of moral responsibility for the routine doing of our job. Eichmann and Milgram's subjects lost the right to be unconcerned with the moral implications of their actions just when the German state and the experimenter's demands became immoral. Milgram's obedient subjects and Hitler's murderers ought to have seen that these institutions were no longer legitimate, could no longer claim their loyalty, and could no longer settle for them the question of moral responsibility. Milgram's subjects, insofar as they accepted the experimenter's explicit or implicit claim to accept responsibility, failed to see what is, from a distance, so obvious.

MORALITY AND THE LEGITIMACY OF AUTHORITY

One might suppose that the failure of Eichmann and the millions like him to perceive the patent immorality of the German state bureaucracy must be different in quality from the failure of Milgram's subjects to see what had become of the experiment. After all, the magnitude of the failure in the Eichmann case is so much greater, the responsibility so much greater, that it would seem that we need different principles to explain it. We want to assume that the German bureaucrats acted out of a deep anti-Semitism, or, perhaps, financial self-interest, or perhaps they just sought to avoid the Russian front. We want to see the German failure as motivated, in a way that the moral failure of Milgram's subjects seems not to be. Further variants of the Milgram experiment address the question of whether we need to assume such motivation.

In one version, the experiment was repeated ostensibly not for the benefit of pure science under the auspices of august Yale, but rather subjects were told it was for a firm of private industrial consultants located in a somewhat run-down commercial building in an office which barely managed to appear respectable. Yet in this setting, nineteen out of forty subjects obeyed fully. Although this is fewer than the twenty-six out of forty at Yale, it is not significantly so. This rather shabby setting in an institution of vague if not questionable aims was not only sufficient to induce subjects to start the experiment, but to keep them going to the end.

A second variant further explores the issue of legitimacy. Subjects in the original condition sometimes reported that the reason that they continued was that the experiment was fair—the learner *had* volunteered to be in the experiment. As an explanation this implies that the subjects would not have obeyed if the experiment had not been fair, at least in this restricted sense. This possible explanation was examined in a condition in which the learner, in the presence of the subject and experimenter, agreed to participate only if the experimenter would stop the experiment if and when he, the learner, wanted it stopped. The experimenter agreed. As in the other conditions, the learner demanded that the experiment be stopped at 150 volts. Sixteen out of forty subjects continued to the end, even though this was in clear violation of the prior arrangement. If anything ought to have undermined the legitimacy of the enterprise, this ought to have done so. It did not. These experiments do not explain *why* institutions keep such a strong presumption of legitimacy, why it is so difficult for people to extract themselves on moral grounds, but it does illustrate that people can treat corrupted institutions as legitimate in cases in which it would not seem possible to do so—even though they have *no* ulterior motive. For people to perceive the Nazi government as legitimate even while it was slaughtering millions, it was not necessary to personally profit by, for example, taking over confiscated Jewish businesses.

Participating in a "legitimate" enterprise allowed subjects and bureaucrats to ignore the immoral implications of their actions in two ways. First, the issue of *moral* responsibility for the goals of the organization just does not come up in legitimate institutions; to do their jobs, people do not have to think about such matters. Second, even if subjects or bureaucrats *had* addressed the question of moral responsibility, bureaucratic structure would have helped them answer the question incorrectly; the relation between an individual's action and the rules and commands of an organization obscures personal responsibility.

RESPONSIBILITY AND INTENT

Typically there is a close relation between responsibility and intent—we are responsible for what we intend to do, what we are *trying* to do. If we accidentally cause something that was not our intent, then we have less or no responsibility. For example, if we accidentally step on someone's toy poodle, we may be guilty of clumsiness but not cruelty to animals since we do not intend to hurt the dog. Lack of intent is a quite common ingredient of excuses in everyday life. An act we do not intend is usually a mistake, an error, an inadvertent consequence, and for these reasons our responsibility for it is usually diminished. In fact, the link between responsibility and intent is even tighter: if we were asked what we are doing at a given moment, we would be likely to reply by mentioning the goal of our action, what we are intending. We would not be likely to point out the constituents or consequences aside from our goal or goals. For example, going to the store to get a loaf of bread is also: putting on our coat, walking down the street, wearing down our shoes, not to mention contributing to the profits of the grocery store owner, providing employment for his clerks, using up the earth's scarce resources, and so forth. However, of all of these, "going for a loaf of bread," our goal, is the only one we are likely to see ourselves as "really" doing. The typical Milgram subject was only trying to be a good subject, and, perhaps, contribute to science; one imagines the German bureaucrat, similarly, as trying only to do his job well, follow the rules, perhaps support his family. In both cases, the evil they did was not intended; it was, perhaps, easy to "feel" that the evil was not their doing, to feel that it had an accidental quality. Moreover, in both cases not only was destroying others not something they were trying to do, not intended, but, as in the case of the poodle who was accidentally stepped on, it was something they *would never* try to do. Carrying out the evil may even have been something they disliked doing while they did it. For all these reasons, it was easy for Milgram's subjects, and at least some bureaucrats, to feel so innocent, so lacking in responsibility for the evil they performed. But feelings aside, they were responsible—not because their protestations of innocent intent were necessarily insincere, but because in *these* cases the question of intent is irrelevant to the question of responsibility. No matter how much the evil that was a part, say, of dispatching the trains, when those trains went from Warsaw to Auschwitz, *felt* accidental, it was not. Eichmann knew what his actions caused. Eichmann may well have been personally indifferent to whether the Jews were annihilated, or sent to Madagascar, or, for that matter, allowed to fulfill the Zionist dream, and in that sense he didn't intend the Holocaust. But he was still responsible because people *are* responsible for all that they *cause* so long as they can see that they cause it and can do otherwise. We may *feel* responsible only for what we intend; we *are* responsible for all that we do. And we know it.

Because our *feelings* of responsibility are grounded in our intentions, and bureaucracies arrange that everyone need only intend to follow the rules, the result is that bureaucracies have a genius for organizing evil. The bureaucrat knows what the rules of the bureaucracy dictate; if he should find some action contrary to his inclinations, he can still act with a clear conscience since he knows the action is contrary to his inclinations and can be divorced from his intentions. Even if he actually does want to bring about the very thing the bureaucracy tells him to do and he suspects that it is wrong, he can still correctly maintain that even though he wanted to do it, he would have refrained in light of its questionable moral status were it not for the fact that he was ordered to do it. Of course this is germane to the question of *intent* but irrelevant to the issue of *responsibility.* Insofar as these concepts are muddled, morality is lost from the bureaucracy as a whole; each and everyone is allowed to *feel* free of responsibility except, perhaps, the person who put it all together.

An important difference between Eichmann and Milgram's subjects is that Eichmann, unlike the obedient subjects who gave every evidence of detesting their role and resisting it, did not obey orders passively, but actively strove to carry them out efficiently, intelligently, creatively, and most important, visibly—after all, his advancement depended on it. And trying to advance was what Eichmann, at least as Arendt tells it, saw himself as doing. Orders from above provided the ready excuse for him to kill millions as his particular pathway to self-advancement. This was why Eichmann was able to complain to his Jewish interrogator of the injustice of his being passed over in his difficult struggle to improve his position. The covering excuse of superior orders allows the individual to pursue personal goals—wealth, status, power—as well as more altruistic goals—providing for his family.

Doing one's duty is an important virtue, something that might justify actions one wouldn't ordinarily do. A professor might fail a student, for example, keeping her out of medical school, thereby inflicting real pain—something ordinarily proscribed—out of a duty to grade fairly; yet we find the professor virtuous, not sadistic. But just as a lack of evil intent does not necessarily absolve one of responsibility, neither does a virtuous intent. If in pursuit of the virtue of punctuality we were to jostle an elderly cripple to the ground or refuse to yield the right of way to an ambulance, then we could not offer as an excuse that punctuality was a virtue. Nor can we excuse Eichmann his genocide because he so well exemplified the virtue of adherence to duty.

Conscience and Desire

How *could* Eichmann find that the dictates of his job had a moral claim that could compete with the injunction not to commit genocide? The bizarre moral climate of Nazi Germany, with its constant propaganda about the "International Jewish Conspiracy directed against the German Volk and Western civilization," was undoubtedly one powerful determinant that led Eichmann to be able to see killing, even of the innocent, as the call of duty, and thus as a justification for genocide. Oddly enough, killing even *felt* like duty, like virtue.

When the orders of "legitimate" authority are themselves immoral, then the ordinary connections among the proper course of action, moral principles, temptation, and desire contribute to the *subversion* of our perception of right and wrong. To see why, let us return to the details of the Milgram experiment.

Why do we expect people not to continue in the Milgram experiment; why did the people Milgram asked predict that subjects would stop? The simple answer is that we expect people to see that it was right to stop, that their conscience wouldn't let them go on. Let us examine more closely the way we think about conscience and its relation to action.

We ordinarily conceive of action, at least potentially evil action, as having its source in desire. The commonsense view of the drama of morality is that it involves the conflict of desire with duty. We think of the child tempted to play with a forbidden toy or the adult tempted by self-interest to cheat on taxes; these desires are opposed by the dictates of their conscience. Conscience finds its place in opposition to desire, egoism, internal drives. Morality, "the content of conscience," is perceived by the individual, in Berger and Luckmann's (1967) terms, as an "objective" phenomenon, i.e., something beyond the individual's wants, interests, moods, and control (see chs. 10 & 11). We speak of people *knowing* what is right and wrong, understanding the moral implications of something, perceiving the moral worth of something. So in the classic conception of moral drama there is a struggle between the drives one has and the duty one knows.

But in the Milgram experiment the source of the subject's wrongdoing is *not* his desire; he correctly perceives himself as *not* wanting to do wrong, *not* wanting to hurt the victim. The demands of the experimenter *like the moral principles that ought to oppose them* are external, objective. Indeed, the experiment is constructed to make them external even to the *experimenter:* if the subject attempts to withdraw the experimenter tells him, "The experiment requires that you continue," not, "I want you to continue." Further, the relation of the experimenter's commands to the purported purpose of the experiment reinforces the view that it is the experiment and the institution of science that require this awful act, not the experimenter's will. The subject obeys, not because he wants to please the experimenter, but because he sees himself as being required by the experiment to continue. The subject is not tempted to shock the victim; if he is tempted at all, it is to stop. If the individual's conscience were to come into play to oppose his temptation, it would only have the effect of suppressing his inclination to *stop* and encourage his duty to participate. Indeed, even defiant subjects didn't attack the experimenter for his immorality, but rather, often apologized for ruining the experiment.

> And just as the law in civilized countries assumes that the voice of conscience tells everybody "Thou shalt not kill," even though man's natural desires and inclinations may at times be murderous, so the law of Hitler's land demanded that the voice of conscience tell everybody: "Thou shalt kill," although the organizers of the massacres knew full well that murder is against the normal desires and inclinations of most people. Evil in the Third Reich had lost the quality by which most people recognize it—the quality of temptation. Many Germans and many Nazis, probably an overwhelming majority of them, must have been tempted *not* to murder, *not* to rob, *not* to let their neighbors go off to their doom (for that the Jews were transported to their doom they knew, of course, even though many of them may not have known the gruesome details), and not to become accomplices in all these crimes by benefiting from them. But, God knows, they had learned how to resist temptation.
>
> (ARENDT, 1965, p. 150)

Entrapment

Moreover, Eichmann didn't decide one day that committing genocide was his calling. Rather, he found himself arranging its logistics as the culmination of his career as a specialist on Jewish affairs. The German people did not decide that their first priority was the eradication of the Jews, and for that reason elected Hitler; the genocide they committed was the outcome, perhaps inevitable, of their political choices. The German bureaucrat, say a dispatcher for the railroad, didn't decide to work on the railroad in order to move the Jews to their death; he found himself doing that among his other duties. In all of these cases a person's evil is not the consequence of a focal decision to do that evil, but rather is a result of a prior commitment. Milgram's obedient "teachers" did not decide to give the learner a lethal shock; they too reached that point through a process of escalating commitments.

Subjects enter the experiment recognizing some obligation to cooperate with the experimenter; they have, after all, agreed to participate, taken his money, and probably to some degree endorse the aims of the advancement of science. When the learner makes his first error, subjects are asked to shock him. The shock level is 15 volts. A 15-volt shock is entirely harmless, even imperceptible. There is no moral issue here. Of course the next shock is more powerful, but only slightly so. Indeed every shock is only slightly more powerful than the last. The quality of the subject's action changes from something entirely blameless to something unconscionable—by degrees. Where exactly should the subject stop? At what point is the divide between these two kinds of actions crossed? How is the subject to know? It is easy to see that there must be a line; it is not so easy to see where that line ought to be. Further, if the subject decides that giving the next shock is not permissible, then, since it is (in every case) only slightly more intense than the last one, what was the justification for administering the last shock he just gave? To deny the propriety of the step he is about to take *is* to undercut the propriety of the step he just took, and this undercuts the subject's own moral position. The subject is trapped by his gradual involvement in the experiment.

Of course, the inevitable drama of the 450-volt level is built into the structure of the experiment from the first shock. Had subjects perceived this, they might have refused to participate or set some level in advance at which they would stop; but apparently they didn't. Hitler's program of extermination similarly advanced by degrees. There was an eight-year progression from the first economic measures against the Jews to the construction of the extermination camps. Here too, however, the inevitability of the last step should have been clear from the first; Hitler had made his plans perfectly clear in *Mein Kampf* in the twenties. But still, in both the escalation in the experiment and the escalation of measures against the Jews, there seemed to be an element of contingency. The learner might not, after all, make enough errors to call for 450 volts, or the experimenter might call it off; respectable Germans believed that Hitler's "excessive" anti-Semitism was just a political ploy, that he would become more restrained once he assumed the burdens of power, that even if he wanted to he couldn't really carry out his program of annihilation. Thus it was possible for people to vote for the Nazi party, financially contribute to its flourishing, or join the government bureaucracy without intending the Final Solution, but by a process of gradual commitment become responsible for the horror in its fullness.

Hitler's own sensitivity to the problem of the necessity of gradual action was demonstrated in a 1937 speech. When the most violent anti-Semites of the Nazi party pressed him to move more forcefully against the Jews, he replied:

> Then: the final aim of our whole policy is quite clear for all of us. Always I am concerned only that I do not take any step from which I will perhaps have to retreat, and not to take any step that will harm us. I tell you that I always go to the outermost limits of risk, but never beyond. For this you need to have a nose more or less to smell out: "What can I still do?" Also in a struggle against an enemy. I do not summon an enemy with force to fight, I don't say: "Fight!" because I want to fight. Instead I say, "I will destroy you! And now, Wisdom, help me, to maneuver you into the corner that you cannot fight back, and then you get the blow right in the heart." That's it.
>
> (KOTZE & KRAUSNICK, cited in Dawidowicz, 1975, pp. 124–25)

BRUTALITY AND EMOTIONAL RESPONSE

There is a powerful objection against our analogy between the behavior of Milgram's subjects and that of the German bureaucrat. The parallel seems especially strained when we focus not on train dispatchers, file clerks, and logistics experts, but on the S.S. members in the camps themselves. Accounts of actual concentration camp life portray repeated accounts of wanton brutality on the part of the S.S. In the Milgram experiment, on the other hand, many subjects showed extreme stress while carrying out the experimenter's orders. They held the shock levers down very briefly to deliver as little shock as possible within the confines of their orders. They tried to resist the experimenter who prodded them into continuing. But the S.S. guards were even more brutal than the extermination plan required. Perhaps this shows that the commands of authority were simply an excuse, not the essence of the psychology of the Holocaust. But even if the commands of authority happened to coincide with what the S.S. wanted to do anyway, still the excuse was an important ingredient in action. As we argued above, there is a gap between wanting to do something and doing it; and by seeming to remove responsibility for action, the commands of authority help close the gap. Second, we should not automatically accept that the egregious brutality of the concentration camps followed from the *inherent* brutality of the guards without considering other possibilities.

To focus this discussion we will set the issue of brutality sharply. We begin with the position that Kogon (1950) develops in his discussion of the camps. In his account, the people who made up the S.S. were the most shiftless, rootless elements of German society. Further, the training that the guards received actively selected against any show of sympathy for the prisoners. The result of this process was that the guards were uniformly sadistic individuals, and by implication, the brutality of the prison camps was a result of sadists having the tacit approval of the camp authorities. This view traces back the brutality of the camps to individual depravity. An opposing view supported by Cohen (1953), for example, is that the nature of the task of working as a camp guard was sufficient to produce that brutality even if the guards were not, to begin with, sadists. These are not mutually exclusive possibilities with regard to the concrete, historical events of the Holocaust; it is likely that each contributed. But for the sake of this analysis, we shall focus on evidence to support the latter view, evidence that circumstances such as concentration camps can produce such effects, and any evidence at all that the people engaged in running the camps were not necessarily sadists from the start.

We begin by reviewing a detail of the Milgram experiment. As we have pointed out, although a majority of subjects obeyed the commands of the experimenter, many of them exhibited signs of emotional stress: they were uncomfortable about the pain they were causing. Even if they did not see the moral imperative that they stop, they suffered from no defect of empathy; their emotions if not their intellect and action were in the right place. Further, this emotional reaction could be controlled by moving the "teacher" either further away or closer to the victim. Moving the victim has no effect on the moral issue of the experiment, nor does it enhance the information the subject has about the victim (except, of course, to let him know that the victim has not passed out or been killed, which from the moral point of view should *increase,* not decrease, obedience). Rather, this variation seems to work by enhancing the subject's direct emotional response to the victim. Closeness, in Arendt's terms, enhances the temptation to disobey.

Is there any evidence that even an S.S. member may be bothered by "destructive emotional reactions," and that the apparatus of extermination took them into account? Consider first the *Einsatzgruppen,* which were the mobile killing squads that Eichmann sent into the East following the German army to perform the on-the-spot slaughter of Jews, gypsies, communists, homosexuals, etc. These units functioned by rounding up the Jews in an area, transporting them to a desolate spot, digging a deep ditch, and then marching the victims to the edge of the ditch, where they were shot in the neck, fell into the ditch, and then were covered over (dead or alive) by dirt. Although this procedure resembles a firing squad, it is different. A firing squad is inefficient; a concession is made to the scruples of the squad members by having several people shoot at once at the victim. This fact, along with the single blank bullet, obscures the question of who exactly killed the victim. The scale of the job of exterminating the Jews excluded the possibility of such sops to emotion; hence each squad member shot at only a single target. Steiner writes about this procedure:

> The new system, on the contrary, personalized the act. Each executioner had "his" victim. . . . Moreover, this personalization of the act was accompanied by a physical proximity, since the executioner stood less than a yard away from his victim. Of course, he did not see him from the front, but it was discovered that necks, like faces, also individualize people. This accumulation of necks—suppliant, proud, fearful, broad, frail, hairy, or tanned—rapidly became intolerable to the executioners, who could not help feeling a certain sense of guilt. Like blind faces, these necks came to haunt their dreams.
>
> (1967, p. 73)

In recognition of the emotional cost to the executioners, they were expected to work for only an hour at a time at this physically not very taxing task. Alcohol was also liberally provided to dull the senses (Musmanno, 1961). According to Steiner's account, this psychological difficulty played a role in the evolution of the concentration camp system.

The solution to this problem, this psychological limitation of even the best-trained and best-selected S.S. men, the most rabid anti-Semites, was the eventual construction of fixed gas chambers. Further, a breakthrough in the solution of this problem was made when it was decided that Jews themselves could be employed to do the loading and unloading of the chambers, thus removing the executioners from the gruesome human facts of their work. This solution posed a problem common to bureaucratic organizations—the problem of labor turnover.

Performing this task involved a certain amount of training. Further, there were certain subsidiary jobs that needed to be done and also required training, e.g., removing the gold from the mouths of the victims; collecting, sorting, and transporting the personal goods the victims brought with them; maintaining the camp constructed for the S.S. staff. To supply this labor a certain number of Jews had to be kept in the camp for a considerable period rather than quickly killed. Thus the concentration camps became places where people lived, for a time, as well as died.

This step in the evolution of the Holocaust could exacerbate the Nazi's psychological problem in that these victims became, or could become, relatively long-term residents of the camp in day-to-day contact with the guards who must eventually kill them. If it is difficult to shoot or shock a total stranger, how much more difficult it must be to do so to someone one has seen over a period of time. It was not possible to increase the physical distance between victim and executioner to lessen the problem, but it was possible to do something else perhaps psychologically more potent. How could the concentration camp guards be shielded from the facts of their treatment of these human beings they were now forced to see, smell, hear, and on occasion even touch?

Part of the answer is that for the Nazis these were not, after all, fully human beings; they were a subhuman species. Nazi propaganda, developing on centuries of anti-Semitic rhetoric, elaborated the theme that Jews were less than human. But even so, most normal individuals find it difficult to mistreat a household pet. How many of us would be comfortable torturing or killing a chimpanzee? Another part of the propaganda was that these captives were dangerous to the Nazi war effort. While stories of the danger may have been compelling to the commandos in the field, such a story pales when the potential enemies are in captivity. Ideological notions of the depravity of these groups remain abstract, compared to the physical sight, smell, and expressions of the victims themselves. The captives must somehow not only be labeled as inferior, but must be made to appear that way. This problem was not insolvable.

Goffman (1959, 1961, 1963a, 1971), in his careful analyses of total institutions, stigma, and self-presentation, calls our attention to the ways that the individual must actively present a "worthy self," and to the fact that the presentation of a worthy self exerts a direct and powerful demand for treatment of a kind. To reduce this demand, to nullify it, to subvert its operation, it is useful, if not necessary, to destroy the individual's capacity to present herself as a human being, i.e., as a self-conscious, reflective agent aware of her own humanity, dignity, moral worth, and capable of the expressivity typical of the species. While the capacity for such performance and such expression may be innate, it is still dependent on circumstances. A constant theme of both the literature on the German concentration camps and Solzhenitsyn's (1963, 1973) accounts of the Russian camps is the perpetual degradation of the inmates.

Starvation (along with reducing the economic burden of the slaves to the slave masters) destroys the body's capacity to produce the range of expressions we take as a sign of affective life. Constant hunger, like constant pain, removes the individual from the social world, fixates his attention on his own internal state, and hence dehumanizes. Further, the extremes of hunger drive the individual to resort to scavenging through garbage, turning informant, fighting with fellow inmates for a scrap of food (and in the process impeding the development of associations among prisoners necessary to organized resistance). Starvation and constant hunger are extremely effective tools of degradation. Des Pres (1976) points out that some of the prisoners recognized these sources of dehumanization in the camps and actively sought to resist it by maintaining standards of cleanliness, sharing packages from home, and preventing suicides.

Perhaps the most potent technique of degradation is to make the individual filthy, to make him stink. As Des Pres and Goffman have emphasized, in modern Western culture, at least, the requirement that one remain clean (both of contamination by mud, dirt, and other environmental sources of pollution and, perhaps more important, of one's own excrement) is a first and central demand on every child who would be a member of the society. But to do this requires not only a psychological and biological capacity, but also social circumstances that make it possible. Baths, showers, and toilets are resources made available by a culture without which it is impossible to maintain the appearance of being a self-conscious, worthy member of the social order. To withdraw these or forbid their use makes it inevitable that the individual will be unable to sustain the immediate, compelling appearance of a worthy self, and makes it easier for another to ignore the moral fact that such a spoiled appearance has no bearing on human worth.

We do not claim that all the camp officials recognized the "desirable" consequences of keeping the prisoners perpetually degraded and planned the camps with that in mind, but at least one official noticed the utility of bestiality, after the fact. In an interview with Franz Stangl, Treblinka's commandant, the issue of why the guards degraded the prisoners became explicit:

> "Why," I asked Stangl, *"if they were going to kill them anyway, what was the point of all the humiliation, why the cruelty?"*
>
> "To condition those who actually had to carry out the policies," he said. "To make it possible for them to do what they did."
>
> (SERENY, cited in Des Pres, 1976, p. 67)

Even if the conditions of the camp made it easier, would people who were not already sadists, who did not derive pleasure from torture, wantonly brutalize prisoners? First consider that in the Milgram experiments some subjects became angry at the "learner." As the experiment progressed they became angry at him for, as they saw it, making the mistakes that caused them to be subjected to such stress. Surely this is an extraordinarily immature response; but we are dealing here with matters of emotion, and it is no surprise when emotional responses are immature. But still, none of the subjects went out of his way to further harm the victim, even if the subject was somewhat angry. On the other hand, the experiment lasted only about an hour, and we do not know how the subjects would have responded were the stress more enduring.

More evidence on this point comes from a study by Zimbardo (1971). Zimbardo's plan was to conduct a two-week simulation of prison experience to examine the reactions of normal subjects who would play the parts of guards and prisoners. The subjects were all college-age males who happened to be in the area of the experiment during the summer, and who answered an ad soliciting paid volunteers. Potential subjects were screened by psychologists using various personality tests; any who were deemed abnormal were excluded.

Zimbardo attempted to capture in the details of his model the degradation present in American prisons; therefore, prisoners were, among other things, forced to give up their personal effects and to wear stocking caps over their heads to obscure their hair styles, a rough and ready equivalent of the shaved heads characteristic of the military and German camps. These male prisoners were given gowns to wear (resembling traditional hospital attire) that looked like, and forced prisoners to walk as if they were wearing, dresses. This costume was designed to make the prisoners appear ludicrous to the guards and themselves, and to induce the prisoners, in order to protect their modesty, to walk, sit, and move as a woman wearing a dress would.

Guards were also costumed for their part. They were given uniforms, billy clubs, and silver sunglasses to prevent eye contact between themselves and their prisoners. They were instructed to refer to the prisoners by number only, further stripping away the prisoners' identity.

A long list of prison regulations: forbade unauthorized talking, required the prisoners to address the guards not by name but with the title "Mr. Correction Officer," forbade the prisoners the use of the bathroom without permission, and required a humiliating stripping and delousing as an entry into prison life.

Although the study was designed to last for two weeks, Zimbardo was forced to stop it after six days due to the level of brutality the guards had reached and the signs of severe psychological distress on the part of several prisoners. The behavior on the part of the guards could be characterized as an escalation of brutality—a moral drift (see ch. 3). The prisoners reacted in an apathetic, despairing way. Both groups seemed to take little account of the fact that it was only an experiment, that they were not really prisoners or guards.

The second day of the experiment was marked by a prisoner rebellion in reaction to which some other features of the concentration camp were imposed (in a minor way). For example, the prisoners were subjected to endless roll calls, taking up the better part of the night. Accounts of concentration camp life almost invariably point to the unnecessarily long assemblies as a feature of daily experience. The prisoners in the experiment were forced to chant songs with content that degraded themselves. This too is a constant theme in the concentration camp literature. Zimbardo's guards took upon themselves the authority to order on-the-spot punishment, to confine to solitary, and to place informants in cells. Prisoners were assigned senseless tasks or were ordered to perform tasks in the most degrading possible way, e.g., cleaning out toilets with their bare hands. Bathroom privileges were withdrawn, and prisoners were forced to use a bucket in their cell; guards, on occasion, would refuse permission to empty it, another torture endemic to concentration camps. Food was occasionally denied, and conversely, a prisoner who refused to eat was force fed. These results strongly suggest that perfectly normal people will, in certain circumstances, treat others in a brutal, inhumane way, even though they know that their victims are ordinary people much like themselves, and that (literally in this case) there but for chance would they be.

It is important to distinguish this result from Milgram's. Milgram's subjects were explicitly ordered to shock the victim; subjects showed little inclination to go beyond the necessary infliction of pain. Indeed, in one condition of the experiment, Milgram told subjects to pick whatever levels of shock they thought best. Although the experimenter tacitly sanctioned any level at all, just by being there and not stopping the subject when he picked a level, only two of forty subjects went beyond 150 volts, the majority staying below 60 volts. In the Zimbardo experiment, again with the tacit approval of the experimenter, subjects innovated their own forms of degradation and punishment. A central difference seems to be that Zimbardo set out to degrade the victims, while Milgram did nothing to degrade the "learner." A further difference is that Zimbardo's guards acted not alone, but in the presence and as part of a group of other guards. We want to know, then, how the presence of peers under at least the passive aegis of an authority might affect one's behavior in this morally significant case.

Milgram (1964), in a variant of his experiment, investigated this matter. The subject met not one but three confederates. As in all conditions, one of the confederates was assigned by a fake lottery to the role of learner, the other two and the subject were to be teachers. The experimenter did not tell them what shock level to use, but rather, told them to decide the proper level among themselves. They were told that they were to give the *lowest* level that any of them wanted; thus the subject had an effective veto on the confederates. As the experiment progressed the two confederates hit upon the idea of increasing the level of shock one 15-volt step with each error; the subject then was faced with the clear option of either passively going along with the plan or using his veto to lower the voltage. One further detail is important: the subject himself was assigned the task of pulling the lever. In this condition about 18 percent of the subjects continued to shock to the end, 45 percent refused to go above 150 volts, and the remaining subjects broke off somewhere in between. If one examines more closely the distribution of shocks that subjects delivered, and compares them to the shock levels that subjects chose when neither instructed by authority nor prodded by confederates, one finds that the subjects' responses in this condition were a compromise between what they would have done were they left to pick their own level and what was proposed by the two confederates. The plans of their peers were not as effective as were the orders of authority (only seven as opposed to twenty-six went to the end), but in this case, with the tacit approval of the authority (he makes no move to interfere) subjects' actions were swayed in the direction of their peers.

How are we to interpret this result? The significance we give it is that the subjects, as shown in the condition in which they were tested alone, had some rough conception of how much shock is appropriate. But as we argued before, how far to go is a matter of degree, and they were not *committed* to some level beyond which they would not go. They encountered in the experiment two other people much like themselves who had a different conception of how to balance the competing claims of the learner and the experiment. The opinions of these other "subjects" influenced their own; their conception of the point beyond which they would not go moved up. Why? If the other subjects had a gun on them we would understand why their behavior would be affected by the other people's opinion, but the confederates had no weapon. As we have suggested elsewhere (see ch. 3), the classic studies by Sherif (1935) are relevant here.

MORAL JUDGMENT AND PEER INFLUENCE

Sherif conducted an experiment in which a subject was asked to fix her attention on a point source of light in a dark room. If you do this you will notice that the light will seem to move, an optical illusion called the autokinetic effect. Sherif then asked the subject how far the light moved. The subject had no frame of reference within which to answer this question, so she made a guess. If the subject is tested over 50 or 100 trials, the answers tend to accumulate about a central value; they do not evenly distribute themselves along the continuum of plausible answers. If you now take three subjects, each of whom has taken part in this procedure and each of whom has reached a mean (some stable idea as to how far the light is moving) and ask them again in each other's presence to say out loud how far the light has moved, you find that the individuals' judgments tend to converge. Subjects do *not* experience this procedure as a stressful one in which someone else is trying to impose her views on them; rather, since each believes that there is a right answer (if you tell them it is an illusion as Alexander et al., 1970, did, no convergence occurs), each knows that she does not know that answer (they can each see that they have very little basis for guessing), and each knows that no one else is sure either, they give weight to others' opinions in forming their own judgment about this ambiguous matter.

If we take this as a model for this latest Milgram experiment, then we might say that when a subject confronted with an ambiguous moral judgment finds two other people who differ about that judgment, he takes into account their views in forming his own opinion. Were the other two subjects in the Sherif experiment known by the third subject to be blind, then we would not expect perceptual convergence; were the two confederates in the Milgram experiment known in advance by the subject to be sadists, we would not expect moral convergence. If this line of thought is correct, then the fact that another sees a behavior as correct or morally tolerable can, in ambiguous situations, influence a person to find the behavior acceptable.

We can also view these results from the perspective of the subject's presentation of his character before the experimenter, the victim, the two confederates, and, of course, himself. The subject's response as a compromise between the judgments of the confederates and the very mild shock that, if he were on his own, he would choose, displays his sensitivity to the learner while showing that he respects the opinion of his fellow teachers. He is in this way sensitive to and responsive to all points of view on the matter. He is not only an effective functionary but a "humane" one.

Before we can apply our analysis of the Sherif experiment to either the Zimbardo findings or the concentration camps, we have two limitations to consider. First, the influence in the Sherif experiment is mutual—a rough compromise occurred. If compromise is what happened in the case of the guards we have been considering, then we must conclude that they were, on the average, sadists since the mean level of viciousness was so high. And second, the Sherif experiment takes place in circumstances of ambiguity—no one could call the behavior of concentration camp guards morally ambiguous.

To deal with the first objection, that the Sherif results indicate convergence to a mean, whereas the phenomenon we are trying to explain involves progressively more extreme behavior, we must examine the Sherif experiment more closely. The opinions of the subjects enter into the process of convergence only because the subjects offer their guesses publicly—they externalize their private views. They do it precisely because they are asked to do so by the experimenter; they stand in no danger of being asked, "Who asked you?" In the Zimbardo experiment, on the other hand, presumably no one asked each of the guards for his opinion about the limits of acceptable compulsion to be used to control the prisoners. As a consequence in the Zimbardo experiment there developed several kinds of guards rather than a group with a shared consensus.

> The guards could be characterized as falling into one of three groupings. There were the tough but fair guards whose orders were always within the prescribed rules of prison operation. Then there were several guards who were the good guys according to the prisoners, who felt genuinely sorry for the prisoners, who did little favors for them and never punished them. And finally, about a third of the guards were extremely hostile, arbitrary, inventive in their forms of degradation and humiliation, and appeared to thoroughly enjoy the power they wielded when they put on the guard uniform and stepped out into the yard, big stick in hand.
>
> (ZIMBARDO, 1971, p. 14)

But the "good guards' " good-heartedness had no apparent effect on the behavior of the more sadistic group. Zimbardo writes:

> In fact, they allowed it to go on, never once interfering with an order by one of the cruel guards. It might even be said that it was the good guards who helped maintain the prison, although the bad guards set the tone.
>
> (1971, p. 16)

The failure of the good guards to act cannot, of course, account for the *inclination* on the part of the others to be brutal; but it does have to do with the absence of group norms, both in the sense of shared understandings about right and wrong and enforceable regulations. Matza (1968) as we mentioned in chapter 3 pointed out a similar drift into brutality in some youth gangs he extensively interviewed. He claimed that individual gang members reported that they privately disavowed the delinquent behavior the gang engaged in but that each was afraid to say this out loud for fear of ridicule. Behavior can deteriorate to the level of the least-restrained members of the group, not because the other members fully endorse that behavior, but because they are unwilling or unable to make their view known. Private views of morality cannot become anchors for the behavior of others unless those views are expressed; there is even the question of whether these views can remain anchors for the individual who holds them unless they are expressed. The Zimbardo experiment lasted six days; could his "good guards" have remained attached to their at least passive unwillingness to take part in the brutality had the experiment continued? It is difficult for people to hold indefinitely to a moral position that they see flaunted by others like them. Of course, they might remain less brutal than the worst guards, but were the worst guards to become worse, the good guards' "temperate" behavior could become quite brutal, indeed.

We propose, then, that in cases where an individual sees others doing what she would not do but doesn't voice her objection, moral drift occurs. The failure to establish publicly the wrongness of a particular action gives it an implicit legitimacy; even those who would be disposed to find it wrong have difficulty in sustaining that view when others, presumably as competent at moral matters as they, give evidence by their actions of finding it acceptable.

Once brutality becomes standard procedure within an institution, it takes on an added legitimacy. As Berger and Luckmann argue, institutions by their very existence are taken by people, at least *prima facie,* to be legitimate. This legitimacy is conferred and reinforced by the process of socialization into the institution. Consider the problem a newcomer to an institution has in dealing with practices within it that she may find distasteful.

A newcomer is typically in the position of someone who doesn't know her way around, and knows it. It is natural to seek to learn from others how things are done here. The fact that everyone else seems to accept, or at least no one opposes, what would appear to naive first glance to be brutality suggests *prima facie* that in the judgment of *other people* the behavior is acceptable, and this suggests that the behavior *is* acceptable. Tillion's account of the "socialization" of a new *Aufseherin* (a female guard) at Ravensbruck, suggests this process at work:

> The beginners usually appeared frightened upon first contact with the camp, and it took some time to attain the level of cruelty and debauchery of their seniors. Some of us made a rather grim little game of measuring the time it took for a new Aufseherin to win her stripes. One little Aufseherin, twenty years old, who was at first so ignorant of proper camp "manners" that she said "excuse

> me" when walking in front of a prisoner, needed exactly four days to adopt the requisite manner, although it was totally new for her. (This little one no doubt had some special gifts in the "arts" we are dealing with here.) As for the others, a week or two, a month at the most, was an average orientation period.
>
> (TILLION, 1975, p. 69)

Tillion claims that the *Aufseherinnen*, unlike the male S.S. guards, were not selected for their brutality. This puts her in accord with Kogon in the claim that the male S.S. was a selected band of sadists, but the similar brutality of the female guards points to the superfluousness of this selection; it appears that the conditions of the camp were sufficient to socialize guards into brutality in a relatively brief period without prior selection.

There is still a gap for us to close. The Sherif illustration deals with cases of ambiguity; no one would call the behavior in the camps ambiguous. Can social influences lead people to view clear-cut moral matters in such a perverse way if they do not have a prior desire to see them that way? Some evidence from a series of experiments conducted by Asch (1952) and also discussed in chapter 3 brings us closer to an answer.

Asch recognized that the Sherif demonstration had to do with an entirely ambiguous matter; he expected that if people were given sufficiently clear cases to judge they would not be subject to such influences. To investigate this he constructed an experiment in which people were asked simply to judge which of three lines was equal in length to a fourth. When people made these judgments alone they erred in only a very few cases. Asch asked other subjects to make the same judgments in the presence of a group. The group contained six confederates who were instructed to give a patently wrong answer on some of the trials. Subjects then were asked to make a judgment about a perfectly clear matter in the presence of other people who, presumably, were judging the same relation. How did subjects react?

All (or nearly all) subjects reacted with signs of tension and confusion. Roughly one-third of the judgments subjects made were in error. Nearly 80 percent of the subjects gave the obviously wrong answer on at least one trial. The perception that a few other people made an absurd judgment of a clear, unambiguous physical matter was a very troubling experience, sufficient to cause doubt, and in some cases conformity. This procedure lasted only an hour or so. How would subjects have stood up had the procedure lasted for even the four days of Tillion's "little one"? Notice too that here the subject is asked to judge a physical relation, something, presumably, our nervous system is wired to perceive directly. While we would agree with Durkheim (1893) that moral matters are objective and external, they are clearly not directly tied to the wiring of the nervous system as is the judgment of line length. As Durkheim saw, for moral norms to have the force they have of inhibiting, limiting, and regulating individual action, they must be elements external to the individual—properties not of internal subjectivity but of the social world. This position confers on moral norms a certain fragility; they are fragile in that others have access to them, they are not private property. Others' statements about them, and perhaps more important, the statements about them implicit in others' behavior must have weight with regard to our own personal view. The assumption of mutuality leads to the most basic and primitive form of social influence: influence that arises from taking into account each other's views of our shared social world.

The guards influenced the level of each other's brutality in a further way. In replicating the Asch work Tuddenham and Mac Bride (1959) asked subjects about their conformity. They were surprised to find that some subjects who had given erroneous judgments reported that they themselves were quite independent of group influence. On further prodding they revealed that, as they understood the situation, the first subject who gave a wrong answer was honestly confused about the right answer, but the other subjects (in reality confederates) who gave that answer were not themselves confused; they were just following the leader like sheep. These naive subjects then went on to say that while the "followers" conformed on *every* trial they themselves gave the wrong answer on only *some* trials. As they saw it, by comparison they were independent. The "independent" behavior of subjects here is similar to the "humane" behavior of the subjects in the Milgram conformity variant.

Consider this account about a "good guard." Karst (1942) is writing about the night of January 23, 1939, in Dachau. A prisoner had escaped and the remaining 12,000 prisoners were forced to stand for twenty-five hours in the assembly square with the temperature at 16 below zero C. Two twenty-minute breaks were allowed. Many of the already starved and exhausted prisoners collapsed. As was the rule in the German camps, other prisoners were not allowed to go their aid. Karst was standing next to an old man who fell over dead. He writes:

> Then the S.S. man moved on, but five minutes later he returned. "Take the body into the hospital," he gave us the order. We were glad that we could move. I bent down to get hold of the body, but I was so stiff that I had absolutely no strength. I could not straighten up and was afraid I would collapse. That would be the end of me: refusal to obey a command. Would the S.S. man draw his revolver? He looked at me, noticed my terror stricken eyes. "Take your time," he said. "Get a cover," he added. I owe to him my life.
>
> (pp. 146–47)

For acts of this sort the guard gained the reputation of a "good guard." This act of simple humanity showed him to be not ignorant or insensitive to human impulses. We recognize the compassion in his action and assess his character accordingly. But still, this was Dachau, a slave labor camp. The institution of Dachau itself rivals all constructions of humanity as an embodiment of evil, and this guard was part of it. We see, and the author saw, and the guard himself saw himself as a kind person; but this perception of him is grounded in the fact that he was personally less brutal than some other guards while working thousands of people to their death. Actions that bespeak an inner self that is pure, "a heart of gold," have a direct and compelling impact on our judgment of the character of an individual. In circumstances where the individual's social world is to some degree humane, we are led to proper conclusions of his moral worth; but when those conditions are the hell of the concentration camp, the judgment that a particular guard is a good person measures only our capacity to appreciate irony.

CODA

The thrust of this chapter has been to bring the phenomena of the camps closer to home, to see how this horror, this inhumanity, could have been the product not only of deranged individuals but of "normal" people placed in deranged circumstances. We have attempted to draw links between what we know the artisans of the Holocaust did and what ordinary people have done in laboratory settings. We have tried to show how this evil is more comprehensible if we analyze it in terms of the influence of authority and of peers on people's moral judgments.

There is a danger in this. The task of making something understandable *is* to make us see how it could have happened by showing how it is akin to something we can already grasp. There is a tendency to slide from understanding to excusing. We are accustomed to think that once we have understood how someone came to do something, we then can forgive. In this case, we cannot allow understanding to mislead us to excuse or forgive. As scientists examining the phenomenon, we are committed to trying to discover its similarities with things that we know, how it follows from fundamental facts of human nature; only when this is done do we have an adequate grasp of the phenomenon. But no matter how well we understand, no matter how clearly we see the behavior as an expression of something basic to human nature, we cannot alter our moral judgment of these actions or of the actors who performed them.

There is a precedent. Greek tragedy is absorbed with the attempt to make evil understandable, to relate it to common flaws in human nature. Our appreciation of how hard it is to do right when fate and circumstances conspire to trick us cannot obscure the fact that the measure of human nature is our capacity to do what is right and resist what is wrong.

CHAPTER FIVE

A Plea for Gossip

Gossip seems unserious. It isn't much of a social problem. It isn't the name of an underlying mental process. Kant didn't deduce its presuppositions. It's a ramicle even Austin didn't trace. Treating gossip seriously, then, needs a defense.

First, it is common. Everyone we know gossips. Gluckman (1963) declared it a cross-cultural universal. If he's right, it's *very* common.[1] But then, so are faculty meetings, and no one defends them. But we do announce them; we don't announce our gossip.

Even though we all gossip, we feel we shouldn't, and we're discreet when we do. Gossip isn't alone in this: remembering Kinsey and his times, we take it more people had affairs than approved of them. Still the pleasures of sex are so apparent and compelling that it is obvious why people are tempted. In contrast, the pleasures of gossip are subtle and elusive; it's not obvious why people are tempted. Gossip is a curious pleasure and sin.

One more brief in our plea: gossip exercises moral talents in an unstudied, natural, easy form with mundane, concrete, and compelling content. Enough of briefs, now to the defendant.

What is gossip? How should we define it? Perhaps we should

1. Prevalence alone isn't much of a reason to study something. But all other things being equal, the common is to be preferred to the rare.

stipulate a meaning for it—give it a definition and move on. But that would be inventing a defendant, not examining one. Inventing a defendant does have advantages. Show trials have defendants of neat character, accused of textbook crimes committed in exemplary circumstances; stipulative definitions, too, are tidy—designed to create exemplary clarity. But show trials are too convenient; the ambiguities of actual trials aren't artifacts, but consequences of the ways trials relate to a world not constructed to suit prosecutors. The ambiguities of our ordinary concepts aren't artifacts either, but consequences of the ways our language relates to a world not constructed to suit scientists. While we might gain simplicity by stipulation, we would leave unclear how our invented gossip is related to the real thing. And after all, it was for the real gossip we set out to make a plea (see Rosnow & Fine, 1976, for a source book).

So then, what is gossip? How can we pursue it? By following some examples, questioning our intuitions, and testing motley theories against circumstantial evidence. A promising lead is what people gossip about. The lead seems easy, straightforward, empirical. It isn't. The reason it's not direct is that gossip won't be separated from its content. For instance, imagine a conversation about tables and chairs; would we call it gossip? Not ordinarily, gossip is about people, not chairs.[2] What if the chair talk is about how shabbily they've been built? And "everybody knows" that Bill just made them to show off his $4,000 Hobby Master tool set. Arrogance, ineptness, and profligacy are in the air, as well as poorly turned teak. Unfortunately, "what everybody knows" isn't picked up by tape recorders; the content of this chair talk won't be separated from its context. Gossip must be *about* people, but telling what an utterance is about (as opposed to what it mentions) requires an insider's background knowledge. Ferreting out targets isn't all that straightforward.

Of course, if Bill were there while the quality of his carpentry was being assessed, then, while delicts—cattiness, cruelty, malice, or pedantry—may have been committed, one of them wasn't gossip. It is odd to talk of "gossiping to someone's

2. Gossip, of course, can be about honorary people—universities, corporations, or governments—as long as they are treated as animated by motives and subject to moral constraint. Clearly these cases are parasitic on our talk about people.

face"—except in lament: at a faculty party you find yourself telling a story about a new visiting professor's gauche tastes, and then discover the subject and recipient of the story match. (So we recommend gossip *in absentia.*)

Does "talk behind a person's back" define gossip? Consider this snippet:

A: Where is Dr. Watson?

B: She's in her office.

It's about a person, and she isn't present, but we wouldn't call it gossip. Why? Because gossip is evaluative as well as, sometimes, informative. The snippet we overheard might look more promising in *this* context: imagine that Dr. Watson, a junior member of the faculty, is notorious for her boycott of all those faculty meetings, and for some reason this has been taken not as a sign of her good sense but of dereliction of her responsibilities. Now suppose the "in her office" were said while she ought to have been attending another measured debate. Here the "in her office" becomes gossip because it implies an evaluation. Any fact, on a suitable occasion, can be found in gossip's company. And just as an innocent content is gossip in some contexts, an evaluation, even a defamatory one, is sometimes innocent of gossip.[3]

Imagine a department of physics considering whether to hire an applicant. The discussion about her qualities as a professor is surely evaluative, certainly behind her back; yet we wouldn't call it gossip, though we do see the similarity. Why wouldn't we call it gossip? Imagine a drift from a discussion of her research, teaching, and administrative potential to talk of her sexual affairs. Some would say the group slid into gossip; others would say her relationships, especially with students, are a legitimate concern. But both groups agree they should mind their own business—not gossip; they disagree over whether her affairs are their business. Is this a rule: is it legitimacy that saves talk's virtue?

Imagine a conversation about Dick: "He sleeps on the job," a fit suspect for gossip. But is it gossip if the discussants are

3. We can use this example to gut a red herring. Suppose the student who learned Dr. Watson was in her office rushed to tell a friend, "She's missing another faculty meeting. That's the fourth this month." If Dr. Watson were in her office, then, while the conversation is gossipy, it is also true. Gossip need not be false, its unreliable reputation notwithstanding.

robbers, Dick is a night watchman, and the talk of his sleeping habits isn't to amuse, but to advance a heist? No. But it isn't legitimate talk. Still, it is pragmatic. So it isn't legitimacy that redeems talk, it's relevance—the relevance of the talk to a plan. So far we've sketched gossip as idle, evaluative talk about someone behind his back.

GOSSIP AND RUMOR

To make our sketch more useful, we shall fill in detail by contrasting gossip with a look-alike—rumor. We have so far treated 'gossip' as if it were the name of a thing, but this is limiting. Now we shall ask: to what point and in what circumstances would we say a person is spreading a rumor? And when would we say he's gossiping?

Suppose you eavesdrop on: "Did you hear about that foreman, Bill? I heard the only way you can get promoted is by paying him off." Is the speaker gossiping or spreading a rumor? Both? What would we be stressing if we said the speaker was "spreading a rumor," and what would we stress by calling it gossip?[4] To see the difference, consider how a person could defend himself against a charge of spreading a rumor. Claiming it's true is a good defense: "It's true. Ann told me she just quit because he told her what her choices were." Now suppose he were defending himself against a charge of gossip. What would be natural? "We're not gossiping. Debbie just got a chance for a transfer, and she needs to know what the story is around here." This defense is not that the story is true, but that it's relevant. It could be true and still be gossip; it could be relevant and still rumor. Calling a story gossip and calling it rumor are both dismissive, but they dismiss in different ways. 'Rumor' attacks the speaker's claim; 'gossip' attacks its idleness.[5] You can, however, attack a claim without calling it a rumor; you might, for example, claim the person is lying. 'Rumor' entails a more specific attack, one on the speaker's credentials. If our friend,

4. One difference between rumor and gossip is that rumors can be about things: "I heard a rumor the dam is breaking." This differs from our "poorly made chair" example of gossip in that talk of the chair was an implicit evaluation of its carpenter; talk of the dam is just a warning.

5. If you hear gossip that Dean Smith is being forced out for peculation and you tell the purchasing department to wait before ordering the Persian rug for his office, you are passing on gossip, not gossiping.

the White House chef, told us the President ordered veal *cordon bleu* for the Camp David meetings between Sadat and Begin, we wouldn't say he was spreading a rumor, even if we doubted him. He should know—he's the chef. We might challenge the truth of his claim, but that would be to call him a liar, not a rumor monger.[6] Either way, he's gossiping.

Rumor and gossip are often entangled in the same conversation—for good reason. The juiciest things to gossip about are, after all, the things we most want to conceal, the things few people are likely to know directly. Thus, we often find occasion to accuse people both of gossiping and spreading rumors. But still, 'gossip' highlights the idleness of talk, and 'rumor' highlights the weakness of the speaker's grounds.

WHY DO PEOPLE GOSSIP?

If gossip is idle why do it? Paine (1967) has an answer, the common one—to advance interests. But this, as Gluckman points out, is paradoxical. If, as we have argued, gossip is idle then how could it be done to advance interests? Yet it seems true that at least sometimes people gossip to advance themselves. How can we and Gluckman square this with our notion that gossip is idle?

Perhaps a distinction will help; a distinction between 'points' and 'purposes'. Points belong to *activities*, purposes to *people*. Chess has a point: mate. To play chess *is* to move your pieces toward this end. The coordinated activity of two people moving with this inspiration makes up the game. But this doesn't tell us why anyone would play chess. Why do they? For money, to kill time, to relax, to impress a friend, to show off intelligence (or at least intellectual tastes), or for its own sake—the pleasures of finding new strategies, of getting out of tough situations, of springing amusing traps, i.e., the pleasures of playing well. Two players may not have the same purpose, then, but if they are to play chess their moves must have the same point—mate.[7]

6. This is perhaps a special case of a more general rule—the conversational rule of best evidence. If you see Nancy stealing a Persian rug and then someone tells you about it, it would be misleading to say to a friend, "I heard that Nancy stole a rug." There is a conversational implication here that you didn't see her steal it but merely heard about it.

7. Even someone trying to lose deliberately (for some reason) must give the appearance of trying to mate, i.e., must make it look as if his moves were directed toward this goal. Even for deliberate losers, the game is organized by the goal of mating.

The point-purpose distinction gives both Paine and Gluckman their due. Paine receives the purpose; Gluckman wins the point. Paine's claim is really about the purposes individuals have in gossiping; but the idleness, we and Gluckman stress, is characteristic of the activity itself. For friends to gossip, we suggest, they must act as if their talk were idle, had no serious intent—were not designed to advance their interests. They must treat their talk, as they talk, as idle, even if each has a serious purpose, e.g., one may be defaming an ex-girlfriend, another checking out whether his next is now available. Still, they must package their serious purposes in the wrappings of idleness. So long as they are willing and able to sustain the facade, they are at once gossiping and reaching their separate ends. If it becomes patent that the idleness was just a facade, then we, and the participants, would say they had not been gossiping, or not just gossiping.

Paine's claim, then, that we gossip only to advance our interests is not ruled out by our commonsense conception of gossip, but it is not a claim about gossip per se. It is a hypothesis about the purposes of gossips. We shall address it on empirical grounds later. For now we pursue the points.

Is idleness the point of gossip, then? Not quite. Rather, idleness is a characterization of all of the varied points instances of gossip have. One piece of gossip may have the point of amazing us with Jim's bizarre life-style, another of expressing disapproval of Ann's work habits. These stories have different points, but both amazing us and expressing disapproval are sufficient reasons to tell a story. Gossip is less like chess playing, where every game has the same point, mating, and more like storytelling, where each story has its own point. The point of chess doesn't tell us why people play it; nor do the points of stories tell us why people tell them. But the points do make sensible the particular moves that were made. Now back to the purpose. When we looked for the purposes people have in playing chess we gave a list of possible extrinsic motives, e.g., impressing friends. But on our list we had one additional entry: for its own sake. And sometimes we tell stories too just for their own sake—the delight in telling an interesting story.

'Interesting' is a criterion we apply to stories to distinguish good from bad, those that give us pleasure from those that don't.[8] Because interesting is a general term that may be applied not only to stories (including gossip), but also to: theories, new acquaintances, fossils, or the latest dance, we can't expect it to tell us much about *what* is good about any one of these interesting kinds of things. Yet if squeezed, 'interesting' may come across with some useful distinctions appropriate to gossip per se, and flesh out our story of why people gossip.

News is interesting, and new facts are sometimes news. Gossip often tries to be news; it trades in new facts about commonly known characters. But what counts as a new fact? If Jerry fell down the plane steps in Washington it might be news; but after Kansas City, Cleveland, Omaha, and Houston, is Des Moines still news? So new facts about old characters are not interesting—unless those facts are helped along.

Glancing at several ways to freshen the news will help us appreciate the delicate nature of 'interesting'. Another case of Jerry's clumsiness can be mentioned if it shows he is clumsy to a degree heretofore not suspected, or in an area of his life not previously implicated, or in a novel, inventive way. People, then, have a reason to notice or invent the hyperbolic—it keeps the gossip going.

Another way to fix up old information is to connect it to new character defects; old news can be retread if it can be related to new, preferably deeper, flaws. Psychoanalysis is of great use to gossip; for example, we all know Tom is sloppy, but mentioning its relation to his toilet training is sure to catch attention. (Personality theories, lay and professional, can rejuvenate tired gossip, since they are continuous with our pretheoretical psychology, i.e., our gossip.)

But there is a way for people to defend themselves against

8. Schachter and Burdick (1955) have shown experimentally that it is really "ambiguity" that makes people gossip (or, as they say, pass on rumors). In their study when a student was removed by the principal from class to go to an unknown place for the rest of the day, her fellow students discussed it. We would prefer to call such an event "interesting" rather than ambiguous since, we suspect, the students did not discuss other ambiguities such as: the ambiguously green-blue sweater she was wearing at the time; whether the principal meant her just to take her coat or to put it on; precisely which books to take, and in which order to stack them.

Events, we claim, are not ambiguous or unambiguous, except with respect to some particular concern. So a student walking dead east is unambiguously walking east although whether she is attempting to step on a snail, walk off a cliff, or see the view below may still be ambiguous. Thus Schachter and Burdick might want to say people gossip about "relevant ambiguity"—but that still sounds like "interesting" to us.

gossip by robbing it of its interest: we can embrace, or at least confess, the flaw we are accused of. Part of the charm of gossiping is sharing a secret (see Simmel, 1950, on secrets). Betty Ford's announcing she is an alcoholic robs talk of her drinking of its interest as gossip. Of course, the announced flaw can still be linked to a deeper, still hidden fault, or a particularly salacious detail can still be traded, but the mere fact no longer has gossip value.

There is another way to press "defective news" into service. Suppose you have been a victim of your roommate—he stole your camera. Telling a friend about it would be evaluative talk, behind the thief's back, and, unless your friend is a: cop, vigilante, camera fence, insurance agent, psychiatrist, or easy touch, it would be idle talk, hence gossip. But even if your story is convincingly idle, you still have a problem if your friend doesn't know your roommate. Good gossip requires that both parties know the main character.[9] Of course, being a friend's roommate confers honorary acquaintance. Still a story about a theft by a merely honorary acquaintance is not very interesting, and you'll have to work to remedy this defect. You can't show he is more of a thief than your friend had imagined since your friend hadn't been imagining your roommate at all; but you can show he is more of a thief than could possibly be imagined. Many interesting stories can be built from this plot.

In one version the teller is bewildered and sharing the experience. Or the teller can be searching to understand how a person could be like that and soliciting enlightenment from the audience. In a more developed form, the advice sought might be about how to treat the thief: "It isn't the camera I care about. It's that his taking it was a cry for help, and I just don't know how to answer." Another way to tell the story of the theft if you've been reading O'Henry is to find the latent irony—when he pushes the shutter the camera will self-destruct; alienation from character can be compensated by tricks of plot. Another traditional technique is to present your story as having a lesson either for your particular audience or for the world. So the tale of the stolen camera has a point, to warn the listener about:

9. Movie stars, politicians, and athletes are a special case of people in some weak sense known to their audience and hence targets of gossip. We see this case as parasitic on the case of gossiping about a neighbor.

roommates, students at North Dakota State School of Mines and Liberal Arts, young adults, people in our day and age, human failings, or nature's red teeth and claws. There's an upbeat version of the moral degeneracy tale—virtue triumphant: "He took it, but I confronted him, took it back, and threw him out." Or, at least, "I'll confront him as soon as he comes back from his Modern Photography vacation." Juicy gossip, then, can be made from wilted news and the proper treatment.

The strategies we've mentioned (as well as some we might, e.g., tales of adventure, amazing coincidences, touching or amusing sorrows) employ dramaturgic devices in the telling of transgressions. Of course, none of these techniques is restricted to victims; anyone who wishes to fashion a story about a transgression can use them. All of these techniques provide explicit points, give the actors using them a way to make their stories interesting, thus giving tellers a reason to tell them and their audiences a reason to listen. Now we are ready to consider Paine's empirical claim about the purposes of people gossiping.

If he doesn't include telling interesting stories among interests to be advanced, his claim wilts. If he includes it, his claim bloats. Further, there are other instances of gossip, even motivated instances, that it would be even more misleading to call advancing interests. For example, you meet an acquaintance, and you have very little in common except he once worked for your boss, so you spend the afternoon trading stories about her. This is the sort of talk that characterizes college reunions, family gatherings, or APA conventions.[10] In these cases, for one reason or another, you have an obligation to talk; and gossip is a pleasant, easy, and universally accepted way to fulfill the obligation.

Is "advancing your interests" to include a case where you've asked a colleague out for a drink, and you think she will be amused by your stories about your antic college roommate?[11]

10. "Catching up" talk—who had a baby, who moved where, who was promoted and who wasn't—is surely news and loosely gossip, though it isn't (necessarily) evaluative. It is distinguished from our prototype by: (1) we readily admit to this sort of talk; and (2) we wouldn't be embarrassed by the subject's overhearing us. (We thank Jacob Nachmias for suggesting this point.)

11. Another fuzzy case. If the talk is about your roommate's antics, then it is evaluative. Still, we have affection for foibles and we often are not really evaluating—foibles aren't very important failings either to us or their host, but they do portray character. 'Foibles' are a sort of evaluation; talking about them is like gossiping. (Henry Gleitman brought foibles to our attention.)

Does Paine's account include both the case where she is twenty-one, very attractive, and eager to form a meaningful relationship and the case where she is sixty-five, not your type, and deeply committed to her husband of forty years? Is it to include a case where your roommate did something so droll that you can't wait to run into someone to tell it to or the case where what he did wasn't very droll, but the way you can put it will be?

People gossip for various reasons, with various motives. Even after we look behind the point of the story to the purpose of the actor, we may find nothing deeper than his desire to meet his obligation to talk to an acquaintance. The irony of Paine's position is that the recognition that people can advance their narrow, material interests through gossip leads him to believe they always do; but were it widely known that people must be advancing their interests by gossiping, then this strategy wouldn't work. The reason it can work sometimes is that ulterior motives are parasitic on more usual and less noxious motives. If gossiping announced its ulterior motive, then those who had an ulterior motive would avoid it, and those who heard it would be forewarned.

GOSSIP'S MORAL CHARACTER

Now that we have identified gossip, we shall pursue its defense by examining its virtues, vices, and character traits. Gossip is a medium of self-disclosure. It involves taking a stance about another's behavior—behavior which could be our own, but isn't. To do that is to dramatize ourselves: our attitudes, values, tastes, temptations, inclination, will, and so forth. Further, gossip is reasonably safe; it's safer, although less heroic, than commenting on someone's behavior to his face (on the difficulties of the face-to-face version see ch. 3).

Gossip has another attraction to the lay moral theorist, in addition to safety. Typically, when we gossip, we tell a story we claim to know to someone who doesn't.[12] This gives us a certain

12. There are two counter-cases here. In one, two people see together the same misbehavior; there's no information to pass on, but there are evaluations, "I couldn't believe he would . . ." In the other case, Tim tells Mary some gossip she already knows, but she plays along; it's polite.

latitude with the material to remove conflicting details, heighten the moral point, improve our role in the matter, or at least remove jarring intimations about our own motives and *faux pas.* We are likely to come off well. Our license isn't absolute; some details of the story may be available to those who would check, but, even so, the danger isn't too great. We all know memory is fallible, so even if our details aren't perfect, this in itself shows nothing more than our human forgetfulness. Further, someone who wants to check may find it difficult because admitting she's heard the story may compromise her. More often, checking involves revealing the source, betraying the secrecy of the gossip and the intimacy of the relationship; if the fact you've checked gets back to the source, you may earn a reputation for being mistrustful. And even if the detail you want to check is a matter of public record, it may just be inconvenient to find it. Lastly, it's not often you'll have a reason to check the details, or if you do, it's likely we knew this when we told you the story, and we made sure our account of these details was exact. So gossip is supple as well as safe.

Gossip has another virtue: it forms instant, if fleeting, bonds, saving effort. Simmel, Gluckman, and Berger (1963) have pointed out that gossip creates an ephemeral intimacy between the people gossiping through the exclusion of the person gossiped about.[13]

Gossip is a "tie sign," a bearer of information about relationships (Goffman, 1971). People display their relationship by gossiping—they display it to each other and to anyone at hand. Not only is gossip a tie sign, but the fact that we gossip creates a need for tie signs. Letting everyone know the fellow you sat next to at the dinner party is an old and dear friend and not just an acquaintance can save trouble, especially if he is wont to eat escargot with his fingers. This caution will save the embarrassment involved in being told what a dolt that fellow was. Thus it is dangerous for newcomers to a community to gossip until they have been filled in on who is related to whom: the stranger

13. Of course, we usually know the people we gossip to; still, gossiping to people we know by sharing evaluations, perceptions, and talking about an overlapping history creates a feeling of intimacy. And part, at least, of our getting to know people is by gossiping, and by having a shared secret about an excluded other the people gossiping are drawn together.

has to know who knows whom well enough to care about the gossip, but not so well as to be offended.[14]

Now to gossip's role in community affairs. Gossip brings ethics home by introducing abstract morality to the mundane. Moral norms are abstract. To decide whether some particular, concrete, unanalyzed action is forbidden, tolerated, encouraged, or required, principles must be applied to the case. But applying principles to cases requires us to realize there is a moral decision to be made, then recognize which principles to apply, and finally apply them correctly. None of these steps is mechanical, infallible, or guaranteed by sincerity (for more on this point see chs. 3 & 4). To see this problem in operation, consider some analogies.

Principles are as important to morality, the social order, as they are to law or physics. But the skill in law and the skill in physics lies not so much in learning the rules as in acquiring the tacit knowledge to apply them. How do lawyers acquire this? By practice at solving legal problems. Only then can they make the law live, i.e., have a place in the actual doings of their clients. Learning physics, too, is a matter of developing intuition, i.e., becoming skilled at applying physical laws to concrete cases. How do commonsense actors come to apply the moral principles their cultures give them?

Well, there's always childhood socialization. Socialization includes learning the rules, coming to care about them, and perhaps, learning some specific applications. Some moral principles come with clear applications.

Religious food laws can, perhaps, be taught along with their application. If the child can be expected to find, as an adult, the same foods he found as a child, socialization can include both the principle to be followed (no meat on Friday, no meat with dairy) and its application (this counts as meat, this counts as dairy). A sexual code can be passed on this way, too. Suppose the principle is "Virginity until marriage"; tolerably clear applications of the notions of virginity and marriage can be taught. But the feasibility of passing on these applications depends on an unchanging conception of virginity and of marriage. Sup-

14. They will also have to know what passes as gossip here. Gossip about padded expense accounts in a community where it is common practice, and commonly known, dramatizes your position as an outsider, not your being in the know.

pose instead the norm to be socialized is "Sex must be part of a meaningful relationship." Would the application of this rule be as easy to pass on as the application of "virginity"? Could anyone teach all the particularities bound up in this concept by pointing to examples?[15]

Could you teach your daughter legal ethics—the line between a fair fee for service and gouging or respect for her colleagues and collusion—in her crib? This is not just because the vocabulary is too difficult or you are unable to borrow law books from your local children's library. Of course, you can teach her to be fair. And it isn't pointless for you to teach this or useless for her to know it. But even if you taught her the proper fee for a 1946 divorce, how does this help her know what to charge for a no-fault divorce? For palimony? How could you teach her how much *pro bono* work she should do? Perhaps these are esoteric examples. Let's consider a more homely case.

You've been *taught* not to bother the neighbors, and you've been *trained* to recognize what counts as bothering the neighbors: playing music too loud after 11:00 p.m. or riding motorcycles without mufflers at night. But now you've moved into a graduate student apartment complex with very thin walls and a neighbor studying for her Ph.D. qualifying exams. She finds your normal sound disruptive of her studying. Your socialized rule that you shouldn't bother the neighbors wasn't applied for you to this new circumstance. Of course, you have principles. Some account will have to be taken of the thin walls, and perhaps, of her special need for quiet. But some account must be taken of your life, too.

Here, gossip can be of help in a double role. If you've been lucky enough to participate, even as a listener, in gossip with other students with thin walls and noisy or nervous neighbors, you may have picked up some specific examples of excessive noise and reasonable lives. And these specifics, like settled cases in common law, can serve as precedents for your construction of a reasonable solution.

15. This isn't just the problem of generativity familiar to linguists. Generative grammar assumes an innate set of unchanging primitives, e.g., syntactic categories, to which rules are applied. But, for example, the evolution of 'usury' as church law painfully accommodated capitalism suggests that the moral primitives of everyday life are neither innate nor unchanging. At a deeper level there might be an innate set of principles, but their appearance is awaited. Of course, we will then have the problem of applying them.

Gossip serves another role. Suppose she sent you a note complaining of your noise, and you sent a note back telling her the balance you struck. Now your concern is not with constructing a solution, but with getting it ratified—with reassuring yourself that you have been reasonable, considerate, and your neighbor oversensitive. One way to do this is to gossip about your neighbor's excessive, neurotic need for quiet. Your story can be counted on to enliven and amuse with the multifaceted nature of your neighbor's personality flaws. Of course, your story will illustrate a flaw of your character, too—excessive altruism. Your moral-characterological discourse will be presented as something else, something casual, an interesting story about your neighbor—and it may be intended as nothing more than that—but it will also be an analysis of the moral problem along with a presentation of your solution—to a public.

Gossip, then, is one method commonsense actors have to externalize, dramatize, and embody their moral perceptions. In gossip moral positions are offered, and typically accepted, as sensible and correct. This acceptance is one way that, to use Berger and Luckmann's (1967) unhappy term, the "facticity" of the moral order is driven home. The appearance, at least, of consensus sustains commonsense actors' beliefs that moral decisions are external, shared, and independent of their personal wants, beliefs, and desires. This taken-for-granted assumption of the externality—objectivity—of the moral order is not only a consequence of gossip but a presupposition.

What sense would calling your neighbor hypersensitive or yourself reasonable have if these characterizations were not to be taken as claims about your neighbor and yourself? The ratification that gossip solicits is not one of standards or facts but of *application:* saying she is hypersensitive because she . . . , and implying I'm reasonable because I . . . , asks for a ratification of an application. Gossip, then, both presupposes and constructs an objective moral order. Just as in evaluating job candidates we presuppose and construct a consensus about what it is to be an acceptable professor. Evaluative talk about people, of which gossip is an important part, spells out the common grounds of our social life.

Gossiping, unfortunately, is a less than perfect way of establishing the correctness, the lack of bias, of our moral judgments. Ideally, we would want to try our judgments out on a select group of morally sensitive, impartial, broadly representative members of the community. But our student with the nervous neighbor picked a different group—her own friends. She can count on them to understand her perceptions of right and wrong; or if they don't she can count on them to be discreet about their disagreements, to let overstatement pass, and not to press for proof or keep perfect track of inconsistencies in the shifting grounds of her account. Because we gossip to friends, and friends are tactful, positions ratified during gossip need not reflect what the audience really believes. And we know it. Our knowing it limits the support we can draw from it.

What someone gossiping agrees with or acknowledges by silence, though not fully informative, is committing: if a friend agrees that life must go on, neighbor's Ph.D. or not, then she will face a problem in complaining about a noisy neighbor herself. Of course, she can still do it, but good manners require some account to be given, albeit indirect, of the relevant difference between the cases. In this way the articulation of the noisy neighbor problem continues.

But gossip isn't the only way to contribute solutions to the common stock of social problems. You could confront the culprit publicly, but direct confrontation is difficult and risky. Anger has a way of escalating. Expressing moral perceptions of a person to the person may disrupt intimate, profitable, or merely cordial relationships and make everyone's day harder; overt confrontation recruits support and hastens factions. Of course, gossip can lead to clique formation too (one reason why monasteries and utopian communities forbid it, see Kinkade, 1973).[16] But because gossip is behind a person's back and because it is supposed to be a secret, partners can be switched from day to day without the issue of betrayal unpleasantly intruding. Gossip lets people air their chest, find support for their outrage, and be heroes of a moral drama with a minimum of

16. The secrecy implicit in gossip is a starting point for the formation of cliques; people gossiping have a shared understanding, necessarily exclusive of the rest of the community. Repeated practice may prove insidious as more content is added to the gossip. This problem is particularly troublesome for groups fostering the notion of openness (Boggs, personal communication).

inconvenience. An account by Wells sheds light on gossip's role in the airing of grievances. In the Polish *shtetl* where he grew up, there was a formal procedure for the airing of grievances:

> It was an accepted custom that if anyone had any grievance against the community or any member of it he could step up to the podium just prior to the reading of the Bible, with the Holy Scrolls lying on the table on the podium. The man had the right to announce that he wouldn't let the scrolls be read until the entire congregation listened to his grievances. Everyone would sit down, and there would be grave silence in the synagogue. Everyone knew that it must be a serious grievance; otherwise no one would take the responsibility for stopping the reading of the Holy Scrolls.
> (1978, pp. 5–6)

The seriousness of invoking this right restricts its usefulness; gossip by waiving the rights of confrontation serves more mundane cases. But why couldn't we institutionalize the airing of trivia? Well, airing requires an audience. We know why Wells's audience came and sat still, but why would they sit still to hear about trivial offenses? You could have a law, but this would surely tax the time and patience of the community. Gossip solves the problem by being restricted to friends and by being amusing. Further, the very seriousness of the synagogue setting dramatizes the accuser's outrage; he knows, and everyone else knows, just how seriously he's treating the complaint. But you can gossip about foibles as well as felonies, or even about flaws whose seriousness you haven't yet determined. And, like the launching of a law suit, a charge before the scrolls must be answered. For serious crimes it's worth the community's energy to resolve right and wrong; but since charge and countercharge, attack and defense, can continue indefinitely, could any community treat all grievances this way? How many Dreyfus Affairs can a community afford—over a noisy stereo? Also the most prudent way to insult someone and continue to do business with her is to insult her behind her back. Unless of course the gossip gets out of control.

Wells's account also illustrates gossip's dangers. One of the grievances he recalls being aired was *about* gossip.

> I remember a time when the butcher, with his loud and raucous voice, complained that there was gossip that he cheated with his

> scales; that would mean to everyone, of course, that he was not true to the Jewish religion, and therefore could not be trusted to be selling truly Kosher meat. He could lose his livelihood through the rumor of dishonesty, of course, and wanted to know who was responsible for it. He wouldn't leave the podium until the community leaders promised to investigate the whole problem.
>
> (1978, p. 6)

Both the virtue and vice of gossip, then, is that one doesn't confront accusers or demand proof.

But even if flawed, gossip expresses moral perception. If people didn't express their perception of transgression, either formally or in gossip, there would be an obvious problem: wrongdoers would get away with their delicts, and potential wrongdoers would lack a deterrent. But Durkheim would notice a deeper problem: moral drift. As we have argued (see chs. 3 & 4), failure to express moral criticism can lead to the erosion of shared social norms and to confusion of the individual as to just what his stance is. Gossip, then, is a means of social control in that it allows individuals to express, articulate, and commit themselves to a moral position in the act of talking about someone publicly. Thus it is a way we come to know what our own evaluations really are.[17]

What we say in gossip, as opposed to what we just think, commits us—after all, we announce it. And we are required by the form of gossip to put it as a coherent story. And when we hear it we may notice how coherent or incoherent it is. Because

17. The notion that we come to know what we really believe by public talk runs counter to a commonsense inclination. We are comfortable with the view that if we were but able to listen in on people's private soliloquy we would know what people really believe. What follows from this is the belief that people always know what they believe since they can listen in on their own soliloquy. But there are two problems with this view: (1) we don't say to ourselves at each moment all the things we believe—we haven't told ourselves that the world is round for several weeks; and (2) we (at least the authors) don't believe all the things that pass through our minds. How do we know whether what we are saying to ourselves is: a strongly held belief, a conjecture, a wish, a fantasy, a fear, something meant ironically, a slip of the mind, a quote, a memory of a former belief? Our mental contents are not always accompanied by labels announcing just how they are meant to be taken. Moreover, the connections among mental sentences, other than before and after, are missing. Are two mental sentences entailed by one another, negations of one another, major premise and conclusion waiting for an empirical minor premise, clang associations? This is a problem that should have made cognitive dissonance theory uneasy. Logical relations among ideas do not appear to be self-announcing. This is unfortunate. If they were, we could resolve whether 'free will' and 'determinism' were inconsistent—dissonant—by entertaining them both in our minds and measuring the discomfort. (To date philosophers have not made use of this interesting tool.)

gossip is public talk, but only to a very selected audience, it is transitional between things merely said to one's self and positions taken in a public domain. Gossip, then, is a training ground for both self-clarification and public moral action.

CHAPTER SIX

Flirtation and Ambiguity

FLIRTATION

Andy and Debbie are lost in a discussion of Kant and the subtleties of the second deduction. An observer can see their enthusiasm, concentration, and excitement. An acute observer, perhaps one who knew them, might notice how odd it is for Andy to find transcendental arguments so involving—he's usually more taken by sophisticated transmissions. Debbie, on the other hand, hasn't found "Kant's just like Plato" insightful since Philo. 1. The shrewd observer might suspect that Kant isn't the only object of their passion. Although much has been written about Kant, little attention, conceptual at least, has been given to their other interest: flirtation. We shall redress the balance. But first we must equip ourselves with some concepts.

Purposes

When we describe, explain, or evaluate actions, the concept 'purpose' is central, along with its relations: 'goals', 'intentions', 'what a person means' or 'means to do', etc. Indeed, 'purpose' separates actions from slips, mistakes, accidents, or tics—the sorts of things that happen to people, not things they do. 'Flirtation' names actions, i.e., we flirt; we're not seized by a fit of flirtation. Yet the relation between someone's purpose while flirting and the flirting itself can be elusive and flimsy. In looking at this, we shall see how the purpose of an action can be, or can be made to be, clear or ambiguous. In this way flirtation is an example of how people act so as to make the purposes they have in acting salient or muted, simple or complex, focal or peripheral. In addition, since an actor's purpose is central to the moral assessment of what she has done, by modulating purposes we shade the moral content of our action as we make it known to ourselves and others. But isn't the purpose of flirtation obvious?

The answer seems so—sex. Still we occasionally flirt even though we have a headache and couldn't imagine having sex at the moment. Indeed, we can imagine flirting with someone in whom we have no sexual interest at all. You might flirt with your boss, though you find her ugly, in the service of your career; or you might flirt with someone you find unattractive just to pass the time; or you might love to flirt but be committed to monogomy. So people who flirt needn't have the goal of sex at the moment—or ever. Have we discovered, then, that sex isn't necessary to flirtation? Perhaps sex is just one of the many reasons people flirt. But this slights the role of sex in flirtation. To see how, let's ask: what would lead us to say you were flirting with your boss?

Recognizing a Flirtation When We See One: Lists, Rules, and Points

How do we recognize a flirtation when we see it? Perhaps we can put together a *list* of flirtatious behaviors. Perhaps we say a person is flirting if, and only if, she exhibits a suitable number of items from the catalogue. Well, the list might have: staring lingeringly in a person's eyes, drawing close, talking softly, dimming the lights. But then is every ophthalmologist flirting with her patients—necessarily? With a little effort we could invent a context to show any behavior to be innocent of flirtation. Also, any list would be too short. Would it include slipping on a banana peel? But couldn't we slip to provoke a laugh, strike up a conversation, and start an enduring relationship with a nearby and attractive orthopedist, i.e., to flirt? The creativity of the species and the flexibility of our concepts guarantee that any list must be too short. But still we can recognize people's flirting. If we don't consult a list of behaviors, how do we do it? Perhaps there is a useful list of abstract *types* of behaviors. To explore this possibility we have to introduce an infelicitous technical term and a more useful model; unfortunately the term and the model are a set. We have to hold off flirtations as we construct the machinery.

Here's the model: chess. The game of chess can be identified by types of behavior. "Bishop along a diagonal" is a type of behavior that is part of chess; "rook along the diagonal" is not. Here's the term: "constitutive rules." The constitutive rules of chess are the rules that tell us how the pieces can move and capture, as well as what it is to win or draw the game. Although we couldn't memorize all the individual behaviors that could enter into a game of chess, we easily manage the small set of constitutive rules.

Perhaps flirtation is similar; perhaps it too has a small set of constitutive rules. After all, we do know flirtation when we see it, but not by identifying purposes (you can flirt with diverse purposes) or by consulting a checklist (any list would be both too long and too short). Let's press the chess analogy to see if constitutive rules solve our problem. One hopeful sign is that there are good and bad moves in both chess and flirtation.

But there are two sorts of chess moves we call bad: moving your knight along a diagonal and exposing your queen to a pawn. The rules of chess *define* the first, but not second, as bad. But the first is *nullified* by the rules; the second is *imprudent* but within the rules. Can we make this distinction in flirtation? You can be imprudent, but in what other sense can you make a bad move? Would it make sense in flirtation to say, "That isn't a legal move, take it back"? But we do talk of people "not playing by the rules" in flirting, e.g., ignoring your date to talk with someone else. It's imprudent. Is it anything more than that? It seems to be a violation, perhaps of an implicit rule we have as commonsense actors. And it is. It is a violation of rules constitutive of gatherings, but it isn't a violation of constitutive rules of flirtation. If it violated constitutive rules of flirtation, it would be senseless to say that, in a particular case, it was a good move. But it does make sense to say: "Ignoring my date was a wonderful strategy in our flirtation. It made her first jealous and then eager." On the other hand, there is no context in which "knight along the diagonal" is a wonderful strategy. It isn't a strategy at all; it isn't part of chess. So there aren't constitutive rules defining flirtation. For the same reason there can't be a list of *behaviors*—anything could be a part of flirtation. Yet there are types of behavior that do constitute flirtation. To get at them we return to chess.

There is more to chess than just a list of allowable moves; chess has a *point:* mating. You have to do more than move the pieces in legal ways to be said to be playing chess; your moves have to be *organized* to avoid being mated and to mate your opponent. Someone who randomly selects allowable moves isn't playing chess. It seems, then, that to play chess is to have a particular purpose: mating. But this is a bit too simple. We need to distinguish the diverse purposes of chess players, the pleasures that attract them, and the point of chess.

Bobby's purpose in playing is making money; mating is a means to that end—thus Bobby never plays without a jackpot. Others play to different ends: to impress their friends with their skill, to appear to be intellectuals, to meet interesting people, or to write computer programs modeled on chess playing to show how Mind works. Yet they are all trying to mate,[1] and it is that attempt that leads us to say they are playing chess. They have different purposes, but their behaviors have the same point: mating. The *point* belongs to chess; *purposes* belong to the players. To call a behavior part of a chess game is to claim that it is directed at mating. We have no need to explore the individual motives of the actors to determine whether they are playing chess. Further, we follow a game, understand a strategy, and criticize a move by seeing it in light of the point of chess. We don't need to speculate about psychological states to determine whether a strategy is a good one or not.

Now the pleasures of chess. If you play chess to make money, the money may afford pleasures, but the pleasures the money affords are hardly pleasures of chess. They could be gotten in

1. Ken's case looks different. After accepting his boss's invitation to play, he discovers two facts: she won't be a good sport about losing, and he plays much better than she. His purpose is now clear—to lose. But he can't just lose; he must appear to be trying to mate. If it becomes obvious that he's throwing the game, or even playing without attention or concern, then he is insulting her. For her to believe she's fulfilling her purpose, displaying her mastery, and for Ken to achieve his, keeping his job, he must appear to try to mate, i.e., appear to have his moves called forth by the structure of chess. So even he cannot ignore the point of chess in trying to lose.

other ways—by work, theft, or inheritance. Even the pleasure of winning, if it is just the joy of victory, could be gotten by winning another game. But the pleasures of seeing a way to fork queen and rook, or break a pin, or even convert a lost game into a draw are bound to chess.[2]

Now we can get the sex back into flirtation. We argued before that you can flirt without having a sexual *purpose*. But sex is not irrelevant to flirtation; it gives flirtation its point. The reason we called your behavior with your ugly boss flirting was that it is something sensible to do to stimulate sexual interest.[3] In saying you were flirting with your boss we remain uncommitted about your ultimate purpose—a raise, hiring your brother, or having fun. We are committed just to the view that your behavior is organized by the goal of stimulating sexual interest. All of what you do that doesn't relate to this end we shouldn't call flirtation. Sex, if not sexual interest, can be gotten nonflirtatiously, of course. The point of flirting is not the sex act but, roughly, getting your partner to acknowledge a desire for sexual intimacy.[4] This is why snubbing your date was part of a flirtation (it was designed to pique interest) and the ophthalmologist's coming close wasn't[5] (although we could see how it might

2. Of course, we might invent another game that had forks to make and pins to evade. This new game would provide pleasures like those of chess. The similarity of the pleasures derives from the similarity of the games.

3. "Stimulating sexual interest" is, of course, too broad. If you propositioned your boss, offered to trade favors for favor, you would not be said to be flirting. When you flirt you are attemtping to stimulate interest in your personality and to present yourself as "stimulated" by hers. Flirtation may really be a "negotiation," as Blau (1964) claims, but it must be a covert one, partially concealed from the negotiators. It is this covert quality, together with the ambiguities we discuss later, that conceals the serious business of flirtation and gives it its attractive playfulness.

4. The point of chess is different in an important sense from that of flirtation. Flirtation's point is psychological; chess's is not. In chess it makes perfect sense to say that your opponent was: chagrined, impressed, given a headache; nonetheless, you won. The point of chess, mating, is specified by the positions of the pieces and how they got there (according to the rules), not by the psychological state of the opponent, although your purpose in playing this game may be just to humiliate him. On the other hand, the point of flirtation involves a psychological state of another player, i.e., the "acknowledgment" of a desire for sexual intimacy. Cooking is another activity defined not by constitutive rules, but by its goal—preparing food to eat. In cooking, as in flirtation, "a good move" is almost anything serving that end (unlike chess). Cooking involves some behaviors tedious in themselves (dicing onion) and others delightful in themselves (smelling spices) and others whose delights are strategic (figuring out which ingredients to combine). You can partake of the pleasures of cooking without partaking of its point—sometimes it's fun to cook even when you are not hungry and won't eat. Flirtation can be fun even when you have no interest in its end.

5. Remember Ken (ftn. 1) who was deliberately losing at chess to improve his chances with his boss. Now let's suppose, having passed this career hurdle, he starts to flirt. His purpose

have been—part of the dramaturgical perils of a gynecological exam, see Emerson, 1970).

Now let's consider some pleasures of flirtation. There is of course the charm of sex itself. But this isn't a pleasure of flirtation per se—rape, masturbation, prostitution, and connubial bliss share this joy. There are other pleasures closely tied to flirtation. First, there is the pleasure of finding another person sexually attracted to you. Second, there are pleasures akin to those of chess—the pleasure involved in carrying off just the right move, of exercising strategic talents, or of deciphering the mysteries of your partner's motives. And finally, there are pleasures associated with flirtation because the things we typically do to flirt are pleasant in their own right, e.g., having an animated conversation, looking at an attractive person, touching.[6] To sum up then: actors have diverse purposes in flirting, but flirtation is defined by its sexual point and is attractive because of its diverse pleasures as well as the various purposes it might serve.

Pleasures, Point, and Ambiguities of Purpose

The interplay of pleasures and points can lend ambiguity to the purposes of someone flirting, for the recipient of the attention and for the flirt himself. Let's return to the chessboard to see why. It would be odd indeed to find someone arranging a pin who didn't know that he was playing chess; yet it would be less odd to find someone startled to discover he was flirting.

Recall first that we found constitutive rules for chess but not for flirtation. In other words, we found types of behavior that made up the game of chess, and we found that the types were identifiable independent of the point of chess, e.g., bishop along the diagonal is a move whether it advances toward check

---

might be to spend the night—his boss is very attractive. But let's suppose he is faithful and has a headache after the chess game anyway. He may still flirt to impress her with his *savoir faire*, distract her from suggesting another game, or see if she'll flirt back (marriages don't last forever and headaches pass). Or he may do it just because it's fun or even a habit. Regardless of his sexual state or intent (immediate or delayed), if he is to flirt (or at least appear to flirt) he shall have to act as if some sexual favor, however slight, were his goal.

6. There are also the unspoken pleasures involved in half realizing we are flirting and suspecting that our partner does also. Some of the animation and vivacity that enlivens Andy and Debbie's not otherwise very engaging discussions derives from this subterranean source.

mate or not. Second, the physical moving of the pieces abstracted from a strategic role is hardly a pleasure. What account could an actor have for pushing a pawn independent of the game? Could he say, "No, I'm not playing chess. I just enjoy moving pawns"? But, as an empirical matter, many of the moves in flirtation are pleasures in themselves, many of the things we might do in flirting are fun. For this reason the flirt can see his flirtatious behavior as sensible even when abstracted from the point or pattern of the flirtation. A person can flirt, then, without seeing any particular behavior as a step toward something else. To see that the pleasures of flirtation allow the flirt to miss that she's flirting, consider this example. Suppose she always goes to Harry's Bar and Grill after work, where there happens to be an attractive, blond young man with whom she always exchanges a word or two. Now suppose he decides to spend his bar time next door, sipping Lotus Blossom tea profoundly at the Incidental Meditation Institute. Oddly, she had never thought of Lotus Blossom tea as a substitute for Wild Turkey or *"Omne Mane Padme Ohum?"* for conversation. But now she eases the trip home from work with meditation. She may find it more difficult to ignore the role of the blond in her reciting the mantra than it was to ignore his role in her stopping for a Wild Turkey. After all, Wild Turkey is an obvious pleasure, mantras are not.[7]

In the bar, her purpose is ambiguous to herself and to others. Further, this ambiguity may not be resolvable. No matter how long we stare at the behavior, no matter how many questionnaires about physical attractiveness or TAT cards we present, no matter how many EEG waves we monitor, we may find ourselves with an unresolved ambiguity. But, after the charms of Incidental Meditation pale, but those of the young man don't, a flirtation is unmistakable. In retrospect, we and she can see her stopping for Wild Turkey as part of the same flirtation—i.e., part of a pattern of behavior leading to a certain goal—but this does not mean that she *intended* her stopping *at the bar* as part of that pattern. Perhaps she formed the intent, developed the motive, conceived the goal of flirting with him only after he

7. If you plan to flirt and hide that fact from yourself, it will be helpful not to have distinct, and especially publicly announced, likes and dislikes. Flirting can lead to an extremely broad collection of newly discovered interests.

formed his new intent, developed his new motive, and conceived his new goal of tranquility.

Talking about her purposes at the bar, then, is confusing just because her purposes *were* confused. Claiming either that she had something more in mind with him or that she didn't would be misleading. But at least in retrospect we can call her actions in the bar her first step in flirting with him without resolving the mysteries of intentionality.[8] Saying it was a first step in her flirtation calls attention to its relation to the point of flirtation without committing ourselves to anything more. Similarly, even while she is at the Institute, where it is clear to all who know her that she is there just because of him, it may not be obvious to us, her friends, or her, just what further plans she has with regard to him. But it is clear to everyone, except perhaps her man, that she's flirting; what makes it clear is the goal her behavior is suited to, although it is not clear she will ever achieve that goal.[9] A concept like flirtation allows us to call attention to the way a particular action is, was, or might be related to a particular goal, without committing ourselves to claiming that the actor intended, or even was aware of, the way the action leads, led, or might lead to the goal (see ch. 5 for a similar analysis of gossip).

Collective Collusion

We have not dealt so far with an obvious feature of flirtation (and chess) that should make it very difficult to not know you are flirting: flirtation needs two people.[10] One very good reason for knowing you are playing chess is that the person across the board is too. It's not just that she's sitting there with you; she's

8. If we are sure she went to the bar and kept going to the bar for reasons other than the blond, although her going might still be a precondition of her later flirtation, we are not likely to call it a first step.

9. One way psychoanalysis has of being misleading is to claim that the actor all along unconsciously intended to pursue that goal. This rests on two mistaken assumptions: (1) that the question of intentionality is one of consciousness, a mistake we take up later; and (2) that intentions, at least unconscious ones, are always unambiguous.

10. We leave aside the question of whether "flirting" is an achievement term, i.e., whether if someone tries and fails to attract another's sexual interest we should say he "flirted" or he "tried to flirt." We treat the more central case where the advances meet with at least some response.

fitting her moves to yours. Flirting, also, often involves another person's fitting behavior to yours. Why doesn't this announce your flirtation? In addition to the reasons above, further features of flirtation keep things ambiguous. When we flirt we often have good reasons not to make an announcement of our intentions and so does our partner. Announcing your goal, if you have one, proclaims your intent and forces the issue of your partner's cooperation, and this may not be wise for a variety of reasons. You might not think your chances are good yet, and you want to wait a while. This will give you time to plan your spontaneity and wit. Besides, you don't want to make a fool of yourself. Or you suspect that your partner will be more amenable on the fifth date, not because you'll look any better on the fifth date, but just because it will be the fifth date—everyone knows that's an appropriate interval to wait. Delay can be useful in another way; perhaps you're not sure yourself what you want to do—in general, you may be married—or just with this particular other, or at this particular time—you are very busy. Or it may be an inauspicious setting for you or your partner to announce intent—neighbors, spouses, and pastors make unsupportive audiences. Perhaps, as an aesthete, you know enough to prolong the dalliance for its own charm. And there are some people delightful to flirt with, but nothing more serious. So there are several advantages in avoiding premature announcement—for both of you.

The tactical infelicity of announcing your plan can affect your ignorance of what you are doing in two ways. First, it gives you a reason to refrain from doing something that ordinarily makes intentions clear: making a public announcement. Let's consider the relation between private intents and public announcements in another domain: you are playing with the idea of going to graduate school, and you have been accepted. You are still unsure but it's April 15, the deadline. Turning down the invitation settles the matter, publicly and privately. On the other hand, accepting complicates things. It would still be possible to back out, but that would be a serious thing to do: reasons could be called for and a reputation earned. So public commitment plays a role in the formation of intent (although one can have a firm private intent without announcing it). Having to declare provides a reason, cause, and a way to clarify intent. Since you don't have to announce you are flirting you don't have to fully intend to; you don't even have to think about it seriously.

Second, because it is unwise to make your intentions too clear to your partner, you have a reason to infuse your flirtatious behavior with ambiguity. This ambiguity veils what you are doing, not only from your partner but from yourself. So while your partner in chess provides further reason for not being able to ignore the fact that you are playing, your partner in flirtation may provide the very conditions of ignorance. Ambiguities are a hallmark of flirtation. Indeed, once intentions are clear, flirtation is over, although its fruit may still remain to be enjoyed.[11]

We now turn to some uses of and confusions of ambiguity, which surrounds the notions of what a person "means" or "means to do." Tracing the ways that behavior can be ambiguous will show us some senses in which actions can "mean things."

AMBIGUITY

Reactions, Actions, and Coincidences

Let's start our exploration of ambiguity with a behavior that often has a place in flirtation: mutual eye contact. Andy and Debbie may find themselves looking into each other's eyes. How could this happen? Andy was looking for Tom and caught Debbie's gaze in the sweep—coincidence. Or he heard her close the top of her cigarette lighter, and he automatically turned in the direction of the sound—reaction. Or he was looking in her eyes to communicate something. The reason eye contact is ambiguous is just because it could be any one of these sorts of

11. Consider a case in which you and your partner announce your passion and your plan to fulfill it immediately. Whatever you do on the way to bed, it isn't flirting. Further, if one of you backs out, the other will have every right to feel used, cheated, or teased, unless a good excuse is at hand. Flirtation, resting on ambiguity, offers no commitment and gives no right to claim abuse. To claim you were teased is to claim your partner went beyond flirting to committing. Of course, the disappointed one may be inclined to see a tease in a flirt. This may be untrue, but 'tease' implies reneging on a commitment. If one party declares intent and the other holds back, there will still be room for flirting—room provided by one still unsettled intent.

behaviors. Flirtation often trades in this ambiguity. It is useful to draw out these distinctions.

In the coincidence case, Andy's behavior was unrelated to Debbie's. Debbie was neither the cause nor the target of his looking her way. In the reaction case, Andy's behavior was caused by Debbie's, although she wasn't its target. Indeed, the class of behaviors we shall call reactions are distinguished by the fact that they are passive, automatic, and caused rather than done to bring something about, e.g., turning in the direction of a sound.[12] Intentional action, on the other hand, is done to achieve some purpose, e.g., looking into Debbie's eyes (if done to communicate something or at least to get some response from her). What is important to the role of a caught eye in flirtation is that as commonsense actors we know that a caught eye could be any one of these three. Here are some examples of other flirtatious behaviors that trade on the ambiguity between coincidence and intention. Three days in a row Debbie bumps into Andy on the corner as she comes out of the office. Is this because she happened to get out of work at the same time, and of course their paths intersect, or was he waiting for her? Or, in another example, Andy appears on Debbie's doorstep sweaty, slightly grease-stained, and apologetic. He asks if she would let him use the phone to call the gas station, and while he waits for the tow truck, they get to talking. Well, fan belts do break—even in Debbie's neighborhood. As a last example, Debbie goes for a ride with Andy and he pulls the venerable "the-car's-out-of-gas" routine. In all of these examples, the actor may be using something that he knows "could" happen by accident as a step in the flirtation. Because it could "just be an accident," its intention is disguised. If it weren't, it would lose its usefulness. We suspect, for this reason, that while cars run out of gas more frequently than they once did, they are less likely to do so at "just the right moment," except when bearing the attractive but deeply naive.[13] Some of the ambiguities in flirtations, and for

12. We do talk of the Declaration of War against Japan as a *reaction* to the bombing of Pearl Harbor; yet it was surely intentional. And this seems to upset our distinction. But note, this term stresses the way the U.S. had *no choice* but to declare war, and acted in a rapid, unpremeditated, albeit coherent way.

13. Or the willing not so naive, but still in need of an excuse (see Whyte, 1943, and the place of cars in Cornerville sex life). Or the even less naive who wants to be seen as the

that matter, in life, are between accident and action; sometimes we are a victim of an ambiguity, sometimes its delighted recipient, and sometimes we exploit it. Now we turn back to the ambiguity between intentional actions and reactions, and the distinction that it blurs. (This distinction parallels Goffman's, 1959, treatment of "expressions given" and "expressions given off"—as does our discussion.)

Smiles, laughs, pitch and rate of speech are the sorts of things that might be just reactions—things that happen to a person. Or they might be intentional.[14] For example, at a party you might ask yourself: was she helpless with laughter at my joke or was she laughing to let me know how things are going? Let's see why we might want to package an intentional action as if it were a reaction.

The expression of intent has two consequences: (1) it allows others to predict our behavior, and (2) it leaves us open to sanctions of various kinds if we don't do what we said we intended to do. Someone flirting may well have an interest in giving his partner a basis for prediction without committing himself; signs that can be spontaneous, or that can be enacted but must nonetheless be treated as spontaneous, are suited to this need. Thus, initiatives can be made and encouragements offered without fear of rejection or precipitous surrender. So regardless of how loud she laughed, the woman at your party has the right to retreat to the posture of someone who did nothing at all. Thus, the distinction between "what we do" and "what's happening to us" is overlaid by a distinction of a different sort, the distinction between what we are accountable for and what we are not.[15]

---

sort of person who must have an excuse. Or the least naive who demands the courtesy of an attempt on the part of the partner to produce some excuse—it's the thoughtfulness that counts. And then imagine the point at which naivete disappears into grace: A believes that B needs A to be the sort of person who wouldn't, without an excuse, and although A gave up excuses with braces and doesn't care whether this is obvious to most people, A is touched by B's need, and so becomes the "grateful" recipient of B's effort.

14. The distinction between intentional action and reactions does not rest on consciousness; in saying he acted intentionally we are not claiming that the goal sought was in mind as the person acted. We are claiming that the person adjusted (or would have adjusted) his action to reach the goal. If this is true, imputing intention has no need of speculation about contents of consciousness. There is a long tradition of analyzing "intention" independent of consciousness, e.g., Tolman (1932), Peters (1958), Ryle (1949).

15. Aristotle considered cases in which these distinctions don't quite overlap. Take the behavior of someone drunk: to a degree, his behavior is more like something that happens to him than something he does. Yet we do not fully excuse him. Aristotle would say that

Even if we are sure that a behavior is either only a reaction or obviously intentional, there may still be ambiguities.

Ambiguities of Reaction

Let's suppose, going back to the party, that the laugh is a spontaneous reaction. Still, what is it a reaction to: the wit of my joke, its patent idiocy, the blueness of my joke, the blueness of my eyes, her discovering that I was the type that would tell such a joke, or the tastelessness of my jacket? Is her conversation so animated because: I'm such a good listener; I'm so witty; my job fascinates her? Or is it because she's on speed, a vacation, or sleep deprivation? There are ambiguities both about what causes a reaction as well as which aspects of the cause are effective—personality or decolletage.

Ambiguities of Intentional Action

We want to consider here ambiguities of actions that are purely intentional. Let's start with those not especially involving language. Suppose you decide that the same woman is staring intentionally at you. Does she mean no one's worn a tie that wide in ten years, or why don't you get me a drink? On her part she might wonder why is he standing so close to me now that he brought me the drink? Is it so we can hear over the music? Why are all those buttons open? Is it the weather or to express an invitation? It's possible to touch someone to greet, guide, or steady them, or to get their attention, but are these intentions also in service of another?

Consider doing a favor, e.g., Debbie offers to help Andy with his car. Surely it's intentional; but is it because she's become interested in transmissions as well as Kant, she's just nice, or she owes him a favor? Or is her offer just a pretext to get close to Andy because she's never had a big brother, this way she can get to know Andy's older brother, or she is interested in deepening her relationship with Andy so they can be good

---

this is because, although he may not be responsible for his actions while drunk, he is responsible for becoming drunk in the first place. And if he is addicted, and therefore not quite responsible for becoming drunk, he is responsible for having become the sort of character that can no longer avoid drunkenness.

friends or lovers? Perhaps she herself has considered all these possibilities and couldn't decide; maybe she never really thought about any of them.

Now let's consider ambiguities of language.[16] Talk removes one ambiguity: we don't talk by accident. Tongues may slip, but not in the sense that you meant to spit and a word came out. You may have meant to say, "I love you," and said, "I glove you"; still, you did mean to say *something*. The topics you pick to talk about and whether you dwell on them or skirt them are more or less intentional. They may reflect your interests, or pretended or hidden interests. General themes, "my feelings about open marriage," and specific facts, "my spouse is a social psychologist doing research in El Salvador for the month," may be introduced for their color, or for more instrumental reasons.

Compliments have an obvious ambiguity, teasing a less obvious one. Compliments may be required—just to be polite—or they may mean admiration. Teasing, a mock insult, is more paradoxical. Putting someone down even playfully seems an odd way to flirt; but in the context of continued interaction, especially otherwise pleasant interaction, the teasing can't be all that serious. Yet if it isn't meant to insult, why do it? Well, for one thing, it shows interest, interest in *your* failings. Further, like handholding, "insulting" is licensed, i.e., it expresses or lays claim to some degree of intimacy.[17] The balance to be struck between the insult's insult and the intimacy implied by making the insult provides an interesting unclarity. So even though language use is intentional and known to be intentional, there is plenty of space for ambiguity about what the person meant in saying what she said even when the literal meaning of the utterance is clear.[18]

16. We ignore the simplest ambiguity that can arise in language: referential opacity. In this sort of ambiguity the referent of a word or phrase is ambiguous.

17. As Goffman (1971) points out, hands are typically held in the context of certain sorts of relationships, but handholding can also act as a "change signal." Taking someone's hand for the first time makes an implicit claim to the sort of relationship that would warrant holding hands, and allowing a hand to be held expresses just that sort of relationship. The taking and allowing create the relationship that will make the next instance of a held hand nonproblematic. Ritual insults work the same way.

18. The notion of 'literal meaning' is inflamed. Let's consider an example borrowed from Searle (1979): you order a Big Mac and your very efficient waiter brings you one—encased in lucite. Has he complied with the literal meaning of your order? Surely you wouldn't pay for it; surely he didn't do what you wanted him to. Indeed, he didn't do what anyone in our culture would see you "asked" him to. You might well complain to the manager that

Handholding illustrates a different sort of ambiguity of intentional action, as well as the problems such ambiguities pose. The ambiguity of handholding rests, in part, on the fact that the same act, physically described, can have different meanings.

A hand held to offer support or comfort can slide into a hand held for different reasons. Not only are there ambiguities in the grasping, but there are ambiguities in the response. Removing a hand holding yours as if it were a cold reptile is clear, but just leaving it there might mean different things: the person might prefer to remove the hand but doesn't want to make an issue of it; or she is relieved that the hands finally met. Part of the problem in interpretation comes from the fact that the meaning of the response to the initiative depends on the sophistication of the target: is it a passive response because she doesn't realize that a more active one is called for, or because this realization has struck home and she gives a passive response for just that reason?

There is another sense of "meaning" we haven't yet considered, one attended by a swarm of ambiguities useful for flirtation. Suppose Andy and his brother drive past Debbie's house, and Andy says to his brother, "The red sedan in the driveway *means* Debbie is home." The sense in which the "red sedan" means that is different from the way language, or even language use, means things. Andy is making an *inference* based on his noticing, for all practical purposes, a constant conjunction between Debbie's location and the red sedan; understanding language isn't a matter of making correct inferences, but of mastering conventions.[19] The red sedan means Debbie is home in a

---

you didn't get your order. But the waiter could have brought you a sock, and that wouldn't comply with your order either. A sock is different from a Big Mac encased in lucite—it wouldn't be funny. In explaining why the even less digestible than usual Big Mac was funny but the sock wasn't, we shall need to refer to something very like "literal meaning."

19. Consider the distinction between meaning by inference and meaning by convention in the context of two ways for students to know whether the material from a particular lecture will be on the exam. In the first case a student asks, "Will today's lecture be on the midterm?" and the instructor says, "No." Her answer means the material won't be on the exam. In the second case let's imagine that an industrious student notices a curious but perfect correlation, i.e., whenever the instructor wears blue slacks, the material from the lecture isn't on the exam. One day this industrious student notices the instructor's blue slacks and says to a friend, "Her blue slacks mean the lecture material won't be on the exam." Wearing blue slacks and answering "no" to a direct question are radically different ways of meaning the material won't be on the test. To see this, imagine that the instructor puts today's lecture on the exam.

If she did this after saying "No," the student would have every right to say she lied, or at least was negligently absentminded. But the industrious student in the second case has

way entirely different from the way Debbie's blush means she is embarrassed. Blushing is built into the species; red sedans aren't. The multiple ambiguities of an act's meaning create challenges, opportunities, pitfalls, and anxieties of interpretation, as well as afford the means to pursue a flirtation.

Consider this fable of the life history of a line: it is the first rainy night since the institution of singles bars. The bar is closing, and since you have one of the few cars in front, you chivalrously offer the lovely lad next to you a lift. In gratitude he invites you up for a drink, which leads to another drink. In our fable, neither you nor he had any particular plans for the night when you offered him a ride. You did it just out of generosity; he just wanted to stay dry. Even if he had inferred an overture behind the offer, still "anyone could see" it might be just a favor, so he would not be announcing he was "that kind of boy" in accepting. Time passes. Your offer turned out to have such a pleasant upshot that you employ it each rainy, foggy, or even dewy night; and it has even caught on with all of your friends. Unfortunately, the success of your line converts its innocent ambiguity into an announcement. "Let me give you a ride" is now not merely grounds for *inferring* intent, but a way to announce that intent. If someone accepts a ride now, he is accepting an invitation for more than a ride; and he knows it and knows that you know it. He realizes that you could rightly call him a tease if he did not follow through. Unfortunately, when a line reaches this state of perfect clarity, it becomes useful for jokes, but worthless for flirtations.

Ambiguities even play a role near flirtation's denouement where the scene would appear to be far from ambiguous. For example, not inviting him up "for a drink" could mean: a temporary personal indisposition; the roommate is home; or the apartment is a mess; or adequate preparations haven't been made—and the drug store's closed. And these may be true and offered as reasons, not true and offered as reasons, or true and not offered as reasons. A lull might also mean: I'm not the kind of person who does that after only . . . ; or not until we have

---

no such right to be offended; he should say that his inference was wrong, not that she misled him. 'Lying', 'misleading', and like terms are tied to the ways we abuse conventions. Mistaken inferences are the responsibility of those who draw them, not those who give evidence for them.

a meaningful relationship; or it might just mean that: a little alcohol, a good meal, a trip to Florence, or a bit of flattery had better be applied. Or it might mean: not with the likes of you; or I've never done this to my partner before and I don't ever plan to; or next week will be better—I'll be alone; or think of the children. And all of these could be offered as reasons and be true, or not offered as reasons and be true, or be offered as reasons and not be true. Each of these reasons or pretexts has meaning in the sense of a place in your, and a place in the other's, plans. The difficulty is not in discerning what they express, but in determining what moves they set up and what moves they foreclose. To get through this calm requires strategy. For instance, you might point out: you are only 'at home' in messy surrounds; how miraculous it is that our relationship has become so meaningful so quickly; "Let's have just one more drink"; or affairs are very good for marriages, my analyst has written several books about it; there is a good deal of research showing that children are hardier than we used to think.

Of course, these are quite sensible answers to concerns, worries, and objections. But they are also parts of strategies and should be interpreted in this way also. So the previous replies might mean: I am fastidious, but I can put up with anything for one night; meaning is a matter of feelings and mine are aroused; one more drink should be enough; I'll help you believe this if you want to. So there are abundant ambiguities even toward the end of love's sweet course.

Ambiguity Is a Resource

The inability to say in every case what a person's purpose is, has appeared to philosophers as a defect in the concept of purpose, one to be corrected. It appears to psychologists as a technical difficulty to be overcome by methodological sophistication. We have treated it as a fact about actions, one that can't be argued or even measured away. Besides people treat it as a resource too valuable to let go.

CHAPTER SEVEN

Procrastination

Harré and Secord (1972), in the tradition of the "philosophy of action" (see White, 1968), model the scientific description of behavior with a refinement of commonsense actors' understanding of behavior. They propose that scientists ought, and commonsense actors do, typically treat behavior as rational and intentional—roughly, that people choose means to suit ends. Yet, there are, clearly, behaviors that do not fit this model.

Some of these orphans the model should not adopt: the untoward behavior exhibited in general paresis, epileptic fits, or retorts missed because of injury to Broca's area are sorts of things we shouldn't expect a model of rational action to shelter. Habits, rituals, and well-learned skills have a place in rational action, but, because they are run off rather than planned and adapted, they deserve an analysis of their own. Here we focus on a rational behavior and a liability that does not, as far as we know, have its source in internal lesion—writing a paper, a clear member of the family of intentional, planned, even deliberated action, and procrastinating writing, a clear liability for this sort of action. Writing a paper typically exhibits the working out of a plan that is extended over time, has a clear goal, and requires sustained attention to the better alternative (the most apt means to an end) at every step. Procrastination cannot, or cannot always, be ascribed to the limitations of the mental machinery; it isn't, or isn't always, a result of a finite memory or attention span; it doesn't always result from fatigue, epinephrine depletion, or a lesion in some hemisphere or other.

Further, procrastination is also puzzling for our notion of self-control (see Secord, 1977; Alston, 1977): the procrastinator is, we shall develop, someone who knows what she wants to do, in some sense can do it, is trying to do it—yet doesn't do it. If a model of rational action is to be general, it must cope with phenomena like procrastination. We shall first try to show that procrastination is necessarily irrational[1] and then show how it can cohabit with a model of rational action.

Procrastination has attractions aside from its interest to the theorist: it is a psychopathology of everyday life, as curious to those who suffer it as to those who would explain it.

> . . . I do not know.
> Why yet I live to say "this thing's to do,"
> Sith, I have cause, and will, and strength, and means,
> To do't. Examples gross as earth exhort me.
> (*Hamlet* 4.4.43–46)

Hamlet's dwelling on incestuous sheets has intrigued one school of thought; his procrastination is at least as curious.

METHODS

We shall employ two methods to probe procrastination. First, to support the thesis that procrastination is necessarily irrational, an anomaly for rational models of people, we shall consider instances of a broader concept, "putting things off," to show that when "putting off" is rational it isn't procrastination.

1. We begin with this conception of rationality: rational action is action suited to fit some goal, given what the actor knows of his circumstances. As we develop the notion of procrastination, we shall see that there are behaviors we call irrational although they meet this criterion.

There is an inevitable circularity involving the concepts of belief and desire, i.e., to get some notion of what a person believes one must start with some belief about what he might want and vice versa. Some have seen this circularity as destructive of the above conception of rationality. But we would suggest that although one can never achieve certainty about beliefs and wants, the conceptual frame of wanting and believing is useful to understanding behavior. However, in some cases it is not useful: sometimes what a person wants is baffled by his procrastination.

We don't apologize for resting our analysis on concepts the certainty of which can never be certified because we are skeptical about whether there are logically necessary and sufficient conditions for the application of any but trivial concepts.

Further traces of the relations between procrastination and rationality will be tracked in analyses of how believing and wanting are distorted in and by procrastinating.

Our second method, akin to that of ideal types, will be to construct some cases of procrastination and classes of procrastinatory behavior that are unmistakably irrational, and clearly procrastination. We shall look for the minimum deviations from rationality that could produce such aberrations, and in that sense explain them.

PUTTING THINGS OFF

Let's entertain some examples of putting things off. Which would we call procrastination and which not? We shall show that rationality does the sorting: in our everyday intuitions we would not say that someone rationally putting something off was procrastinating.

First, imagine someone putting off something onerous in hopes of getting out of it. Suppose he were *sure* he would get out of it; would anyone say he is procrastinating? But what if there were only a *chance* he'd get away with it? Well, while we have no inclination to legislate how unlikely the indulgence must be for "waiting to see what happens" to become procrastination, we do claim that the better the odds the more rational the stalling, and the less inclined we should be to say the person is procrastinating. Of course, perceptions of odds are notoriously distorted in the direction of wants. Anticipating a *deus ex machina* with the confidence appropriate to the rising of the sun is one way of irrationally putting things off, one way to procrastinate. It is one liability of intentional action: motivation can drive belief. Furthermore, it is one long studied in the psychological tradition, e.g., cognitive dissonance (see Festinger, 1957).

What shall we say about someone who puts something off she knows she won't get out of? Judy has only the weekend to do a paper. Tom invites her to the movies for Saturday night. She says to herself, "I'll just work very hard on Sunday, and do it then." Is she procrastinating? Is she acting rationally? Could her putting off be both? We need to know more. Suppose this is the ninth weekly paper for her course, and she has written the previous eight "A" papers in six hours? Duties must be fit to pleasures; she has good reason to trust the fit. Wouldn't we say she is neither procrastinating nor acting irrationally? Putting things off even until the last moment isn't procrastination if there is reason to believe they will take only that moment. Indeed, sacrificing pleasures to do things at the first moment, when they clearly could just as well be done later, is itself a form of irrationality—a rare species, one we know only by rumor.[2]

But suppose she doesn't get the paper done. Imagine that this one turned out to be more difficult than the others or that her work was interrupted by firemen extinguishing the blaze in her study. Judy might, in retrospect, reproach herself for procrastinating, but we, and on reflection Judy, should realize she had been unfair. Her putting off wasn't procrastination. So, a "putting off" resulting in a late or bad job need not be procrastination—if done with reason.[3] This case illustrates a liability of action, but not one that challenges Judy's rationality. Rather, it reminds us that people act, and can only act, in the absence of perfect knowledge.

Debbie is a pre-med with a paper due in her English course. She knows she needs Saturday night and all day Sunday to do the paper well. But Tom asks her to go out on Saturday night. She accepts, knowing her paper will be late or mediocre. But after all, it's just a requirement she's meeting. Here we have another rational, deliberate putting off—not procrastination. Perhaps even a pre-med should be serious about English, but she isn't and, therefore, acts rationally.

Now let's complicate Debbie's story. Her mother does not share her view of the English requirement, or Tom, and believes Tom ought to be sacrificed to cummings. So Debbie says, "I've plenty of time to do it on Sunday"—knowing she won't.

2. Our informant, Hillary Glick, suggests that this form of irrationality is often a result of a fear of the anxiety that approaching a deadline would produce. Here even if the anxiety is irrational, the premature work is a sensible way to cope with it.

3. A more interesting case is one in which Judy has no reason to expect some *particular* disruption, but she has reason to believe that something will come up—whether it is a long phone call, a friend stopping by, or a neighbor asking for a favor. The excuse: "How was I to know *that* would happen?" is sometimes pale, not because the person should have known *that* would happen, but because the person should have known that *something* distracting would occur.

This makes Debbie devious, not irrational, and her sin is not procrastination.[4] Her sin is the sacrifice of an obligation to a pleasure. Moreover, Tom's attractiveness isn't a side effect of the alternatives she faces; she'd go out with him even if she didn't have a paper to do. Her choice of Tom over the paper may make her foolish, hedonistic, shortsighted. Still, anyone appreciating Debbie's priorities and Tom's widely known charms can understand her choice.

To come closer to procrastination's irrationalities, let's consider a putting off unmarred by pleasure. Dave believes people should have clean apartments. He also has an important paper due in two days. Is his vacuuming the rug, dusting the credenza, and washing the windows procrastination? What details let us decide? Details concerning Dave's wants and beliefs matter. Suppose we ask Dave what is more important to him—a clean rug or a completed paper? And he says, "Dirty apartments spread the plague." It would be hard to make a charge of procrastination stick. His belief might be odd, but his actions follow from his wants and beliefs. His irrationality is not procrastination; his not working on his paper follows from his priorities. But suppose Dave's concern about the plague has a sporadic course, breaking out only when he recognizes that he ought to be writing a paper. Although Dave's vacuuming follows from his beliefs and wants, in this case we would be inclined to call him procrastinating. Thus, correspondence among beliefs, wants, and actions is not a sufficient defense against the charge of procrastination. What makes this sporadic fear of the plague procrastination is that it is caused by Dave's recognition of what he ought to do—the paper. In this way, the irrationality of procrastination is rooted in rationality: it is dependent on a person's knowing what to do. Here we have a case in which action is criticized as being irrational even though it is in the pursuit of some goal. So perhaps we should insist that for action to be rational its goal must be chosen rationally. But this is too stringent; explanations in terms of goals must come to an end somewhere. Still the example seems to

4. Debbie's "lie" may not be to her mother but to herself: she may be in "bad faith." This form of irrationality infects putting off and procrastination as it does the rest of our moral-rational affairs.

show that *some* ways of coming to have goals are irrational. A fully developed model of action as rational must include some distinctions among sorts of goals.

Changed desires induced by obligations are not *always* procrastination. Bob has always valued being a househusband, but he also has a tug toward getting a master's degree. His assignment to compare Lacan's and Sartre's revisions of psychoanalysis sends him once more in search of the vacuum bags. But this time while vacuuming, Bob realizes that he would really rather be a full-time househusband than an academic; he belongs in the home, not with Lacan. Or, perhaps, although he acknowledges his calling to structuralism, the pain of reading Lacan is so intense that he resigns himself to the kitchen. If this decision is not a transient eruption, we would see his vacuuming in the face of the paper as conversion, not procrastination. So a discussion of the rationality of goals will also have to consider the fit between those goals and the abilities, propensities, and values of the person who comes to have them independent of the causal path they followed in entering the person's life. In both Bob's and Dave's case the recognition of the necessity to do the paper was causal in having a new goal; yet Dave's sporadically cleaning house is irrational and procrastination, while Bob's devotion to housework is neither.

We have found, then, that putting offs are procrastination only when they are irrational, and the irrationality is caused by recognizing (or fancying) what one ought to be doing.[5] The irrationality can be a self-serving *belief* (e.g., an obligation will go away if ignored) or a free-floating ulterior *want* (e.g., a transient desire to have a spotless house only near deadlines). Thus only agents capable of recognizing what they ought to do are capable of procrastinating; it is an irrationality parasitic on rationality.

5. We include "fancied obligation" to cover two cases. An executive sees herself as obliged to fire an employee. She puts off the act through some convenient self-deception. Saying, "She recognized an obligation to fire him," implies that she ought to. But this may not be so—perhaps he is a victim of a blacklist. What makes her postponing really procrastination is her *fancying* that she had an obligation to fire him.

The second case is one in which, say, a student procrastinates writing a paper he wants to write, and anyone sees he can write, because he imagines himself to have an obligation to write the definitive work in the field rather than the sort of paper expected of him and within his competence. It isn't the difficulty of the task he has that makes him procrastinate, but the difficulty of the task he imagines. (We are indebted to Mark Boggs for this example.)

To understand the features of procrastination and how they might arise, we probe for the specific places where the parasites feed.

PROCRASTINATION'S FIRST STRAIN

We return to Dave, sporadically plagued by the demand for a clean apartment. Surely he is procrastinating, but *how* does the deadline get him to fear the plague and clean the house? A commonsense actor might say of Dave that he is cleaning *in order to not* write the paper. We take this explanation as a starting point of our analysis.

Ordinarily, when we say that a person is doing something in order to ' . . . ', the ' . . . ' specifies some state of affairs. We use the 'in order to . . . ' to claim that the person will pick a path to that state of affairs that appears efficient, pleasant, easy, etc. (at least within the bounds of moral constraint and convention). But "not doing the paper" doesn't specify *a* state of affairs; it specifies the infinite set of all states of affairs save doing the paper, and of this set cleaning the house could hardly appear to be the easiest or most pleasant. But this doesn't mean that the expression "he is doing x in order not to do y" is necessarily meaningless or vague. To understand this we must repair to context.[6]

Let's consider a context in which "Tim is doing x not to do y" is explanatory. "Tim is taking Seventh Avenue in order not to get stuck in traffic on the Eastside Drive." What is the force of this eminently sensible account? Tim can get to his destination using either Seventh Avenue or the Eastside Drive. But if he took the George Washington Bridge, which doesn't get him there, then "He is taking the George Washington Bridge in order not to get stuck on the Eastside Drive" would, at first blush, be mystifying. Similarly, "Dave is cleaning the house in order not to do the paper" is either arch, mystifying, or in need of a suitable context. Let's try to find one.

First, note that having a clean house and writing a good pa-

6. We might say in this case that Dave decided not to do the paper *and* is doing his housecleaning since it is the next most important thing, but then we would not say he was procrastinating. Only in a case in which the housecleaning has more to do with the paper than this would we say he is procrastinating.

per are both accomplishments, ways of displaying one's worth. In this sense, they both lead to the same goal. And vacuuming is less demanding. But if this is so, why ever write a paper? Because clean houses and well-written papers, although both accomplishments, are not interchangeable—even though they may fit in some larger general category. Unless housework and school work offered the same satisfactions to Dave, saying, "He's cleaning the house in order to not do the paper," falls through as an explanation. If the explanation had force it would be because it accuses Dave of fooling himself into believing that being a good housekeeper is at the moment more important than writing a good paper. If Dave does this then it is understandable why he is doing housework instead of the paper. It seems, then, that one of the defects to which rational action is prey is a confusion about the substitutability of ends. Can we develop an account of how this confusion could come about?

Well, it seems common that people invest themselves in different areas of their lives—jobs, relationships, hobbies—and sometimes when a return on one investment is slow, commitments can be shifted. So some trade-off is sensible. But there are limits to this strategy, limits that Dave's procrastination oversteps. A clean house isn't a good trade for a flunked course. Dave's housecleaning, then, is irrational, but only as an exaggeration of a common and benign strategy.[7]

A SECOND STRAIN

Some ways of procrastinating are hardly confusions about self-esteem. Take Ed. When he has a paper due, he decides to watch television for just ten minutes. He turns on *Lust for Life*, certain he will turn it off by the first commercial. Yet curiously, the eleven o'clock news finds Ed still at the TV. Other times, Ed decides to play just one game of pinball, to relax, but later finds himself ten dollars and one night poorer. What makes Ed's be-

7. There is another way of getting the house clean while writing a paper. Before Dave can start to write, he has to clear the clutter of books and magazines from his desk. He can't put them on the floor—that would be messy. So he has to put them on the bookshelf. But he has to put them away in order; he can't shove them in any old place. This means he has to arrange the bookshelf since it's been quite a while since he's straightened it out, but he can't arrange it yet because it's so dusty. Yet there is no point in dusting the shelves if he is not going to vacuum the floor. Unlike the previous case, Dave never exactly decided to clean the house.

havior procrastination and not pleasant dereliction is his unrevoked decision to work. By eleven o'clock, Ed himself may be bewildered by his own behavior and wonder why he hadn't stopped. Let's see if we can help him.

Imagine you have two days to write a paper. You believe it will take about six hours. To avoid being rushed, you decide to get to work. Further assume that writing the paper is itself unpleasant, or unpleasant because of the evaluation attached to it. Now suppose you had to decide what to do for just the next five minutes—either work on the paper or play one game of pinball. The paper can wait one game; there is little long-term cost. In the short run, five minutes of pinball is far more pleasurable than five minutes of paper writing, and after all, how much of a paper can you do in five minutes? Pinball is the obvious choice. The game is over so you must decide about the next five minutes. The situation is only trivially changed, so you will reach the same result. Once you've taken the possibility of playing pinball seriously and fragmented your night into five minute intervals, you may be doomed to play until you run out of money, the machine breaks, or someone meaner than you wants to play. Or you might realize that even five minutes has a real cost to the paper.[8] Because a single game of pinball is brief, it is particularly seductive. Other activities have similar allure. You may decide to watch ten minutes of television, listen to just one cut of a record, or read just one article in *Car and Driver*. One of the ways of being irrational and procrastinating is to act on *rational* calculations for intervals that are irrationally short. So one further liability to which rational action is prey arises from the interesting multiplicity of time intervals over which calculations can be made. A model that would capture rational action must not only show how means are fit to goals, but also show how appropriate intervals for calculation are picked.[9]

8. There are other ways out: pinball may get boring, or you may find yourself growing anxious and then realize you are anxious about your paper even though five minutes still don't matter—but anxiety does. Or you may catch on to the insidious logic of your situation. Or you may have a general policy to stop after just one game since you've found that if you don't, you'll find your evening will be taken from you. (We thank Art Levy for insights into procrastinating with pleasures.)

9. Stories about dentists may illustrate some niceties of calculation. In the first story you have a toothache and are passing by your dentist's office. You conclude that you will surely save yourself pain by having the root canal job now. So you decide to go in, but find as

The real curiosity of Ed's case is not that he spent the night pursuing pleasure instead of his paper—although that's what happened. Had he decided to leave the paper for pleasure he would have called Debbie for a date, not played pinball. He found himself with pinball in the first place out of virtue: when Debbie called he had said, "Sorry I can't go to the movies tonight. I have to work on my paper." When we procrastinate we are particularly likely to find ourselves sticking to things that are brief or can be dropped at any moment—not only ephemeral pleasures, like pinball, but also ephemeral chores.

A THIRD STRAIN

A different account will be needed for a person who finds himself fitfully reading cereal box labels or stockmarket quotations, or even alphabetizing the spice rack. As baffling as it might be to explain that you disappointed Debbie and didn't do your paper (though you did play pinball all night), it would be more perplexing, even demeaning, to find that you alphabetized your spice rack. Let's see if we can incorporate this oddness, too.

A person working smoothly on a paper has a goal, getting the paper done. If for some reason she were called upon to show her devotion, she would have the best possible evidence, the product. But suppose she becomes stymied. If she were called upon to show her devotion she would have to use other signs: the time spent sitting at her desk, the books piled up, the pleasures forsworn, her expressions of intense concentration and bafflement. The same signs are available to convince *herself* she is really working, or at least sincerely committed. Her need to externalize involvement, even to herself, contributes to her curious behavior. To see how, we have to set the scene.

Ann sits down to write her paper, works for a while, but then

---

you approach the door that the anticipation of the drill makes you unable to live up to your decision. You suffer a failure of courage. Sometimes as you back out you are accompanied by the comforting belief that you were wrong—teeth often heal themselves without dental attention. Sometimes you decide, on the run, that it isn't really pain you are feeling, it's more like a tickle—something you could live with. Sometimes you just run without the accompaniment of a comforting explanation. These are all irrational, all procrastination, all weaknesses of will. And all have to do with pain's ability to confuse. A model of rational action will have to take account of pain (and pleasure), not only as elements in a calculus, but as forces that distort it.

doesn't know what to write next. So she gets up; pacing helps her think. Then her eye is caught by last month's stockmarket report, on her desk because it had been used as a wrapping for a new ashtray. At this moment Ann can continue to pace, thinking about her paper, or she can browse through the financial news. Thinking about her paper is unpleasant; she's stuck, and even frightened because the paper is due soon. TastyKake's planned merger with Citibank isn't frightening, at least, and in this context it is a serviceable distraction. So she reads a line or two. One might explain Ann's uncharacteristic interest in the future of TastyKake by saying that she *chose* to read it rather than work on her paper, but this would be misleading.

We shouldn't allow a model of rational action to become promiscuous. We should distinguish choosing to do things from other ways of coming to do them; otherwise our model will mislead. For example, suppose Ann *decided* she needed a break from her pacing. She could have considered the many things available for her to do; she could have chosen one that was pleasant or useful. But this isn't what happened. Ann never *decided* to leave off pacing. She didn't consider watering her plants or cleaning her nails. Even to consider them would have shown that she was not working, and Ann knows she can't afford to take a break. Either she continues to pace or she distracts herself with whatever falls to hand. She is prey to capture by anything that requires a minimal commitment, doesn't take her from the scene, and isn't immediately painful. Ann needs both to avoid commitment to her distractions, lest she find herself not working, and to find distractions, since she is not working. This tension explains the fitful quality of her behavior.

The same conflict is expressed in other misfortunes of procrastination, for instance, bringing your books on vacation although you don't open them. Or on vacation in Bermuda you decline an invitation to play tennis in order to work on your paper, and then find you've neither worked nor played tennis. Escorting your books and declining tennis do not get work done, but they do dramatize commitment to it. They are tokens of sincerity if not proofs of accomplishment. We might say these irrationalities of procrastination are attempts to maintain oneself in readiness to work, in what might be called a "procrastination field."[10] Ann may come to feel that she doesn't really want to work, "After all, if I wanted to do it, I'd just do it." So there is a distinction between acting in order to reach a goal and, as Goffman (1959) points out, acting in a way to dramatize an attempt to reach a goal. Happily these often coincide, but when they don't, trade-offs can be made. Sometimes choices are made, and sometimes dramatic postures are taken.

PROCRASTINATION AND MOTIVATION

The irony is: Ann's efforts to portray herself as working force her to the distractions of trivia and her efforts eventually backfire; they make it all the harder to see herself as really wanting to do the project she's doing. If Ann had abandoned herself to the movies then at least she could imagine that although she really wanted to do the paper, this evening she wanted to go to the movies more. But just how much does she want to do the paper if she preferred to alphabetize the spice rack? Had she succumbed to the movies, she might see herself as undisciplined, giving in to an obvious temptation. But how tempting is learning TastyKake's corporate plans or putting the allspice before the basil? Reflection on these activities may convince her she is neurotic or loathes the topic she is writing on, even though she had thought it was her favorite. And even worse, there is something right about her reasoning.

There are close conceptual ties between wanting and doing, ties emphasized in the model of intentional action. It isn't that one collapses on the other. We can say with perfect sense that a person wanted to drive to work but didn't: he found that his car had been stolen or his tires mysteriously slashed. In these

10. Consider how well maintaining the "procrastination field" matches what you would do while waiting on a corner for a friend who is ten minutes late. This experience is unpleasant, not just because corners are sometimes snowy, wet, and windy—some corners are quite pleasant or would be if you were not waiting. In fact, a given corner might be surrounded by the best coffee house in the city, an art gallery you've always wanted to visit, and a cut-rate book store. Unfortunately, you cannot both wait in a prominent place and pursue these attractions. After all, while you are pursuing, you might miss your friend. What you may do is read all the billboards, look in shop windows—even for maternity clothes though you are not expecting, and note the number of green cars passing by. If you have the *Times* you might try to read it. You may skim a sentence or two, but then you'll look up just to check if he's coming. So a fitfulness like procrastination is forced on anyone who has to wait, anyone who must pay attention to something they don't find involving (see Goffman, 1963, for a related discussion of attention, involvement, obligations, and drama).

cases, we can point to a specific liability, and therefore it makes sense to say he wanted to but didn't. But what liability could Ann find to fit the wanting with the not doing?

Yet she knows, acknowledges, and affirms she ought to get to work. She certainly is not pursuing some other pleasure; she would be relieved and delighted if she finally found herself working, and in fact, she tries to get to work. She did after all get the books from the library, sharpen her pencils, and put the paper in the typewriter, things which would lead us to say she wanted to work. Hence, it is both sensible and misleading to say she wanted to get to work but couldn't, or to say that she didn't want to. And we cannot hope that new facts about her real goals could settle the issue one way or the other. We shall see, however, that further considerations may relieve us of our feeling that she either wants or doesn't want to work.

Some of our confusion arises from the tension between her genuine efforts to accomplish something and her mysterious failure to do anything. We address this failure in considering another way of procrastinating—perseveration.

One way that Ann didn't write the paper was by collecting references in excess of what even she knew she needed. This way of procrastinating is by perseveration at a particular stage of a task. Why was Ann unable to move on to writing her paper on the French Revolution?

RECIPES AND CRITERIA: A FOURTH STRAIN

Assume that she has at least narrowed her topic to the French Revolution. But what exactly about the French Revolution—which years, 1789 or 1793, and on the Sans Culottes or the Vendee? She knows this is a critical choice. But what grounds for decision does she have? Perhaps she would be best off rolling a die. But how could she for a serious decision? She would procrastinate less in a world in which the seriousness of a decision matched the compellingness of its grounds.

Eventually having been taken by the Sans Culottes, she's set to begin work. How should she proceed? She might take to heart her teacher's injunction: "Do what you want as long as it is creative, integrated, and sheds some new light on the subject." But how does this help? She has, at best, criteria to tell when she's done it well, not a *recipe* to follow (see Schutz, 1973, for a discussion on recipe knowledge). So how can she start? She knows she has to read some books, assess some claims, cull some facts, and put them together to tell a coherent story. And since she's an intelligent and involved student, she knows good books from bad, how to assess claims, and when facts fit stories. If she could work backward, she wouldn't have a problem: if she knew the story she wanted to tell, the story would provide a guide to relevant books, claims, and facts, and focus her attention. But until the story is sketched, how can she distinguish relevant from irrelevant? She must focus; she knows that pursuing one lead precludes following others. Now, how would this same assignment present itself to a student prepared to take a gentlewoman's C?

The multiplicity of options promises exactly what she needs: a large number of points, facts, opinions, and analyses to be strung together as a serviceable paper. Almost no starting point will prove unacceptable, and even if it should, say, by being about the theater in the French Revolution, this will announce itself quickly. Her indifference and her coarse and tolerant criteria give her a simple recipe: gather diverse facts starting from 1789 and put them in chronological order to the fall of Robespierre.

There is a way of making stew by combining in any order whatever is at hand . . . it has a simple recipe and a tolerant criterion. Bordelaise sauce, however, has a stricter criterion, allows less substitution, and requires each ingredient to be treated in its own way in the proper order; the recipe is correspondingly demanding. The involved student must find just the right recipe; the student content with the C can make do with a recipe that will serve for any occasion. Our involved student may find herself waiting for inspiration; the C student doesn't need any. Not knowing specifically what to do next, and waiting for inspiration is a way to fall into perseveration; at least she knows how to continue to do what she's doing: gathering references. She may even find herself reading boxtops or stockmarket reports while waiting. And sometimes annunciations do happen: a teacher may give a hint or a flash of insight may descend. What then is the rational solution to our not knowing what to do next?

Her problem is that she is confronted with a variety of unmarked paths. She knows that some lead to the outcome she wants and some don't, but she doesn't know which. Each has a cost: while she pursues one path, she can't follow another. A solution is to give up trying to pick among the paths and take any, perhaps randomly. Having started in one way, she can put to good use those skills and sensitivities that are only of use once a path has been chosen. This is a difficult solution to use because it requires ignoring the overwhelming facts that no particular path is compelling, that another might be much better, that each has a cost. She must come to realize the paradox that it is not rational to make all decisions rationally. Rationality is not served by, much less constituted by, deliberating each decision. One of the liabilities a rational and intentional model must allow, then, comes from not knowing precisely what to do next *and* knowing one doesn't know, and eschewing, in the interest of rationality, trial and error. Humans, with their commitment to rationality, may perseverate where rats, unconcerned by such standards, might more rationally flail.

REVIEW

By considering cases of "putting things off," we defended the thesis that procrastination is inherently irrational. At least in the cases we considered, if a putting off was rational, or to the degree it was rational, it was not procrastination. Our case studies led us to conclude that a person is procrastinating if she is irrationally putting off and if this irrationality is caused by recognizing or fancying what she ought to be doing.[11]

We isolated four aspects of procrastination and suggested an explanation of each. First, we considered a case in which someone meets a less important obligation in order to procrastinate a more important obligation. We tied this to a particular liability of rational action unwittingly treating self-worth as homogeneous, i.e., kinds of accomplishments as interchangeable. In the second case, a person sacrifices a substantial pleasure to his obligation but finds he has frittered away the time, entrapped

11. Our last case doesn't appear to fit this definition, but it does. Ann perseverates (but the C student doesn't) because she recognizes the demands of a good paper. If she did not, she would not perseverate.

by some minor pleasure. We show how this can result from rational calculations within an irrational frame—periods of time that are irrationally short. In the third case, the procrastinator exhibits fits of involvement that we show can follow from the aversiveness of the task conjoined with an attempt to dramatize oneself to oneself as diligently working.

Diligence and fitfulness are comingled in procrastination in another way: procrastinators while not working, often keep themselves in readiness to work "at any moment" by doing things that require only ephemeral involvements. They are busy maintaining a "procrastination field" instead of working.

In the last case, we considered a general feature of procrastination: procrastination is most likely when actors know what they are to do in the sense of having criteria to tell if they have done it, but don't know what to do in that they lack a recipe to follow. Perseverating is a common result.

Along the way we found various liabilities of rational, intentional action that crop up in procrastination. Following Austin (1957), we suggest that these liabilities point to places where the machinery of action can slip and places where theorists interested in developing a model of intentional action may wish to start.

CHAPTER EIGHT

Character: The Moral Aspects of Traits

On occasion we call someone: smart, kind, generous, crafty, dishonest, greedy, venomous, untidy. If we're prudent we just think it. These trait words sketch character or at least they are cartoons for finished portraits. We are concerned with these cartoons—the uses commonsense actors make of trait language, the rules they follow in drawing their sketches, and the effects they produce when they talk about character.

Professional psychology precedes us in analyzing these techniques. There is, we believe, a widely shared professional assumption about the naive use of trait language. Rather than present this view ourselves, perhaps sloppily, we shall let a member of this school speak:

> Traits refer to relatively stable behavioral dispositions that individuals exhibit over time. To take physical height as an example, people can be characterized as short, average, or tall because their height remains relatively stable over time compared to the variation in height among different people. If individuals were much shorter than others on one day and much taller on the next, height would be useless as a dimension for characterizing individuals. Likewise, height would be of no value in characterizing individuals if individuals remained as stable in height as they currently do but all individuals were of identical height . . .
>
> In real life, we identify people by their behavioral attributes much as we do by their physical attributes. If we failed to do so,

> or did so inaccurately, we would pay a serious price as we would not know what to expect of individuals and how to act toward them. We would be recognized as insensitive or as poor judges of character. Traits, as judged in everyday life, are informal assessments of relatively broad and enduring response dispositions, hopefully inferred from a large sample of behavior. They imply the ability to predict, on the average, what can be expected of an individual over many events. To the extent that an observer can make such assessments accurately, he or she has extremely important information. It is not necessary for the observer to predict accurately in every situation for his or her construct to be useful. There is a considerable payoff, whether one is gambling for money or taking one's chances in interpersonal relationships, in being right most of the time. I considered the woman I was to marry to be a warm, considerate person. This does not mean I believed she would never get angry at me or would never misunderstand me. If her behavior were that invariant across situations, she would be rigid, a robot. It does mean that according to my assessment, her behavior, in general, would place her high on these attributes, high enough to make me willing to gamble my future happiness on my estimates, which fortunately were accurate. Note that in essence what was involved was being exposed to a sample of events from which a prediction was made of the average behavior in another sample of events.
>
> (EPSTEIN, Traits are alive and well, 1977, pp. 83–84)

Trait words, then, in psychology's picture, are used by ordinary people as predictors; for Epstein, calling his wife warm is equivalent to predicting her behavior. Further, people need trait concepts to know what to expect of others and therefore how to act toward them.

We think Epstein's view is lucid and representative. We think that those who debunk traits (e.g., Mischel, 1968) as well as those who defend them, at least in a chastened form (e.g., Bem, 1978; and Magnusson & Endler, 1977) share the view that traits are, or should be, just predictors, i.e., if a trait word doesn't predict it is useless. (Insofar as psychologists are uninterested in commonsense uses of trait language and are only interested in professional uses, our arguments do not touch their work.) Epstein, at least, is interested in showing a continuity between the commonsense use of trait language and the professional use. Indeed, he argues that the professional use grows out of ordinary actors' needs.[1]

Goffman outlines a different model of character language, a "moral model," one absent from the psychological perspective (1959, 1971, and esp. 1967, pp. 214–39). In this more dramatic portrait, characters are earned and squandered; they are warranted by behavior, although not necessarily predictive of behavior. Our character language is rooted in our needs to encourage and discourage, praise and blame, reward and punish, ourselves and others.[2]

We shall be concerned with the contrast between these two models as well as the inadequacies of both. We want to come to a conception of character that will embrace the virtues and shun the faults of each. But our path is crooked; this is so because the view of trait words as predictors seems so natural that dislodging it requires us to approach it from various directions. So a map and some forbearance will be helpful. We shall supply the map.

A MAP

1. We start with a point about predictions per se that will be called upon in our analysis.

2. Then we examine an instance in which trait language is used to make a prediction. We do this to show that our interpretation of this use as prediction depends not only on the words but on the contexts in which they are used. If the predictive use of trait words is tied to particular contexts, then, perhaps in other contexts they have other uses.

3. Goffman provides a hint about another possible use, a moral use. We draw out this view by considering a paradigmatic case of a moral label, 'murderer'. We contrast 'murderer' as a predictor with 'murderer' as a moral label.

1. As to the central issue among Block (1977), Bem & Funder (1978), and Mischel (1968), i.e., whether there are stabilities in individual differences and, if so, of what kind and breadth, we have no opinion. We are concerned only with whether broad stable patterns are presupposed by trait talk: whether ordinary trait talk necessarily involves prediction.

2. Of course, 'need', here, does not refer to needs of an individual at all times when he talks but rather to needs of cultures that have shaped our forms of talk. Neither Epstein nor we are making claims about the immediate needs of speakers when they are using trait talk.

4. We take an ordinary trait word, 'greedy', and see where it fits the predictive and moral paradigms.

5. We point out that there is at least one function of 'greedy', as a warning, that both paradigms leave out.

6. One argument for a predictivist model is that people are reluctant to ascribe character on the basis of a single act. We attempt to show why this does not compel us to accept the notion of trait use as implicit prediction. So other models are still in the running.

7. We consider arguments against both the predictivist and moral views arising from the fact that a person's character is sometimes seen to change.

8. Finally, in response to the conceptual problems of character change, we sketch a typology of character different from the moral and predictivist views, one that allows the possibility of change.

1. The Notion of Prediction

Perhaps we should stop to note that if someone predicts something and it doesn't happen, then she was wrong *when she said it:* if she predicts in March that the Yankees will win the pennant, and if in October they are in last place, then she was wrong in March when she made the prediction. Predictions have a forward-looking character; their worth, like 'promises' remains to be seen. And predictions rely on future circumstances for more than establishing their worth.

If a fan bets us on a Yankee victory, but a players' strike cancels the season, we should give him his money back. He wasn't wrong; his prediction couldn't be tested. For predictions to be sensible, they must be made in the context of shared, implicit assumptions about relevant tests.[3] Sometimes, when we use trait language, it is obvious what the relevant tests are; in just those cases it is sensible to say that 'traits' are used as predictors. Here is an example.

3. Of course, a prediction about the pennant by a labor expert or a fortune-teller would not be canceled by the strike—for somewhat different reasons. Labor experts claim to know about this sort of disturbance. Fortune-tellers claim to know about everything including disturbances.

2. Traits, Predictions, and Context

Suppose a friend asks, "I'm thinking of doing independent study with Dr. Smith next term, and I know you did last year. What's she like?" And you say, "She's really kind and considerate and quite interesting." It is easy to hear the prediction in this use of trait language. But this prediction is not announced by words alone; context supports the interpretation. In answering the question you know not only what the words mean, but the *point* of the question: why your friend asked and what use she plans to make of the answer. Moreover, you know she knows that you know all this (see Schutz, 1964, and Grice, 1969, who develop this point, each in his own way). This gives her license to treat your answer as a prediction.[4]

We constructed an example of trait words used as predictors, one fitting Epstein's analysis. It fits his analysis by relying on certain contextual details, in particular, the patency of the point of the discussion. Can all examples of trait language use be fit to this model? We think not.[5] To see why not we want to look at an example of the use of a description of a person that is distant from Epstein's model.

Oddly, the concept we shall use doesn't refer to a psychological trait, but then neither does 'height', the example Epstein started with. 'Height' had a useful role; it captured succinctly what Epstein claimed are essential features of psychological trait concepts without being one itself. We shall use 'murderer' to the same end.

4. Furthermore, these details of context define the prediction. The prediction needs definition because 'kind', 'considerate', and 'interesting' are broad terms. Dr. Smith could be kind to her family, friends, students; considerate of their rights, interests, or feelings; interesting about art, sports, or history. Regrettably people who are kind to their family needn't be to their friends or students; people who are considerate of their friends' feelings needn't be of their rights; and people who tell interesting baseball stories are not necessarily engaging about post-impressionism.

Suppose your friend discovers that Dr. Smith is cruel to her husband, inconsiderate of her friends' investments, and has only cliches for discussions of Cezanne; would she have reason to fault you for using the traits you applied to Dr. Smith? If the independent study turned out well? Broad trait words can be used to make narrow predictions in disciplined contexts; in permissive environments they succumb to overgeneralization.

Calling a pianist talented makes no prediction about the draftsmanship of her sketches. Our using concepts such as talented, kind, considerate, and so forth, doesn't commit us to believing in broad consistencies in behavior. Monkey wrenches are useful in a broad range of circumstances, but this doesn't mean all bolts have the same size head (or the same *underlying* head size).

5. We don't define 'trait'. We trust our examples are uncontroversial, and any trait theorist would also have to give them a home.

3. 'Murderer', 'Height', and Trait Language

Imagine that Mary kills her uncle for his millions. In calling her a murderer are we predicting she *will* murder again? Suppose, as it happened, she thoughtfully armed the bomb, but stood thoughtlessly close, becoming quadraplegic. Is it wrong to call her a murderer? It would be, if it were a prediction. After all, it's hardly likely she'll murder again. On the face of it, then, calling someone a murderer isn't a prediction. But perhaps it's very much like making a prediction. Perhaps it's predicting what she would do if she could; maybe it's like the bet on the Yankees, with paralysis, not a strike, calling the prediction off. Let's note some differences between the strike and the paralysis.

First, if the fan knew there would be no season, his offering to bet would be senseless, but what's senseless about calling Mary a murderer even though you know her season has been called?[6] Second, as we mentioned, predictions have a forward-looking quality: their worth remains to be tested. Saying, "the Yankees will win," is a *prediction* only if its worth hasn't been tested. Calling Mary a murderer after we know she has killed her uncle isn't a prediction, because its worth has been settled. It's true no matter what else she ever does; it is intelligible in contexts where future murders are impossible and is tested by facts already at hand when the claim is made. Moreover, calling someone a murderer would be wrong—unfair—in some cases where the prediction "she will murder" is (turns out to be) true.

Suppose we discover that 95 percent of murderers have a certain protein in their blood and 95 percent of those with the protein murder. Predicting that a protein bearer will kill is a good bet, but surely it would be unfair to call a one-year-old a murderer, even one with the protein. We reserve this title for those who have earned it. Because having *earned it* is necessary and sufficient for being called a murderer; 'murderer' is ideal for

6. Still, it would not be senseless to talk about who *would* have won the pennant had there been a season. Whatever this counterfactual is, it isn't a prediction. What could the prediction be in Mary's case? Perhaps calling her a murderer predicts what she would do were her paralysis miraculously reversed. But note that several things would have to happen: not only would she have to be restored to health, but she also would have to lose her uncle's money, and then, to supply a motive, her uncle would have to be resurrected and restored to wealth. Why would we predict the sequelae to several miracles?

Goffman's model of character language in the way 'height' is for Epstein's. Let's keep 'murderer' in mind as we consider a real trait word and see if it's earned or predicted.

4. Greedy: Earned or Predicted

Greedy is a trait word, and it is about character. Let's see how it's used. Suppose you meet a friend, who mentions she saw one of your co-workers, Helen, today, and you say: "I've had it with Helen! She's so greedy. Someone from the Wintergarden came to the office today and gave Helen twelve tickets to a play for all of us, and she kept all twelve for herself!" Were you using 'greedy' as a prediction? Is Helen's future behavior what you're talking about? Her future behavior with theater tickets? How often are theater tickets distributed? Who would want to predict that? Perhaps you were predicting Helen's average behavior, "in general," in all situations where 'greed' would be relevant. This would appear to be more useful than predicting what she's likely to do with free theater tickets. But there are quite a few situations where Helen might be greedy, i.e., take more than her due. She might take more than her share of: tickets, coupons, money, food, love, sex, attention, talking time in a conversation, space on the shared arm-rest in a movie theater, viewing time in front of a Picasso at the crowded M.O.M.A. exhibit, free samples from a sidewalk distributor, beer from a pitcher, paper clips from the department's supply, graduate students, pages in a journal, attention from a mentor, time on a tennis court, room in a swimming pool, art books from a library, and so forth. Indeed it is not easy to imagine situations in which a person couldn't be greedy. Were you attempting to predict all these delicts? Were you being vague? Unlike the conversation about Dr. Smith, the context here didn't pick out what your prediction was about. Yet you didn't sound vague. Could you have gotten your meaning across better by being more specific? Or perhaps you weren't predicting.

We suggest that you were pointing to something about Helen, a particular flaw, which makes your "having had it with her" *fair*. The fairness of treating Helen this way is independent of predictions of her future behavior; we are entitled to punish greedy friends (or murderers) not by what they probably will do but by what they surely have done. (Similarly, we might suggest, Epstein's applying 'traits' to his future wife was a way of praising her. It wasn't, or wasn't just, a way of bringing his friends a list of predictions.)[7]

We have suggested that you may have been doing something other than predicting in labeling Helen; you may have been justifying your treatment of her. In calling Helen greedy, you weren't attempting to edify your office mates about greed, even though that was a by-product. You were saying something focally about Helen. Still, you may have been giving a warning, not about greed, but about Helen.

Warnings, like predictions, look to the future; both are senseless about quadraplegic murderers. Is giving a warning, then, a use of trait language different from predicting? Have we found a third use of trait language, or are warnings just a special type of prediction?

5. Are Warnings Predictions?

Suppose you knew your friend was planning a business venture with Helen. You might call Helen greedy as a warning about her. Would warning your friend about Helen be predicting her behavior? How do we assess predictions? What rules should people honor in making them?

One can give narrow, simple answers to these questions, or one can give broad, complex answers. We shall argue that if you give the simple answers, then: (1) the claim that trait words are used to predict, on this construal of prediction, is forceful and important, but (2) warnings, then, are not predictions. If you give the complex answers on the other hand, then: (1) warnings are predictions, but (2) the claim that trait words are used to predict is, on this construal of prediction, trivial. Start with the simple, forceful answers, and then see if warnings are predictions.

7. But, it might be objected, isn't shunning greedy co-workers sensible just because greedy people are more likely to act in greedy ways in the future? No. There would be a point in shunning greedy co-workers even if they were no more likely than others to be greedy in the future. It would at least serve as a deterrent and a public reminder (see Sabini & Silver, 1978, *inter alia* to this point). (Presumably the jurists at the Nuremberg Trial were not concerned that those particular defendants would or could repeat their crimes; they were concerned to make out the limits of international law so that such horrors would not be repeated.) Punishment and praise make an example of people for others to heed.

The simple answers are: predictions are assessed only in terms of 'true' and 'false', and the rules of prediction are the rules of inference. Now let's consider a warning: the Surgeon General's. Suppose it turns out cigarette smoking is not hazardous to your health, and suppose the only evidence he had to think so was the death of three asthmatic Canadian rats who smoked ten packs a day. How would we assess his warning? Well, we might call it rash, ill-considered, or stupid. Now suppose that although the only evidence he had at the time was the three nicotine-stained carcasses, later research showed that two-pack-a-day humans die, too. His warning was still defective; it was precipitous. Suppose he had very good evidence of danger, but fortunately for smokers that very good evidence was misleading—as it turns out cigarettes aren't dangerous. As a prediction it failed; contra the claim, cigarettes don't kill. Still as a warning it was prudent—in light of the very good evidence. Now suppose there turned out to be a real danger from smoking—hangnails. Here the prediction that there is a danger is true, but the warning is overblown. So warnings are assessed with a range of terms, not just (not even) with 'true' and 'false'.

Further, often we have an obligation to warn against unlikely events—the odds are the child will *not* fall through the ice *this* time.[8] So the rules a person should honor in a warning are broader than the rules of inference.[9] To give proper warnings you not only rely on predictions but also must take into account what will happen if you give the warning and how important that is, and what will happen if you don't, and how important that is. Moreover, you shall have to take into account your particular position: lifeguards have different obligations with regard to warnings about undertows than do balloon vendors. So if you give the simple answers, warnings aren't predictions, and we have another use for trait language than predictions.

On the other hand, suppose you say that all of the criticisms you made of warnings can also be made of predictions—they

8. One also ought to know the relation between the frying pan and the fire before warning someone to quit the first because of the heat.

9. Recommendations work similarly. We don't criticize a professor for recommending someone for graduate school if the latter drops out because he married an anthropologist and had to follow her to the Andaman Islands. One reason for not criticizing the recommendation is: we don't expect, or even allow, professors to investigate the private lives of their students.

can be rash, ill-conceived, stupid, precipitous, or overblown—so the fact that warnings can be criticized this way doesn't show they're not really predictions. In specific contexts you shall have to take into account all sorts of things in making predictions, just as you must to give a proper warning. But if you say this you have given up the simple, narrow, forceful notion of prediction that gave your claim, that trait language was used to predict, bite. You have expanded the notion of prediction until it can be assessed in any way thinking can be assessed, and its rules include all those a person should honor to think straight. Moreover, in making predictions, your thinking will have to take account of diverse facts about the world, your position in it, and what your culture values. Once you have expanded the notion of prediction this way, how does the claim that people use trait language to make predictions help? What does it rule out? Of course predictions, narrowly defined, do have a role in warning, a subsidiary one.

Were it not so that we can more or less predict what will happen, we would have no reason to either issue or pay attention to warnings. Still, given that we can, particular warnings are justified or attacked independent of the fate of particular predictions. Further, warnings try to be self-defeating as predictions. If you get your friend to heed your warning, the point, after all, of what you are doing—back out of the deal with Helen—your prediction about her greed will not be tested. Would you call this warning defective?

So we have other uses for trait language than predicting. We can use these terms, for instance, to *justify* or *warn*. Now we shall examine an important objection against our modeling trait language use on justifying or warning.

6. Does One Slip a Trait Make?

As commonsense actors we are comfortable with the notion that just because a person murdered once she is a murderer, but the idea that Helen is a greedy person just because of the ticket incident seems forced. We want to say there's more to being a greedy person than one overindulgence in theater tickets. And this might lead Epstein to say that being a greedy person involves a *stable pattern of such behavior*. If to be a greedy person is, necessarily, to show a stable pattern of greedy acts, then it seems right that there are conceptual links between character ascription and prediction.

Our hesitancy to call Helen greedy just because of her sleight of hand with the tickets has one source that has nothing to do with whether she earns the title 'greedy' in a single bout, i.e., we award the title only on the basis of a legitimate instance. Perhaps Helen took the tickets through a misunderstanding, thinking they were for her; perhaps she meant to share them but forgot; perhaps she gave them away anonymously to a charitable organization. In all of these cases we wouldn't call her greedy, but then she didn't do anything that was greedy, although at first blush she seemed to. And if there was really no act of greed, then there is no reason to call her greedy. This is a feature 'murderer' and 'greedy' *share*.[10] Yet there is a place for repetition in the assessment of greedy character.

It is *improbable* that if a person repeatedly acts in a *prima facie* greedy way, she still has a redeeming account ready for each act. But it is logically possible that someone could act in a *prima facie* greedy way over and over and yet have a valid excuse for each. The real question is this: if we were confident, say, beyond the shadow of a doubt, that someone was guilty of a particular greedy action, could we withhold the title 'greedy'? Is there a way to defend Helen against the charge of being greedy that does not also attack the claim that her act was greedy? Insofar as our reasons for withholding 'greedy' have to do with ambiguities in the nature of the act per se, they leave the analogy between 'murderer' and 'greedy' untouched.

10. One difference between murder and greed is in the area of *mitigations,* see Austin (1970a) and Goffman (1971). An excuse claims, "I couldn't have done otherwise." If successful, an excuse relieves the actor of all opprobrium. A mitigation cites an extenuating circumstance, i.e., a circumstance that affects how much the act reflects on the self. "I missed class because I was in a coma," is an excuse; comas generally preclude class attendance. On the other hand, "I didn't come to class because my girlfriend proposed last night, and I spent the morning telling the guys," *claims* extenuation. After all, even an engaged person *can* come to class. The engagement makes the delict less severe, his self less tainted.

Mitigations blend into excuses. Also, as Austin pointed out, what counts as a mitigation or excuse depends on the seriousness of the delict; so, to use his example, inadvertence is an excuse for stepping on a snail but not on a baby. We are prepared to treat many mitigations for an act of greed as if they were excuses; we slide less easily for murders. (We say all of this with apologies to Goffman's twenty-four ways of driving through a red light, 1971, p. 102, fn. 6.)

Acting out of Character and Predictions

But what about this rejoinder to the Helen story, "I've known Helen for years and she just isn't a greedy person"? Doesn't this defend Helen without denying her act was greedy? Epstein could claim it does: it reminds us we need an adequate sample to make a valid prediction. "I've seen lots of instances of her behavior and I wouldn't predict she'd act greedily in the future." For cases where we have other evidence that prediction is the point of the trait talk, e.g., Dr. Smith's considerateness, this is a compelling account of the logic of the defense. But is the availability of such a defense enough to convince us that prediction is the *only* model for trait talk? How else could the rejoinder be taken?

While the rejoinder might be a counsel of prudence, it needn't counsel against the perils of prediction; it might be about the requirements of fairness. It might mean, "Because of Helen's exemplary past, fairness requires that we be cautious in judging her. There may be an excuse for her behavior that we don't know about." In addition, the rejoinder can bear character witness for Helen: "She's not the sort of person who would do that." But character witnesses are of little help to defendants caught in the act, at least until sentencing time.

Perhaps her defender might say, "I've known Helen for years. She isn't greedy. But she does have this thing about the theater. She's crazy about going to the theater, especially with her friends." Here taking the tickets is admittedly greedy, and so was Helen, but the charge is confined to Broadway. Her sin stands but her flaw is contained.[11]

Or her defender might say, "Okay, I'll admit that was greedy, but I've known her for years and she's always been very generous." What does this do for Helen? After all, it does concede she was greedy in taking all the tickets. This seems a clear

11. A special form of, "She has this thing about theater since she was maltreated as a child by never being allowed to go to a play," jams the crack between excuses, mitigations, and explanations. We might treat it as an excuse and say, "She couldn't have helped herself but to take the tickets because of her tragic childhood," or as a mitigation, "Now that I understand the source of her great love for the theater, I can see just how hard it would have been for her to resist. She's not such a bad person after all," or just as an explanation, "So that's why she's so greedy." Freud (1935), Merton (1949), and Sondheim (1957) have all contributed to jamming this crack. (For a cogent review of the arguments in the field we recommend the song "Officer Krupke" from the musical *West Side Story*, 1957.)

claim that Helen is "not really like that," she acted out of character. Is this a plea for a better sample? Not necessarily, it might also be one for fairness. Fairness requires that if we paint a likeness, it be balanced.[12] The plea isn't that the charge against Helen is false, but the characterization of her is misleading. Epstein might agree. Certainly it's misleading; it misleads prediction because there are more instances of generosity than greed from which to predict. Still, we appreciate balance and object to its absence in places where prediction is unemployable. It is hard to see what prediction we could make about Sienese art, but the unfairness of characterizing *trecento* and *quattrocentro* Siena as inferior—far behind Florence in the realistic treatment of perspective and the humanistic portrayal of emotion—is vivid. It isn't that Siena *wasn't* far behind in these ways; it's that fairness requires us to go on to say that Sienese masters were unsurpassed in their use of color. Balance is a general requirement of judgment—predictive or otherwise.

Modeling character assessment on aesthetics or morality, however, seems to set adrift thought from action—we don't have to do much about Sienese art, but we do have to deal with greedy colleagues. We act *pragmatically* in taking into account well-grounded predictions; we act *morally* in taking into account the requirements of fairness. Sometimes one need dominates, sometimes the other, and sometimes they conflict.[13] Our thinking about people shows its roots in both requirements of action. Both prediction and fairness rebel at ascriptions from single instances (unless the single instance is especially important, e.g., a single murder *does* a murderer make). So our unwillingness to ascribe character on the basis of a single case

12. There is also a locution, "Well, she has always been very generous to me." This has several uses. First, it might challenge the veracity or the accuracy of the person who made the charge. Or it might claim there must be something special about the person who made the charge that provoked the behavior. The "to me" can also stress the unfairness of "my" treating Helen as a greedy person—since she has been generous to me—without denying that the person who made the charge is entitled to treat Helen that way. In this last use, the "to me" is a way to avoid confronting the speaker, and still not treat Helen as a greedy person. The difficulty a person has when he has a particular reason to be grateful to someone who is evil is shown in Speer's (1970) constant confusion in thinking about, talking about, writing about, and acting toward Hitler. Despite Speer's heroic bad faith, Hitler's monstrousness finally intruded on Speer's personal debt of gratitude.

13. One place the conflict is in flames is in the rooms of admission committees of graduate and professional schools. They must select on the basis of their predictions, but that's not all they must do. They are also handing out a scarce resource to those who have earned it. The grounds of prediction and the grounds of fairness need not overlap.

does not win the argument for the predictivist. But it doesn't refute predictivism either. We turn now to an embarrassment to both models of character based on 'height' and 'murderer.'

7. Character Change and Predictions

Let's take, "I've known Helen for years. She's just not a greedy person," one step further. Suppose you agreed and said, "She sure has changed." The notion that people change causes unrest for both models of character talk. What are the roots of the unrest? How does each model attempt to quell its disturbances?

For Goffman's model, the unrest is close to the surface: if you are tarred by a single greedy act, how could you ever be made clean? We shall take this up below, but first we shall look at character change from a predictive perspective. The restiveness isn't as obvious, but it is as threatening. Suppose after we decided that Helen was greedy, she never again took advantage of her co-workers, although there were many opportunities. If calling her greedy was a prediction, then surely it has been falsified. Therefore, we were wrong all along, *even at the time we first said* Helen was greedy. The problem is not that Helen's new behavior shows she has stopped being greedy, which is true, but that it shows she wasn't a greedy person when she took the tickets, which is false. In the predictivist view, Helen's future behavior proves that our interpretation (of what the ticket taking meant about her character) was incorrect—even if our evidence that her *act* was greedy remained unshaken. If at some time in the future, Mrs. Epstein stops acting in a kind way, then Mr. Epstein should conclude by his theory that he had been wrong in calling her kind at the time he did. But couldn't she have changed? Couldn't it be right to call Helen greedy and yet find, sometime later, that she is no longer a greedy person? But can't character change be fit to a predictivist model? Why couldn't we say, "Helen has changed," means "we should now change our predictions about her"?

Suppose she wins a million dollars. Would we still predict she'd be greedy with her co-workers? If she quits her job? If she became paralyzed and could no longer take tickets? Is all of this character change? A predictivist might answer, "No, she hasn't really changed, but we wouldn't change our predictions about her either. But we're not being inconsistent: when we called her greedy we meant that she would take more than her due when there was some point to it, when she was able, and so forth. And we still say if it had a point and she were able, she'd do it." This seems reasonable. But how about a case in which circumstances and ability don't change—Helen just stops acting greedily? Could a predictivist call this character change? No. And this is the embarrassment. In this case, her new behavior shows his old claim wrong—she wasn't greedy all along, since she isn't acting greedily now. Therefore, there is no change in Helen, although there is a change from a false to a new prediction. To talk of changed character because of changed behavior, the predictivist has to show that the changed behavior is really in accord with his prior prediction. So he needs to distinguish sorts of changes that falsify his previous predictions from those that don't, i.e., he needs to distinguish real changes in character from changes in response to winning a million dollars. But to make this distinction *is* to have a notion of character *independent* of predictions.[14] Yet it was predictions the predictivist offered as a replacement for the notion of character. So the problem of character change is as serious a threat to Epstein's view as it is to Goffman's.

8. Character Change and Description: Types of Traits

To quell the problem of character change, we start from a lacuna in our discussion. We want to provide in broad strokes the start of a positive account of 'character'. Our account holds to one side both Goffman's and Epstein's views, and begins with some distinctions among terms that enter into our discussion of character. We shall attempt to sketch an account that can allow (logically) for character change.

A natural way to explain what you were doing when you called Helen greedy would be to say, "I was describing her

14. Perhaps we are being unfair to Epstein (1977) in claiming he treats 'traits' as a way to make predictions. After all he says, "Traits refer to relatively stable dispositions . . ." (83) And dispositions are not quite predictions. Yet just as one cannot distinguish between a falsified prediction and a changed character without an independent notion of character, we cannot distinguish among: not having had a disposition all along, not realizing the disposition in these particular circumstances, and just having changed an old disposition for a new one.

character." This seems to capture what you do when you talk about a person, think about what she is like, or reflect on what you are like—especially when you are not called upon to predict, justify, warn, recommend, or praise. A natural way to do this, to respond to, for example, "Describe your fiancee to me," is to use trait words. Why have we shied away from the obvious notion that trait words *describe* character?

How could you describe character? Character belongs to a person, but not like his nose, his car, or even his height. It is shown by behavior, but behavior is evidence of character, not character itself; character endures over time, but it is not a thing.

The urge to treat trait words as predictors of behavior arises from this elusiveness of 'character'. Since predictions of behavior are: about a person, tested by behavior, enduring over time, not a part of a person, and not behavior or a thing, they embody the elusive features of 'character' in a concrete, simple, well-understood medium. Further, predictions are in favor with science.[15] But there are other ways to capture these elusive features.

Capacities

For instance, *capacities* belong to a person, are tied to behavior, and endure over time (see Alston, 1976; Goffman, 1967; Harré & Secord, 1972). To say someone can do something is not to predict they will; it is perfectly sensible to say that a person can do something they have neither done nor will do. But then, how can we be sure what capacities people have (how are capacities conceptually tied to behavior)? Well, if they do it, then we are sure they can, although we can't be sure they can't if they don't.[16] Still to the degree they have a reason to do it, we have a reason to say they can't if they don't. If we offer you a

15. Logical positivism, too.

16. Of course, you have to show the person really did it. Repeated success gives evidence he did, but then Clever Hans got a lot of problems right. So repetition without an understanding of how a person, or horse, could solve the problem in a simpler way, have memorized the right answer, be using subtle cues only correlated with the right answers, or be using the techniques of magicians is not such good evidence after all. And if you do know the ways a person could seem to do it without really doing it, and if you have eliminated these ways, what do you need repetition for? Of course, if you have to test a thousand people, equating repetition with capacity is not a bad rule.

free vacation in Baltimore or Philadelphia if you sing on key, and you're still flat, we have little reason to believe you couldn't do it; if we promise a vacation in New York or Florence, on the other hand, and you're still flat, "unwilling" is more convincingly replaced by 'unable'. Some character talk, some trait language, is about capacities (or incapacities), e.g., smart, stupid, talented, and all their specifics—brilliant pianist, math whiz, illiterate, and so forth.

Motives

Other trait words have to do with *motivation*—the goals a person is inclined to seek out. 'Adventurous' and 'curious' are examples. 'Adventurous' is related to behavior, but does not predict an adventure. For a motive to emerge as behavior there must be opportunity. Someone obliged to take care of dependent children, parents, or perhaps pets, and therefore not able to spend her time on the Wall of Yosemite may still be adventurous, though we wouldn't predict she'd have an adventure. (Notice that the father responsible for his children *can't* go on an adventure, but the 'can't' refers not to a physical incapacity; it depends on shared understandings of obligations and their importance.) Sometimes an adventurous person chooses to pass up an adventure: an aspiring actor offered a part in *Othello*, starting on the same day the plane leaves for Katmandu (where he was to meet his crew of Sherpas) might not go, but still be adventurous. So, passing up an adventure doesn't mean you're not adventurous. Still, if you pass up an opportunity to climb Everest to see the Super Bowl, your adventurousness is in serious doubt. On the other hand, if you risk fame, limb, and future to climb Annapurna, even without royalties, you are an adventurer. Motives are tied to behavior, but the attachments are indirect. We may be motivated to act, but not act because of a lack of opportunity, an incapacity, or the presence of a more important and incompatible goal.

Moreover, we could predict you will have an adventure without saying you are adventurous: suppose you join the police because they pay well, you have a large family to support, and you want to retire after twenty years. Choosing a life that involves, even inevitable, adventures does not make you adventurous. You are adventurous only if it is the adventure that attracts you. Specifying a person's motive is tricky, but the logic of it is clear: if the direction of a person's behavior changes in response to new information about his relation to some putative goal, we have some reason to believe the goal is his—it's his motive. Since our policeman would continue in his job even though it lost its adventure and wouldn't even ask for a transfer to a hotter shift (but he would quit if they dropped the retirement benefits), it isn't adventure that is his motive but security (see Peters, 1958, for an extensive development of this point).

Style

In describing people we might find use for another notion: personality style. "My friend, Charlie, is really frenetic." Why might we call 'frenetic' a style? What is a style? Let's start with a style simpler than a life's, Chris Evert Lloyd's two-handed backhand style. At one time a two-handed backhand wasn't called a style; it was called a mistake. But she demonstrated it could be effective, very effective. So it was promoted from a mistake to a style; this promotion suggests it is now considered to be one way to hit a backhand. If we were teaching someone to play tennis, we wouldn't correct him if he adopted it. Similarly what we want to say about Charlie's ways is that doing things frenetically is one way to do them, and like a two-handed backhand, is neither good nor bad in itself. But there is a difference between freneticism and a two-handed backhand. Some things should be done frenetically, e.g., boogieing, or signaling to the gentleman across the way he just set his pants afire with his cigarette. But in other cases freneticism is somewhat out of place, e.g., when ordering a cup of coffee in a restaurant. Then there are cases where freneticism is "just a matter of style," e.g., extending congratulations, taking a solitary walk, or making love. So we couldn't call a frenetic style good or bad across the board, as we wouldn't call a two-handed backhand good or bad. But note this difference: the reason we wouldn't call freneticism good or bad *tout court* is not because it's an equally good approach in all circumstances, as the two-handed backhand is, but rather because it's sometimes better, sometimes worse, and sometimes neither. If Charlie were only frenetic in the right circumstances he would be better off, but he would no longer have a style. We reserve 'personality style' for broad characteristics that are sometimes advantages, sometimes liabilities.

Notice that terms denoting families of useful characteristics, such as intelligence, perceptiveness, or dexterity, are not called styles; unlike freneticism they are very generally useful and almost never in the way. 'Stupid' isn't a style either, for the reverse reason. But what sort of characteristics can be part of a style? Look at freneticism. Very roughly, freneticism has to do with broad inclinations and aversions (preferring the fast pace to the slow), or capacities and liabilities.[17] Also the expressions of style are spontaneous: if we say that someone has a frenetic style we imply he is *spontaneously* frenetic. Of course, frenetic people can sometimes deliberately stifle the freneticism of their reactions, or deliberately enhance them, or even deliberately force them, merely to live up to their personality. Insofar as we realize this, these calculated cases aren't evidence of a style; at best they are neutral and often debunking.

Defects of Will

Helen's greed isn't a capacity, motive, or style. We wouldn't call her greedy just because she had a capacity to take more than her due—presumably we all have that. Nor is it an incapacity. If she literally can't restrain herself from taking the theater tickets then she is not greedy in the ordinary sense: typically 'greed' pins a moral failing, it doesn't excuse it, as 'kleptomania' does. (Incapacities are fine excuses.)[18] Greedy doesn't name a motive or a goal people seek, either. Helen wasn't trying to be greedy in taking all those tickets; if she could have

17. The notion of a cognitive style is interesting in this light. The use of the term is meant to call up, like Chris Evert Lloyd's backhand, an optional approach to a problem; it is meant to suggest there are several equally good ways to solve a problem. But, it often turns out, some problems require one technique and other problems another, although some problems have multiple successful approaches. If a person always uses the best way to solve a problem, then she uses different approaches on different occasions and has no broad strategies; she has particular strategies suited to particular problems. Hence, she has *no* style. A person who does use a single approach consistently has a style; but this means she doesn't use the most (or only) effective approach when she should, which implies she has an incapacity or, at least, a weakness. And this isn't where we started.

18. We are claiming, here, that our use of 'greedy' presupposes that wills are ordinarily free. Perhaps they are not. But then, debunking free will debunks our ordinary trait talk.

gotten them without being greedy she would have. Greedy is a title she risks, not a goal she seeks.[19] But Helen did have a motive: getting the tickets. Perhaps calling her greedy says she has a stronger motive than everyone else. But suppose she hocked her engagement ring to buy the tickets. This would show a strong motive, but not greed. Then again maybe she wouldn't even have been willing to hock her dented eggbeater to get the tickets—a very weak motive. It's just that as little as she cared about the tickets, she cared about her co-workers' rights even less. So 'greedy' doesn't specify the intensity of a motive; it criticizes how well it is controlled.

'Greedy' describes a defect of character or will. To say a person is greedy is to say the person is unwilling to restrain himself from taking more than his due. To show he was unwilling to restrain himself is to show he knew he ought, but didn't.[20] There is a parallel between the way moral traits, like 'greedy', and capacities are tied to behavior: the best evidence that you can press 200 pounds is pressing it, and the best evidence that you are greedy is transgressing. Goffman's model captures this. 'Strong' and 'greedy' continue in parallel. Your not pressing 200 pounds (or your not acting greedily) does not show you are weak (or restrained). Motives count. You may have had a reason not to lift the weight or a pragmatic motive not to take the tickets: you were more afraid of getting caught or afraid of what others would think of you.[21]

Now we have assembled the pieces to deal with character change. At least some capacities are part of character. When do we say they change? Can we avoid the circularity the predictiv-

19. A person might try to be greedy. Suppose there is a club that admits only greedy people, and you know it. And, let's say, there is a very attractive person you would like to get to know in the club. You might try to become greedy to get into the club. But this is not the usual case of a person's being greedy; this is a case in which greed *is* a motive.

20. "He knew he ought to but didn't" is too strong here, as it often is in moral discourse; we often rely on "he ought to have known that he ought to but didn't." Claiming you were so bedazzled by the temptation that you forgot your obligations doesn't excuse. But it may mitigate. It is especially likely to mitigate when you also offer an account of how you blamelessly became the sort of person easily overcome by greed—you are "depraved because you were deprived"—how the allure was such that resisting would be a sign of saintliness—you're depraved because you are human, only human. If the mitigation works, the self is less tainted by the act.

21. There is a nice problem hidden here: suppose a person refrains from doing what she knows she shouldn't do to avoid the uncomfortable internal sensations of guilt. Or even more nicely: suppose she refrains just in order not to see what it makes her? Are these moral reasons or not?

ist falls into? Yes. Suppose a weight-lifting friend lifts 200 pounds on Tuesday; on Wednesday he lifts only 150 pounds. To encourage him and provide a better test of his capacities, we threaten to shoot him if he doesn't lift 200 pounds. If he fails we have excellent reason to believe he couldn't, that his abilities had changed. Of course, if he doesn't it is possible he had decided to end it all and thought this was as good a way as any. Or perhaps his fear of death temporarily lessened his capacities. These possibilities can be excluded empirically, and in principle so could each further sensible objection. (For a more developed treatment of this problem, see ch. 9.) Whatever uncertainties arise in assessing *changing* capacities are the familiar uncertainties of assessing capacities. Change isn't the issue. Nor is it the issue with character change at the level of motivation. Although there are uncertainties in describing motivation, they are not peculiar to changes in motivation.

But how can we tell if a character defect has changed? How could Helen convince us that she is no longer greedy? (Can our Goffman model quell this disturbance?) Refraining from further instances of greed is not quite enough to convince us she's no longer greedy. Suppose she is never tempted again, or if she is it's only while she is under surveillance. For us to be convinced her character has changed we must be convinced she was tempted to act in a greedy way and restrained herself for moral reasons alone. This can be arranged, but it is difficult. How can Helen arrange it? She can refrain and show that her restraint was motivated by moral concerns, not, for example, by the fact that our knowing about it will lead us to withdraw the label. It would be best if her resistance to temptation were in private, and she knew no one could ever learn of it. But then again, it must become known if it's to convince us—a delicate problem. Because of this, character change must often be shown with indirect evidence. After all, how many opportunities will a convicted murderer have to portray compellingly his resistance to the temptation to murder? Where will he find the opportunity? But on occasion we are moved to say a person's character has changed. (Caryl Chessman comes to mind.) How could a murderer move us? He might display a generalized moral sensitivity—the Birdman of Alcatraz patched up animals. Sincerity is useful because it is difficult to test and easy to display. Feigned tokens of real moral fortitude may have to be forged. For example, someone who has lamentably run over his grandmother might try: being born again, writing a book emotionally baring his past missteps, or perhaps both. Thus, character change is anchored in the changed relation the individual can demonstrate to the moral order.

We have carried our analysis through in terms of greedy, but is greedy unique or does the analysis have a broader scope? Well, we suggest a similar analysis for: proud, envious, lazy, gluttonous, lecherous, choleric; we might then go on to: prudent, courageous, temperate, just, loyal, generous, patient; then we might try: trustworthy, courteous, kind, warm, thrifty, spiteful, inconsiderate, lax, persevering, manipulative, open, cheap, punctual, and gossipy—as a start.

CHAPTER NINE

Anger

In the name of science, I (J.S.) once bullied a young woman. She was sitting at the time in a moderately crowded Lexington Avenue I.R.T. headed downtown. I walked up to her and snapped, "That's my seat." She replied, "What?" I pressed, "That's my seat. I saw it first." She protested, "I'm sitting here." I ordered, "Get up, give me that seat." She gave up and left the car. I took her seat.

A minute or so later, a man, about fifty years old with a slight accent, addressed me: "That wasn't a nice thing to do." His tone was firm but not threatening, so I thought it would be interesting to see what would happen if I offered no apology, though it was clear that an apology was called for. He reacted more intensely with, "How would you like it if *I* told *you* to get up?" I fumbled, and sputtered. I was becoming less "interested" in his responses and more concerned by them. I was unprepared for what he did next: he crouched down, looked me in the eye, and screamed, "Someday somebody could kill you for that!" Then he lifted me out of the seat while screaming, somewhat redundantly, "Get up!" He sat in the seat he rescued from me for about fifteen seconds, then, perhaps because he recognized the incongruity of his position—sitting in the stolen seat—he got up and yelled, "The lady who was sitting here, come and take your seat!" Regrettably his restoration failed since the lady, our cohort, had left the car.

The science this experiment was meant to serve was an analysis of when people will morally reproach others, a topic we treat elsewhere (see Sabini & Silver, 1978; see also ch. 3). In the interest of safety—passengers' and experimenters'—we were forced to a different approach. We recall this fragment of our past not because it became a datum, but because it was an authentic outburst of anger, a reasonable place to start our discussion.

TWO STORIES OF ANGER

Two different accounts of the nature of anger can be made to fit this story. One would stress the slow build-up and explosive release of anger. It would call attention to the mild way the angered person began, "That wasn't a nice thing to do," and how, frustrated by my unwillingness to apologize, he lost control, burst into rage, and then became violent. The other account stresses that his outrage was not gratuitous but a response to a clear-cut transgression—a bully's intimidation of a young woman. It would further point out that what he produced was not just "angry noise," but a "moral reproach,"[1] and that even his violence was not merely explosive, but had a point—separating the bully from his gains.

We might call the first account "hydraulic": anger builds in the face of frustration until civilized constraints burst. Constraints can be rational, but anger is brute, unmeasured, irrational. We shall call our second account moral: it treats anger as a social, moral phenomenon. In this account, anger has to do with transgressions and retributions, not dikes and torrents.

It is these two accounts of anger we shall consider here. The hydraulic story has been predominant in social science over the last fifty years. In this period, we believe, the moral story of anger has been overlooked (cf. Averill, 1978, for a prominent exception). This, we believe, has distorted the conception of anger (and emotion). We first want to restore the balance (and morality to its place in anger) by critically considering the hydraulic story, in particular how it tried to deal with the moral

1. The characterization of an action as not nice combined with an appeal to reciprocity, "How would you like it if I told you to get up?" makes clear the moral force of the reproach. In Sabini and Silver (1978), we develop a characterization of what a moral reproach is.

side of anger. Second, we shall draw out a moral story and criticize it on grounds attractive to the hydraulic story and then show why these criticisms fail. Third, we shall assess each in response to this criticism: both miss the phenomenon of anger itself, its mental quality.

The hydraulic story surfaced in the late 1930s in the form of a psychological theory drawing on Freudian insight and Hullian mechanics. Dollard, Doob, Miller, Mowrer, and Sears (1939) proposed, in the original and boldest form of this theory, that frustration always causes "aggression" and that all aggression is a product of frustration. Aggression was taken to be a "drive," roiled by repeated frustrations and released in aggressive behavior.

The Vocabulary of Frustration-Aggression and Anger

Frustration-aggression as an account of anger appears wanting; it doesn't even mention the word 'anger'. But this omission should not be taken too seriously. After all, the authors of this theory were old-fashioned behaviorists, too circumspect to be seen in the company of 'anger', a word tainted with mentalism.[2] But in their behavior, if not in their language, it was anger, or angry reactions, that concerned them. We can tell it was anger they wanted to talk about by looking at what their account professed to explain, i.e., what kinds of aggression were left after they chipped away those kinds their account was *not* meant to explain.

Strangely, they denied interest in the causes of: armed robbery, invasion of another country, killing your aunt to get her millions, or calmly but randomly murdering pedestrians because of a brain lesion—all things we might call aggression. But they *did* include in their story of "aggression": screaming at someone who deliberately steps on your toe, punching a rapist harder than is necessary to ensure separation, or the desserts of my bullying. The kinds of acts their account *excludes* are all instances of aggression without anger; yet they *include* cases of anger without aggression (for example, those we've just mentioned). We conclude from this that it was really anger they

2. Notice the moral story, too, is about actions, not mental contents. This is not a difference between the two accounts, although the hydraulic story needs to insist it is.

talked about, or at least angry reactions. We shall take the Dollard et al. behaviorist account, then, to be our example of a hydraulic account of anger. How did it deal with the moral aspect of anger?

In truth, it didn't, except obliquely. The reasons behaviorist theory missed the moral aspect are the reasons it misunderstood anger and even angry action. We approach these reasons by examining the theory's mishandling of its central term—aggression.

Aggression

Aggression is an unhappy word to do the job the theory needed.[3] "Germany committed aggression against Poland" is more natural to English than, "The mugger committed aggression against the old lady." Ordinarily 'aggression' is applied to nations, not persons. Further, arguments about who was the aggressor in the Vietnam War were not about who was using violence—this was obvious—but about who started it, and who was right in fighting it.[4] So, if we were to extend 'aggression' to individuals, it would carry a reproach. While it's odd to say, "The mugger committed aggression against the old lady," it's scandalous to say, "The old lady committed aggression against the mugger," even if, because he frustrated her desire to keep her purse, she poked him with her cane. It's scandalous because the term aggression has moral force, and this force is also turned against the victim. Why this looseness with language? Why did the hydraulic account take the moral term aggression rather than 'hostility' or 'violence' if it wanted a neutral term as fit for the victim as for the mugger?[5]

3. In science, ordinary words are often given a special theoretical sense, and sometimes this is harmless. But we argue that frustration-aggression theory needed the ordinary English word, aggression, to make the theory seem to be about phenomena of importance to human nature and to call up the usual moral force of the word in English, while denying morality a formal place in the theory. For this reason, we focus on the ordinary use of the word aggression. We want to see what frustration-aggression theory was dragging behind it.

4. There is another word, aggressive, which is an *a*moral relative of 'aggression'. It makes sense to say that someone is an aggressive altruist (e.g., she is vigorous in her fundraising for pacifist activities), but aggressive action in this sense has no place in a theory of aggression.

5. The words violence and, to a lesser degree, hostility have a hot feel to them, and ordinarily we use them in contexts in which we are disapproving. 'Aggression' has a colder,

Even scientists like to be relevant. Aggression is a social problem, something we would all condemn. Hostility is another matter. Some we condemn, the mugger's, some we condone, the old lady's. Hostility is not per se a social problem; aggression is. 'Aggression' is a relevant-sounding euphemism for anger. But how could behaviorists use the moral word aggression for the welling up of a neutral drive? Weren't they worried about contaminating value-free science with morally loaded language?[6] They weren't worried because they knew that whatever connotation aggression might have, its meaning *could not* be moral. They could enjoy the connotation without danger from its meaning. How could they believe this?

Morality as Feeling

For the behaviorist all moral notions were subjective—personal reactions with emotional connotations—not objective, verifiable claims that could be included in a proper scientific theory. This 'fact' about morality was not a discovery of empirical research, but a presupposition, a gift from the philosophy of the time—logical positivism.[7]

If one takes the view that morality is subjective, then 'aggression', 'violence', and 'hostility' are synonyms; they differ only in connotation or the subjective emotional reaction they provoke, rather than in denotation, and the theorist is free to use whichever one pleases him to describe behavior. The same

---

blander, more bureaucratic feel. Still, we could say, "In the context of widespread misery and exploitation, the violence of the El Salvadorean peasantry is morally correct." If we had said, "The *aggression* of the El Salvadorean peasantry," we would either be speaking ironically, a member of the ruling class speaking sincerely, a Reaganite, or someone who believed violence never to be justified.

6. Perhaps 'violence' and 'hostility' and 'aggression' are all morally loaded, contra our earlier claim. But this doesn't help frustration-aggression theory. Why didn't theorists invent a morally neutral term to keep it value-free? Scientists often invent terms to avoid excess baggage.

7. But hydraulic theorists are also, sometimes, commonsense actors who can tell the difference between the old lady and the mugger. Was a philosophical dispensation sufficient to launder 'aggression' of its moral import? The behaviorist might try another line of defense. He might argue that 'aggression', as commonsense actors use it, both describes behaviors and calls up an emotional reaction to them, e.g., disgust or outrage. While some of the *behaviors* of the old lady and the mugger were the same, people only have a negative emotional reaction to the latter; hence they only use 'aggression' for the mugger. But since frustration-aggression theory was only about behavior, and not about emotional reactions to it, it was free to use 'aggression' to denote just what the mugger and the old lady shared. But this defense relies on morality's being an emotion. It isn't.

view of morality that gives the theorist value-free aggression settles the status of the moral story of anger. The very features the moral story wishes to call to attention have been dispatched in advance as subjective contributions of the observer, not properties of anger or aggression.

Values and Rocks

There is something alluring about this position that morality is subjective, unfit for science. After all, there is a great difference between the *hardness* of a rock and the *wrongness* of pounding it on someone's head. And we might want to say the difference is between the objective (physical) and the subjective (moral). But is this real difference a difference between the objective (the public, verifiable, unbiased, what any competent person would see) and the subjective (the private, incorrigible, biased, personal)? Well, is the *wrongness* of hitting an old lady on the head with a rock private, incorrigible, biased, and personal? No, but it is cultural.

Cultural facts are not universal, like the hardness of a rock; they are not facts that anyone with intact senses from *any* culture would notice. They are still facts, like the "professorness" of a professor, facts that anyone with intact competence in our culture would see. It might be pleasant if psychological laws could be expressed in terms of universal concepts like hardness. But first there is the empirical question: are there such laws? There need not be any. Science doesn't require universality only objectivity. The moral story does not depend on the universality of moral notions, merely on their objectivity. If moral talk is objective, then moral force *can* be included in psychological theory and *cannot* be rejected as a subjective connotation of ordinary concepts like aggression. Advocates of the moral story would argue that frustration-aggression theorists haven't just wiped a subjective connotation off an English word; they have chopped off part of its (objective) meaning. (These claims require amplification, see chs. 10 & 11.)

The hydraulic theory, then, did not seriously deal with the moral side of anger because it found moral talk too disreputable to include in its theorizing.[8] We want to restore morality to its

8. Berkowitz (1962) attempted to incorporate the moral story within the frustration-aggression frame. He claimed that frustration always leads to anger. Pastore (1952) pointed out

place in anger by considering and developing an important version of the moral story—Aristotle's.[9]

Aristotle's Moral Account

In the *Rhetoric* Aristotle says:

> Anger may be defined as an impulse, accompanied by pain, to a conspicuous revenge for a conspicuous slight directed without justification towards what concerns oneself or towards what concerns one's friends. . . . It must always be attended by a certain pleasure—that which arises from the expectation of revenge.
>
> (Book 2, ch. 2)

How are we to take Aristotle's definition? It isn't one people offer, but it might explain their use of 'anger': An adequate definition would include just those features of a situation that anyone could use to show that his belief that someone is angry is correct. Does Aristotle's definition meet this test? We will need some cases of anger to tell. If we find examples the definition doesn't include, or some that it includes that aren't anger, then Aristotle is wrong. But how shall we find our cases of anger in the first place? A straightforward way would be to ask people to describe instances of their anger and then test Aristotle's definition against them.

Imagine someone told us she was angry with Tom. When we asked, "What are you angry about?" she said, "Tom gave me a

---

that whether you became angry at a bus-driver who passed you by depended on whether the bus had an "Out of Service" sign on it or not. Whether it did or not, it was equally frustrating, but if it did, then it was a justified frustration; if it didn't, it was unjustified (he called it arbitrary). Pastore claimed that we became angry at "arbitrary," but not justified frustrations.

Berkowitz answered Pastore in the following way. First, following Pastore, he calls the distinction between unjustified and justified a distinction between the arbitrary and the justified. Then he takes arbitrary to mean *unexpected.* And, of course, unexpected frustrations are more frustrating. But how was the bus that was out of service more expected than the one that wasn't? Next, Berkowitz decides that you really would be angry but not show it. This sometimes happens. But suppose you're frustrated by someone who misses an appointment because his mother died. Couldn't you just feel pity? Does he deny this possibility?

He also claims it is your interpretation of the frustration that counts. But this is rampantly circular. Then he claims that among the ongoing, goal-directed activities we are always engaged in are, "the internal responses oriented toward the preservation of security and comfort" or "impulses of self assertion" (1962, p. 30). For a behaviorist, he certainly does multiply internal, mental entities. We find these ad hoc accounts shaggy. We recommend Ockam's razor.

9. Of course, Aristotle has had some successors, even contemporary ones. For instance, Peters (1972), Melden (1961), Kenny (1963), Bedford (1964), Ryle (1949), Averill (1978), and many others.

million dollars." Then we asked, "What do you want to do to Tom?" to which she replied, "I would do anything I could to help him; I introduce him to all of my friends as a wonderful fellow, and I like spending time with him." Suppose we asked, "Then why do you say you are angry with him?" and she answered, "I know I'm angry, I just have that feeling." Would we believe her? Wouldn't we say that she isn't really angry with him? Isn't our saying this based on our understanding of her pattern of inclinations and her assessments of Tom's character as incompatible with anger?[10]

So we're not compelled to believe that anyone who sincerely says she is angry is angry.[11] What we need for our definition is the pattern of circumstances, reactions, actions, and inclinations to act that would convince us someone was angry, whether they said so or not. This is the standard we shall measure Aristotle's claim against. We shall consider Aristotle's complex definition bit by bit.[12]

We start with pleasure and pain. The source of anger is a slight; its object is revenge. Slights are painful to remember; revenge is pleasant to anticipate. Is Aristotle right? Are slights painful? Is revenge sweet? His account, at least, spares us arguments about whether anger is positive or negative, painful or pleasurable by showing how it is both.[13] Now let's turn to Aristotle's account of the source of anger, a slight.

Suppose someone stole your car but was thoughtful enough to leave a note: "I stole your car because it is the classiest I've

10. A Freudian might find "deep anger" hidden under her behavior. This is at least a sensible claim. To support it, the Freudian must show how at a deeper level the behavior really does meet commonsense criteria of anger; the same criteria are used, just applied to different levels. What makes "deep anger," anger is just what makes anger, anger.

11. This is not to say people are not sometimes, often, or even nearly always right about what emotion they are experiencing; rather, it is to say that as a logical matter a person *could* be wrong.

12. Schachter and Singer's (1962) account of anger seems similar to Aristotle's. They also include a perception and a reaction. However, they are systematically vague about whether their theory concerns how people label their emotions or the emotions people have. Gordon (1978) spells out the ways this theory is vague.

13. The notion that the same experience has both painful and pleasurable sides relates to the psychoanalytic (and commonsense) notion of ambivalence; it is, perhaps, worthwhile to see the difference. Consider someone who is offered a very good job that involves moving from a city she loves. Taking the job has two aspects. But this does not mean the person is ambivalent: she may be firm in her determination to take it. Thus, cognitive dissonance theory notwithstanding, she can see and be affected by both aspects of the same act, taking the job. The ambivalent person not only perceives both sides, but can't decide, or make a commitment to one or the other path.

ever seen. You have excellent taste. Please accept my congratulations." Though we might not say the victim had been slighted, we would still understand her anger. So 'slight' is too narrow.[14] While this theft is not a slight, it is a *transgression of the owner's rights*. Recall that the angry outburst with which we began had its source in a transgression, though not of the *angry person's* rights. So anger has its source in transgressions, not slights.

Returning to the example of the angry millionaire, we see why her anger was incomprehensible. Ordinarily, giving someone a million dollars isn't a transgression. We can imagine a circumstance where it is, but that is also a circumstance where we understand the anger, e.g., the million is hot and the police near. The other reason the example is confusing concerns her impulses.

Aristotle claims the impulse of anger serves revenge, but she has impulses we could not recognize as directed toward revenge—unless, of course, she knew her friends to be deadly bores.

Take another case. Bill believed that Sam called him "cheap"; actually, Sam called him "deep" and Bill misunderstood. Once we learn what Bill *thought he heard* we understand his anger. So even mistaken anger must invoke transgression; throttling someone because you mistakenly believe he's your best friend isn't anger. It's something deeper or darker.

Some Objections

We shall consider three objections to Aristotle's account. First, this account includes a causal claim, i.e., transgressions lead to impulses for revenge. But he had no data. Perhaps, as a matter of fact, the perception of transgression doesn't lead, or doesn't always lead, to an impulse for revenge. Doesn't this show that anger is really caused by something else? No. There are two sorts of cases to consider: hostility without a perception of

14. So is Aristotle's notion that anger must be directed against those who slight one's self or one's friends. While this makes sense, probably more sense in fourth century Athens than twentieth century New York, still it betrays an undemocratic sentiment. While anger at transgressions against the self or friends may be more common than anger against those who transgress strangers, still our subway hero's reaction was sensible as anger.

Our wanting Greek leaves us to the mercy of Aristotle's translators; since we are more interested in anger than Aristotle, we can, at least, be fair to anger, if not Aristotle.

transgression and the perception of transgression without hostility. As we shall see, an Aristotelian would say that these are not, or not simply, cases of anger. In this way the claim is circular. After all, what else could a definition be? Must it be a defective definition because it includes a causal claim?

The concept sunburn includes a causal hypothesis; yet we use it happily though we are conceptually disbarred from discovering that sunburn is also caused by moon rays, fog, or overexertion (see Gordon, 1978).[15] Still, isn't it the job of scientists, not philologists, to discover causes? Hasn't language pre-empted the terrain? It hasn't; there is plenty left to discover. Ask any dermatologist. Although anger must involve a transgression, perhaps only some transgressions cause anger. Some people don't get sunburn; perhaps some don't get angry, or angry very often. Or burned very badly. These are real empirical questions not pre-empted by Aristotle's definition. And there are others.

Transgression is the name of a class, not a particular. (In the same way, fathers are men, but this does not resolve which men are fathers or which man is the father of which child.) Which transgressions cause anger? What transgression caused *this* anger? So there is still work to be done.

Another scientific question about anger is: what neural networks are involved in the perception of transgression? Presumably one day we shall have something to say about this; now we don't. On the response side, neural-humoral stories *are* available about some of the manifestations of anger, especially arousal. But the behavioral manifestations of anger are not merely diverse; the class of angry responses is open. Some angry responses, e.g., sweating or trembling, are symptomatic of anger, but they are not unique to anger (it could be the flu). Other responses, like yelling, "Someday somebody could kill you for that!" while hurling an offender across a train, are, perhaps, unique to anger, but called forth by rather rare circumstances. No matter how long a list of angry responses we drew

15. This is, perhaps, an important fact about ordinary language overlooked by psychologists: the useful terms of the language have grown up in the context of centuries of observation of human action. As Kovesi (1967) points out, it is often important to tell another not only what a person did, but why he did it; some of the words in the language include some degree of specification of cause. The emotion words seem, generally, to fit this pattern. One reason for suggesting that social psychologists ought not bother attempting to discover general causal laws of human behavior is that the language has already taken account of them.

up, someone could always add a new one; there are always new ways to insult, demean, injure, revile, bore, or betray—as transgression or revenge.

Another way to express this, as Wittgenstein would, is that anger is not an *ingredient* of angry responses. Indeed, the only thing angry responses have in common is their direction toward revenge, and that *is not an ingredient but a goal.* Thus, there is no shared element in angry behavior. So, whatever neural account can be given cannot be expected to be strikingly simple.

A cognitive story of anger is not disbarred. Perhaps an account can be given of how people come to recognize a particular act as a transgression, not by specifying neural activity, but by documenting the 'cognitive processes' occurring, i.e., specifying something akin to a computer program (not computer wiring—that's the neurological story) that can decide whether a transgression has happened, and then, in light of the situation, what sort of revenge can be taken (see Sabini & Silver, 1981).[16]

A Second Threat

A second, more serious threat to Aristotle's definition is that his anger seems to inhabit a world of rational, cool-headed, Greek moral philosophers.

This temperance of the Aristotelian account makes us uneasy with it and tempts us to think of anger in terms of drives, frustrations, and hydraulic mishaps. Aristotle's notion seems to rule out the possibility that our anger *could be* irrational, that we could lose our head. How can the Aristotelian account be fit to cases in which someone's anger is intemperate?

Consider the following example. Someone rushing off to work tries to start her car. It won't. So she curses it, kicks it, and screams at it. Wouldn't we say she is angry? Could we say the car transgressed, or she mistook the car for the sort of thing

16. We are unaware of any arguments showing that there must in principle be such an account, but there are no arguments for why there can't be. The proof of this pudding awaits the baking. And, when the pudding is baked, if it is baked, we will be in a position to see whether anger processes are like *electromagnetic* processes, in that their mechanisms are understood in reference to a single set of principles, or like *digestive processes* that have little in common except their involvement in digestion. We content ourselves in this paper with an investigation into what anger is; perhaps that will prove useful to those wanting a cognitive account of anger.

that could transgress? This seems to be a clear case of frustration leading to anger and even aggression (although it is odd to talk of aggressing against a car). This anger does not seem to fit rational Greeks or their definitions. But before abandoning Aristotle perhaps we should recall a principle proposed by a more recent philosopher.

Austin (1970a) asked whether we should say that a person who sat down in his chair, in the usual way, did so intentionally. He proposed that saying, "He sat down intentionally," is misleading. It is misleading because we use adverbs, including 'intentionally', only in circumstances where something is aberrant about an act; in this case there was nothing in the slightest aberrant about the way he sat down. That is not to say that he sat down *unintentionally* since that too suggests some aberration in the sitting down—perhaps he tripped, slid, or was pushed. Austin proposed, "No modification without aberration," i.e., we should not add modifiers to a description of an action unless there is something noteworthy about the action. Here we endorse the reverse rule—no aberration without modification, i.e., if the act is aberrant, it is misleading to describe it without modification.

Let's return to thrashing the car. There is something aberrant about treating a car this way: it is immature. Let's look back on the case in more detail. What leads us to call the woman angry? Not just her hitting or kicking the car, or even vigorously hitting or kicking—that might be the only way to start it. We call her angry because she is cursing, villifying, or "punishing" the car, i.e., she is treating the car as if it were an agent that had transgressed her. And this is what is immature.[17]

Note, in contrast to a case where someone mistakenly *believes* he has been offended, this commuter doesn't *believe* she has been transgressed. If you ask her, she would surely say the car really isn't making fun of her, trying to get her, or being spiteful or malicious in not starting. Immature emotions are defective, not crazy; they remain rooted in some features of the objective situation. Getting angry at a car that *does* start is crazy,

17. Further, the judgment of immaturity is not a judgment about the futility of the response; although hitting a car is futile, so too might be becoming enraged at the repressions of a government. But futility alone does not make an emotional response immature.

not immature.[18] Emotions can be defective, immature, in other ways.

Immature anger often lacks perspective, for instance, through an overestimate of one's due. A person may fancy a slight because he assumes more is owed him than an uninvolved observer would. Or someone may take herself to be the target of criticism or ridicule aimed elsewhere. Or someone may blow things out of proportion by giving accidents, mistakes, errors, or slips their worst possible reading (see Goffman, 1971, on virtual offenses). Overblown reactions are not always indicative of a spoiled character; sometimes they just mean it's been a bad day. You don't have to be immature to have a bad day.

When we are touchy, grumpy, or cross, we are likely to flare up, lash out, explode. Of course, we rarely flare up at nothing; rather, we blow up at trifles, at what we'd ordinarily perceive as a minor transgression or even an excusable accident or slip. That's what it means to be in a bad mood; just as being in a good mood suggests we are more forgiving, tolerant, or indulgent than we are ordinarily. So blowing up because your four-year-old has left his blocks just where you ordinarily trip on them, even though you have happily stumbled over them for the past three months, is a good sign of a bad mood. Still he should have put them away; your explosion wasn't measured, but it had its reasons.[19] If you blow up at your wife for making the broccoli mushy but it's really because she wears the same

18. And perhaps this is more generally true: immature thought, emotion, and action are defective in limited ways. Immature thinking is limited especially in the sense that it lacks perspective. Puppy love, an immature emotion, is among other things focused on the attractive features of the object in disregard of other features and, sometimes, of the absurdity of the attraction viewed in broader perspective. Perhaps, just because of this oddness of focus, emotions can be subtle, sometimes more acute. Puppy love will make one more attuned to signs of attention, interest, or change of mood in a ninth grade teacher than an uninvolved perception would. A narrow view will, on occasion, be more revealing than a broader, more inclusive one.

The hydraulic treatment of anger treats beating up the car as a central case, as showing what is essential, important, and typical of anger. The Aristotelian treatment sees the immaturity of this case as an important fact not about anger per se, but about emotion more generally. For that reason, it doesn't occupy the same place in the Aristotelian account as it does in the hydraulic.

19. It is not only moods that show such exacerbations. Sometimes we display not a temporary readiness to see the world in a particular light, but a habitual sensitivity to the behavior of particular people. Parents and children, wives and husbands, often lock themselves into attitudes that construe almost all accidents, omissions, lapses of memory, as well as peccadilloes and harmless fun, as insults, challenges, threats—as transgressions which lead to immediate and practiced anger.

perfume as your boss—who was particularly unfair to you that day—then hydraulic theorists talk of displacement, an unconsciously focused bad mood. If such things happen, and perhaps they do, they are still overblown reactions to a minor transgression.

The moral story, then, deals with hydraulic cases by pointing out that although they share some elements of anger, they diverge from central cases of anger in one way or another. "Hydraulic phenomena" could do damage to Aristotle's story only if there were hydraulic cases of anger we would not independently judge to be defective anger.[20] Perhaps there are some. But the obvious examples of hydraulic anger are all defective; they are at once separate, yet draw their identity as anger, from the ways they are like central cases.

A Third Objection

Now for the third attack, one that can be lodged against both the moral and hydraulic stories: they have missed the essence of anger. They busy themselves with external causes and results without ever getting to the heart of the matter, what anger *really* is—a feeling, a mental state. A critic might say, "If someone didn't *feel* angry, have anger as a content of consciousness, he wouldn't be angry even if frustrated or slighted, no matter how he behaved. The feeling, the mental state, is what is distinctive, and distinctively human, about anger. A dog might attack someone after he took away his food, but we wouldn't seriously call the beast angry. His behavior might look like ours when we are angry, but he can't be angry because he doesn't have the same feelings, the same mental contents, we do."

20. Consider an analogy: suppose Bill wanted to claim that, among other things, a car is a self-propelled vehicle and Fred raised as a counterexample his car, which was at the moment in the garage having a new engine put in. At the moment it was not self-propelled—still it is a car. Is this a counterexample? Wouldn't we say that having no motor is a defect in a car? And for this reason, we would not allow Fred's car as a counterexample. For a real counterexample, we would need a car that would not be independently judged as defective, but which was not self-propelled. About a "car," we are not forced just to say it is either a car or it is not; we can also say it is a defective car. Our conception of what it is to be a car should show us just what is defective about Fred's. In parallel, "getting angry at one's car" is neither just an example of anger nor not an example of anger, but an example of defective, immature anger. Conceiving of anger as a response to transgression shows us *just how* this reaction is defective. On the frustration-aggression account, there is nothing odd or immature about our commuter. In fact, it can draw no distinction between the commuter's beating her car and Spartikus' slaying his master. Aristotle, on the other hand, naturally picks out righteous and defective anger.

Although we suspect the dog is not angry, we reject the mentalist reasons for this conclusion.[21] Hydraulic theorists have neither grounds nor instigations to reject a frustrated dog as angry; the terms of this theory apply equally well to dogs and humans. If Aristotle too has slighted the human *experience* of anger, then he too shall have to pay.

How did our mentalist know that dogs don't have the right mental contents? He has no access to the beast's mind. So he has no reason to believe one way or the other. But this agnosticism doesn't capture his position. He wanted to say dogs aren't angry, not that he had his doubts; he wanted to say dogs *can't* have the right mental content, not that they *might* not have it. If the mentalist were really relying on mental content, then he should doubt another person's anger as he doubts the dog's. After all, he doesn't have access to another person's mind either.

There can only be one case of anger the mentalist is certain of—his own—and only one reason for his certainty—specific angry mental contents. So we shall let him root in his own mind to tell us if he comes upon a mental content necessary to his anger.

Suppose someone deeply insulted him with a racial slur, and he reacted by punching the racist in the nose. Imagine three cases: (1) as he punches him in the nose he says to himself, "You dirty bastard"; (2) he sees a red patch as he punches him; and (3) as he punches him he says aloud, "You dirty bastard," but nothing "goes through his mind." Surely we would call him angry in all three cases, and so would he; yet there were different contents in his mind in two cases, and nothing went through his mind in one. Does the mentalist believe *screaming* "dirty bastard" is not a token of anger but *thinking* it is? So there is no requisite mental content for his own anger. Then why should he require one for a dog?[22]

21. Of course, ordinary speakers often say that dogs are angry. And we understand them. We even understand how to confirm their statement or show that they are wrong, e.g., although the dog is barking, his tail is wagging. But this does not mean that the dog is angry in the same sense its master is; there is an overlap in the two senses, of course, but they are not identical. We are not attempting to challenge this usage—nor would we want to; we just call attention to how it differs from the human case.

22. Someone might reply: "Yes, but there is an unconscious mental accompaniment to his anger. You have been using mental only in the conscious sense." But if this is true, when I say I am angry in the third case I am making an *inference* about an unconscious mental

Access to consciousness—a dog's or a person's—won't settle whether he is angry since there is no particular angry content. Indeed, there may be *no* content on an angry person's mind.

We have been trailing two things: a mind and a hound. The trails diverge. We shall come back to the mind after finishing with the hound. How might Aristotle deal with whether dogs can be angry? He might first ask whether the dog can distinguish between a transgression per se and a frustration. If it could not he would call it incapable of anger. He would wonder whether the dog can seek revenge rather than merely be hostile. These questions are *empirical* and can be resolved by evidence.

Oliver Wendell Holmes once claimed that even a dog can tell whether it's been stepped on intentionally or by accident. Let's assume he was right, i.e., a dog can tell the difference between someone's deliberately stepping on his tail and an accidental mis-step, and furthermore, responds violently only to the former. This evidence supports the claim that dogs get angry, but it doesn't settle the case. The dog would have to show that it can tell pains in its paw caused by transgressions from those caused by mistakes (his master in attempting to save him from the attack of another dog steps on *his* paw by mistake) or justified medical interventions (his master has to pull a thorn from his paw). The dog would also have to show it can appreciate mitigating and exacerbating circumstances. If a dog can do all these things, then it can be angry. In our experience with dogs, these talents have not been apparent, but it is an empirical matter and further research is needed.[23]

We leave hounds and return to minds. Although rooting around in consciousness has found nothing special on the minds of angry people, still what you are thinking *may* have to do with whether you are angry or not. A person who seems to be angry may only be pretending, and perhaps the only difference between his pretense and the real thing is what he has on his mind. But the relations between mental reserve and pretense are intricate. To unravel them we start from a simple case, a pretended action, and work toward emotion.

---

accompaniment to my screaming, and if this is just an inference, it might be wrong. If this is so, I don't know I am angry in the third case although I do in the first case. And this is queer because I am just as sure I am angry in both cases. So we still don't have a principled basis to distinguish the dog's anger from our own, save that it just isn't human.

23. There is a lot passed over here. Bennett (1964) is extremely useful in seeing just what, especially in his notion of fake and frozen intelligence.

As Bedford (1964) argues, one can pretend just so far. I may say passionately and repeatedly both to you and myself that I am only pretending to murder you as I load the gun, aim, cock, and pull the trigger. But no matter how vivid my mental content, "I'm pretending to murder you" is, as I stoop over your dead body, I will have murdered you, not pretended. Bedford attempted a like analysis for emotion. In his account, no matter how pacific the mental accompaniment, one can pretend to be angry just so far; if he goes further, then he just *is* angry. But anger's mental accompaniment is not as easily dismissed as murder's. Let us examine a story in which you go beyond Bedford's limit, but are still only pretending to be angry.

A captured spy must convince the enemy that he is angry at me, a fellow spy, to persuade them that he is on their side. If he fails to convince them they will blow up New York—even the Metropolitan Museum. Our agent sincerely believes the loss of all those New Yorkers would be regrettable, and the loss of those Velasquezes and El Grecos unthinkable. The enemy puts him to the test: they give him a gun. He knows if he kills me angrily they will spare New York, but if he doesn't they will blow it up. So he kills me, and as he does so he says to himself, "Sorry, old chap," while pretending to be angry. There is no question that he killed me, and, depending on your view of New Yorkers, pragmatist or consequentialist ethics, and Spanish art, you will or will not say he murdered me. But this much is clear: it wasn't out of anger, in anger, or while angry. The distinction between pretending anger and being angry isn't one of degree. What went through his mind, his "Sorry, old chap," plays a part in this story, suggesting that mental contents are important to anger. Still, before leaping to the mentalist position, let us examine the precise role of the mental content and the way it must be mental to get the part.

Considerable staging was necessary to sustain the role of the mental accompaniment. First we had to give the spy a motive to pretend, i.e., something his pretense would accomplish or avoid—otherwise, "Sorry, old chap" would be pointless and irrelevant to our drama. And by itself it would not, as Bedford realizes, convince us he was pretending. Second, the motive is commensurate with his action. His mental "sorry" would be merely ironic if he were trying to save two Keene's, a Norman Rockwell, and a Renoir. We need to know not only our killer's motive and whether it was commensurate, but how attached and committed he was to it. If he were attempting to save New York, but would have abandoned the effort for a free, all-expense-paid round trip to Atlantic City, then his "sorry" would have been hollow.

We are acquainted with some of the staging necessary for "sorry" to have force. But why must this "sorry" be mental to have this force? Couldn't it have been said aloud? Of course, saying it aloud would not have been prudent. The mental "sorry" was *private;* that's why it won the part. But, if it were not for the surveillance, if the killing had been done in private, then he could have said his "Sorry, old chap," *aloud*—a more poignant performance. Given the circumstances, he had to make do with a mental stand-in. Saying it to himself was just a way to ensure privacy. It had no other virtue: a soliloquy, if the spy story had adopted Elizabethan convention, or a private diary would have been equally effective.[24] So the virtues of the mental—convenience, privacy, tact, secrecy—are social, not psychological.

For dogs and spies, and presumably others, we do not have to assay mental contents in order to determine anger; contents of consciousness, contra the mentalist critique of Aristotle, have no special status although they may play a role in special circumstances where privacy is useful.

24. Suppose someone said: "Perhaps every case of emotional display is like the spy's—maybe everyone is always pretending. We can never tell whether people are 'really' angry or in any other emotional state. Perhaps in every case, save our own, when somebody seems to be angry they really aren't." How might we reply? Well, let's see what's involved in this claim. It assumes that if we knew all there was to know about people displaying emotion we would always find unnoticed, powerful reasons for them to pretend. And this is logically possible but implausible; what payoff could the fellow on the subway have had for pretending to be angry? This possible but implausible claim is not restricted to emotions.

Consider this case: you're having lunch in a restaurant; on your way out someone asks you, "What were the *other* people in the restaurant doing?" After you recover from the apparent pointlessness of the question, you might answer, somewhat tentatively, "Having lunch?" Now suppose when you leave you find that there are Kleig lights, a script girl, a make-up boy, etc. Now, we would say all these people weren't really having lunch, even though they were really eating the food. It could (logically) be true that there is more to life (not just emotion) than meets the eye (how else could psychoanalysis get going?). It is logically possible that the world, save us, is a stage, but this amounts to the claim the Kleig lights are more prevalent than we had imagined.

Note that nothing about this depends on what the people eating lunch said to themselves consciously, unconsciously, mentally, or otherwise. It depends on real Kleig lights, script girls, and make-up boys. Next, notice that as a customer in the restaurant we were never uncertain about whether the people were eating lunch. Before we discovered the movie set we were certain they were eating lunch; afterward, we realized they weren't. But never were we uncertain.

SOME IMPLICATIONS

We featured anger on the subway as a sample for both theories. We owe a report on how the theories fared. How did the moral account do? How did the hydraulic account do?

The hydraulic account is surely right in that subways are frustrating—they can be hot, noisy, and jarring. And the outburst we reported was on the subway. However, the careful reader will have noticed the outburst was not to the heat, noise, or bumps. Rather it was to a bully. Of course, bullying can be very frustrating—to its victim. But how was it frustrating to the observer, our hero? Perhaps it frustrated his sense of fair play, his drive to live in a just world. Of course the hydraulic story could be put this way, but, if it is, the concepts of drive and frustration become so elastic that they enclose any possible story—even the moral one. Let us grant that at least for some frustrations there is an outburst. But an outburst against whom? Floods don't discriminate between those who have stirred up the waters and those innocently on the bank. Say our subway hero was in some way frustrated by the offense. Why shouldn't he pummel the old lady on his right? Hydraulics could be made to answer this, but not without adding ad hoc principles: more elastic.

The moral account, on the other hand, picks out the bully as the likely source of the outburst rather than the noise, heat, or bumps. And only the bully could be the target of the urge for conspicuous revenge.

Of course, if Aristotle had been on the train he might not have understood the outburst. Why should a peripatetic philosopher understand that on the subway "I saw the seat first" doesn't give someone a right to the seat but "I'm sitting here" does? But this is not a problem because on Aristotle's theory no purely psychological account of anger could be given, since his conception of anger gives a role to transgression. And the concept of transgression implies notions such as culture, shared norms, common understanding. Hydraulics, on the other hand, drowns these social constituents.

Unfortunately, frustrations are not confined to the subway. The frustration of the need for food, clothing, shelter, and medical care for a substantial portion of the world's population has been constant throughout history. But these frustrations often lead to despair, helplessness, submission to the will of the Lord, i.e., quiescence, not anger. The perception of wants frustrated by a transgression is what leads to anger. Social movements fighting injustice often must show how "a morally neutral fact of nature," that one is born in the wrong caste or class, is in fact a human-made transgression. It is hard to become angry about hurricanes, the laws of nature, or even the laws of economics (if you believe they are like the laws of nature). It is sensible to become angered at exploitation but not at marginal utility of labor curves. But starving because you are exploited is no more frustrating than starving because the marginal utility of labor curves "show" that you can't be employed. Yet one case is reserved for anger, the other depression.

Insofar as we see anger and violence as merely reactions to frustrations, then our goal for a just society is to reduce frustration and, where this is impossible, to train the individual to moderate, even contain, his natural reactions.[25] But this can't be a prescription for the just society since it doesn't distinguish those frustrations to which we *ought* respond from those we ought endure.[26] Once we realize that "frustration produces aggression" has been confused with "transgression produces anger," then instead of training people to resist frustration and avoid anger, we shall train them to become angry—carefully.

25. This view would seem to be in accord with the Catholic tradition, which sees anger as one of the deadly sins. But why is anger a deadly sin? First, note that the other deadly sins, save envy (see ch. 3): avarice, gluttony, lust, and so on, do not forbid classes of actions entirely. Rather, they forbid actions done inappropriately—in the wrong context or to excess. Perhaps the prohibition against anger is this sort of injunction. And, as Aristotle points out, anger includes a desire for revenge (see Averill, 1978, for an illuminating discussion on this general theme). It is a peculiarity of Christian dogma that the desire for revenge on earth is itself sinful, an abrogation of God's rights. So the sinfulness of anger may result from this special doctrine of Christianity.

26. What could frustration-aggression theory say about educating anger—or could it say anything? Perhaps people could learn to inhibit anger, or better, direct it, but the anger itself is brute. But Aristotle has a way for anger to be educated. Moral training—teaching people to perceive clearly what their rights are and what other people's rights are; how their actions affect other people; how other people's views, wants, and needs matter, and how they don't—is at the same time the education of morality and the education of anger (see Peters, 1972).

CHAPTER TEN

The Subjective, the Objective, and the Ambiguous

As students of the social life, we are warned: our work is insufficiently objective—science must transcend the subjective; our work is only objective—psychology can't ignore the subjective; our work is in vain—the objectivity of science is incompatible with the subjectivity of experience. All of this sounds important.

As commonsense actors we hear: you can't really say Cezanne is better than Tiepolo—art is just subjective; abortion may be right for me but wrong for you—morality is subjective; no one else can really understand what I'm feeling—emotions are subjective. And this sounds important too.

Some philosophers have hinted: pain or knowledge or causality or meaning or the world is subjective. And this sounds threatening.

One's urge on hearing all of these is to agree; then one wants to disagree. Or in a different mood, the urge to disagree may come first. Here we shall succumb to neither. Instead, we shall look for various ways that something can be subjective. Then when someone tells us something is subjective, we shall want to say, "Yes, in a sense. But in your sense how is that subjectivity threatening—or important?" We suspect that notions of subjectivity are individually harmless, but dangerous in a mob, so dangerous that when 'subjective' is used without its particular sense being clear, it threatens aesthetics, science, ethics, morality, and our understanding of ourselves and others. We shall now pursue the senses, pull them apart, and keep them quarantined.

SENSES OF SUBJECTIVITY

Sense 1: The Subjectivity of Any Point of View

To start with the concrete, consider a tree. We take it that people treat and understand trees as objective, i.e., as something that not only they, but anyone, can see, touch, smell. We assume that if a tree fancier were to call her friend's attention to the beauty of a white birch or the stench of a fruiting ginkgo, she would take it for granted that he would see or smell the same tree. If not, how would "calling attention" make sense? Yet something about a tree is subjective: anyone's view of it, and hence, everyone's view of it.

What a person can see about a tree is tied to her vantage: two people standing in different positions relative to the tree will see different parts of it. In this sense, views of a tree are subjective. The "subjective" here calls attention to the way the view is tied to the position of the person; someone standing somewhere else would have a different view of the tree. The subjectivity of the views does not shake anyone's belief in the objectivity of the tree. The subjectivity of the views supports our belief that the tree is objective. We would be astounded, shaken in our belief in the tree's objectivity, if it had the same appearance from every vantage—even a perfectly symmetrical tree would look different from an airplane than from any side. Hence, the subjectivity of the views supports the objectivity of the tree.

Our belief in the reality of the tree is grounded in the fact that as points of view differ, appearances differ in an intelligible way; our belief in the objectivity of the world is sustained not so often by agreement as by an orchestration of difference. So there is no inconsistency between the belief that there is an *object*, the tree, and that views of it are subjective, i.e., from a point of view. They are intertwined concepts. Subjectivity is neither a defect nor a virtue of a view, but part of what it means to be a view. Even God's point of view, if God can be said to have one, must be subjective in this sense.

Sense 2: The Objectivity of a Single Point of View

In the sense we have just discussed, all descriptions are subjective, but in another sense each is objective. When our tree fancier describes what she sees from her point of view, she takes it for granted that, were a friend to take her position, her friend would see not only the same tree, but the features she described, e.g., the branches crossing at a certain height. We find it natural that descriptions differ in intelligible ways with points of view and that descriptions from the same point of view are the same: this is what it means to see an *object*. Our notion of an object, then, is sustained by both a subjectivity and an objectivity of description.

Visual illusions are intermediate cases in which a view is objective, in that anyone would have it, but it doesn't fit with other views from different positions. For example, suppose a traveler in a desert sees a water hole and wishes to check his perception. He calls a friend, who also sees it. But as they approach, the water hole retreats. They now realize they have seen a mirage, not an oasis. We might say that in one sense their claim to have seen a water hole *was* objective—anyone would have seen what they saw—but *not* objective in another sense—as they moved toward it, their views did not change the way views of a real water hole do. Because of this conflict illusions are different from hallucinations. Because their descriptions fit the concept of an object in one way but not another, we have use for the distinction between hallucinations and mirages.

Sense 3: The Subjectivity of Distortion

There is a sense in which we say that some views of things are objective in opposition to others that are subjective. To call a view subjective *in this sense* is, at least, to call it distorted. This use is brought out in an advertisement for a book on wine.

> Because sensory responses are easily influenced by various physiological, psychological, and cultural factors, wine evaluation can be a highly subjective process. *Wines: Their Sensory Evaluation* tells how to minimize these factors so that more consistent, objective evaluations can be made.
>
> (1979)

Against this sense of subjective, but not the first, we are advised to be objective in our descriptions and opinions. Note that although we may treat someone's claim as subjective in this sense, we still treat him as making an objective claim in the second sense, i.e., he is making a claim about what anyone would see—a claim that is wrong. The fact that both we and he take his claim to be objective (in sense 2) makes it sensible for us to correct him, and gives him a reason to pay attention to our correction. (It is a reason to consult wine books.)

With these distinctions in mind let us examine Nagel's introduction to his article on objectivity and subjectivity.

> The problem is one of opposition between subjective and objective points of view. There is a tendency to seek an objective account of everything before admitting its reality. But often what appears to a more subjective point of view cannot be accounted for in this way. So either the objective conception of the world is incomplete, or the subjective involves illusions that should be rejected.
>
> (1979, p. 196)

Nagel, here, appears to be opposing the subjectivity tied to points of view with some objectivity. If Nagel were using sense 1, we would understand what it means to have a *subjective* point of view, although we would find the "subjective" redundant,[1] since all points of view are equally subjective in that sense. But, how could there be an objective point of view to *oppose* it? In sense 3, there *is* an opposition between subjective and objective, but this opposition is not much of a problem—no one treasures distortion. Of course we want an objective, undistorted account of something before admitting its reality. Nagel seems to slide between senses 1 and 3. This is easy. In both senses of subjective, as in the others we shall consider, experiences are tied to individuals. But distortions are tied differently than points of view.

Further on in his paper, Nagel equates more objective with more encompassing (see 1979, pp. 206–7). We are not sure why more encompassing should be more objective, although we can see how at times a more encompassing view can be more *useful* than a more limited view. But sometimes it isn't. A view is better or worse depending on our purpose at hand. Near is

1. If one examines both the lay and social science literature closely, one finds that 'subjective' is very often used in just this redundant way. It does provide emphasis.

clearly better, though more limited, than far, if we wish to make out the texture of a bark; far is better if we are interested instead in the pattern of branching. Perhaps Nagel is not really urging us to adopt a more encompassing view, but to build a better, more extensive model: one that represents more of reality.

Consider a model of a tree. Imagine that we take photos of a tree from several different points of view and construct a plastic model. We might say that the model is more encompassing than any one picture. But notice that the model is not a point of view at all, indeed, to use the model, one must take a point of view toward *it*. Our model should be objective, undistorted, but since it is not a point of view it isn't an objective one. Nor is it a subjective one. The "problem" of the opposition between objective and subjective views arises no more with models than trees.

Perhaps we're being too literal. Perhaps Nagel doesn't mean *objective point of view* in a specifically visual sense. But he does claim that as our view becomes more encompassing it loses something, and this draws upon a visual metaphor. If point of view means something like a model or system of beliefs, then it is clear why a more encompassing one is better—all other things being equal, it is better to know more than less. But why need there be a trade-off between the encompassing and the close? What do we lose as we know more? But, perhaps, as we "unpack" further senses of subjective and objective, Nagel's problem will become clearer to us.

Senses 4 and 5: Subjectivity of Ends, and Objectivity of Means Suiting Ends

How can we extend our analysis of subjectivity to senses more interesting to a social psychologist than to a botanist? We shall do this by considering what Weber (see Gerth & Mills, 1958) and those following him (see Schutz, 1973; Berger & Luckmann, 1966), at least sometimes, intend by the "subjective meaning" of something. What is the subjective meaning of a shoe? Weber seeks the subjective meaning of a shoe for someone (or some group) by seeing how the shoe is related to the person's motives, i.e., his goals or purposes. Thus, a shoe has different "subjective meanings" for two people if the shoe differs in how it will advance their distinct interests. The subjective meaning of a shoe to a person who wants to walk somewhere is distinct from the subjective meaning of the shoe to the owner of a shoe factory, a shoe fetishist, or someone who has no other way to drive a nail. In both sense 4 and sense 1, something is connected to an individual. In both senses, subjectivity is ubiquitous: all views and meanings are subjective. And, just as even God would have to have a subjective view of a tree, were God to have a view, so too, in order for something to have meaning to God—i.e., a place in God's plans—it would have to be a subjective meaning.

Just as *claims* about subjective views in the first sense are treated as objective in the second—i.e., it is taken for granted that were others to take the same position they would see the same tree—so too is there a sense of objective (sense 5) in which claims about subjective meaning are treated as objective. To see this, consider the claim that the "subjective meaning" of a shoe to someone wishing to walk somewhere is that it permits the walking without pain or danger. This claim is objective in that the person making it asserts that the shoe will *in fact* fit with that goal. Objective claims (senses 2 or 5) can be wrong, of course. The claim that a cubic centimeter of air has that protective subjective meaning for the individual is equally objective (in this sense 5), but it is wrong. This means that *ordinarily* a person who asserted that a cubic centimeter of air had that particular subjective meaning would simply be wrong about the shoe's subjective meaning. But this is too simple.

Consider more closely the hiker who chooses the cubic centimeter of air to protect his feet. We said that his claim, that the "meaning of air" for him (sense 4) was to protect his feet, was objective (sense 5), but wrong, i.e., air did not have this subjective meaning for him. But suppose that right after he puts on his socks he searches for his cubic centimeter; he won't go out of the house until he finds it. If this is part of his routine, we would have to say that he believes the cubic centimeter of air has the effect of protecting his feet, i.e., it has this subjective meaning for him.

Consider this case in relation to hallucinations. Suppose someone stares at a blank wall and announces that he sees someone about to attack him with a meat axe. What we say about this will depend on what he now does. If he ignores it, we won't know how to take his utterance—perhaps he is just repeating a phrase he learned. But if he runs away, then we might well say he had a hallucination of a killer, and we might call this perception subjective. But the subjective, here, does double work. It both ties the "perception" to the individual (in a way similar to the way "points of view" ties perceptions to individuals) and points out the error he is making. Similarly, the subjective meaning of the cubic centimeter is doubly subjective. It is used to show that he believes the air protects and, at the same time, that he is mistaken.

There are cases analogous to our mirage also. Consider a culture in which garlic is worn to ward off colds. Not only does the individual believe it, but it is something everyone in his position (culture) believes. Thus, like a mirage the belief meets a test of objectivity, but also like a mirage it fails to articulate with other beliefs (or it could in principle be shown to).

Sense 6: The Subjectivity of Bias

There is a sixth sense, bias, in which the meaning someone attaches to something can be subjective. As does the third sense, it carries the force of distortion and has as a contrast objective. It is particularly relevant to judgments. To appreciate this sense, imagine a judge is asked to hear a case in which the defendant is his wife's paramour. Assuming traditional sentiments on the judge's part, a defense counsel might search for a judge with a more objective view of the case—meaning a judge without a personal interest. Because of the judge's likely purpose (revenge) he is likely to err in his treatment of the defendant. There is a conflict between the subjective purposes the judge *may* have and the interest he *ought* to have: procedural justice. An objective judge in this sense is not without an interest in the case (sleeping judges may be common, but they are not for that reason objective). Objective judges in sense 6 attach a subjective meaning to the proceedings (sense 4), but the subjective meaning is the one the proceedings *ought* to have. In sense 6, then, subjective judgments are distorted, biased, or confused because of the values or goals of the actor; objective judgments, on the other hand, are guided by *appropriate* goals or values.[2] Just as an objective view of a tree in sense 3 (undistorted) is subjective in sense 1 (from a point of view), so is an objective view of guilt or innocence, in our present sense, subjective in sense 4 (subjectivity of ends).

To return to Nagel, he rightly sees that the perception of objects in the world from the point of view of an agent's plans or goals is subjective, or as he puts it "internal."[3] He looks for an objective point of view about, say, the meaning of life "in detachment from specific or general human purposes" (1979, pp. 196–97). But just as point of view is intertwined with subjective in sense 1, so too is meaning intertwined with subjective in sense 4. Just as it is confusing to ask for an objective point of view (sense 1), it is confusing to ask for objective meaning in sense 4.

Sense 7: Emotion

Another common use of subjective is in connection with emotion. This use is closely related to sense 4 (the subjectivity of ends), as Weber realized. To understand someone's emotional reaction to an event is to understand how the event relates to his goals. Crying at the death of a friend is understood because we understand the role of a friend in the life of an individual. But emotions are subjective, personal in a further way.

We call emotions subjective not only to relate the actor's reaction to *his* situation, but also to stress that he is affected by it. Nonetheless, given the point of view, the goals, and the nature of the reaction, *which* emotion the actor is having *is* objective (see ch. 2, on envy, and ch. 9, on anger, for a development of this).

Sense 8: Cartesian Subjectivity

So far we have found a tidy heap of "subjectives" and "objectives" without intruding upon Cartesian privacy. But there is

2. Lysenko is an interesting case. Biologists forced by Stalin to treat Lysenko's Lamarckian claims as sensible were thinking and acting in a biased, distorted way. Yet we would not call their bias subjective; nor would we call their judgment objective. Subjective, in this as in the other senses, carries the force of "personal"; while Russian biology was a distortion, it wasn't, for the most part, a personal one.

3. Just as there is a swarm of senses of subjective and objective, which it pays us to keep distinct, so too are there distinct senses of internal and external—closely related to subjective and objective. Elsewhere we have made some effort to keep them distinct (Sabini & Silver, 1981a).

an eighth sense of subjective in which sensations are subjective. The experience I have when I look at a red patch is subjective in this sense. In this sense the question "Is your experience of red and my experience of red the same?" involves two subjectivities—yours and mine. We, as social psychologists, have little to say about this sense, as troubling as it may be to metaphysicians; we suspect that commonsense actors have very little use for it (save perhaps, pain reports).

All the other senses of subjectivity are tied to social, corrigible claims about perspectives on objects, ways to goals, deviations from fair standards, distortions of correct judgments; this sense of subjectivity is not. Fitting the other subjectivities to this sense would be Procrustean. As social psychologists interested in describing and exploring commonsense thought, we shall continue to steer a path around this eighth sense.[4]

EVALUATIONS: A CENSUS OF THE SENSES

Colleagues and students sometimes tell us that evaluations are subjective. We want to see, using the various senses we have articulated, the ways they are subjective and what would lead people to want to say they are *really* subjective.

People often use subjective and objective as if each had a single contrasting sense. As we have seen they do not. Perhaps this is innocuous; perhaps subjective evaluations in one sense will happen to be subjective in all senses, perhaps not. We shall be especially concerned to compare evaluations with descriptions, since descriptions, or at least good ones, are taken to be objective (see Jones & Nisbett, 1972, for a subjective evaluation of the subjectivity of evaluations).

Let us take a specific case—the evaluation that a "paper is poorly typed"—and see how the senses line up.

Well, in sense 1 (from a point of view) my judgment that this

4. Of course sometimes pragmatic commonsense actors can't avoid this sense. You have been asked to volunteer for an experiment. It involves the following: you will be given curare so all your muscles will be paralyzed; an instrument will be passed down your mouth past your vocal cords; ordinarily you would gag and shriek in pain, but you have been paralyzed. Behaviorists want to argue that you wouldn't be in pain since you could not exhibit pain behavior. But, it might be argued, you still will sense the pain, and this can be shown by your reporting it later. But that can be fixed too, valium or scopolamine will provide amnesia. There then will be no reaction on your part to the pain—now or later. Some claim that Wittgenstein (1953) would argue that in this case there is no pain. (But we doubt he'd volunteer.) As Dennet (1978) points out, we don't know that current anesthesia does not work just like this.

paper is poorly typed is subjective. I am looking at the paper from a certain angle in good light, and so forth. But then my judgment is objective in sense 2 (objectivity of a point of view); after all, I claim that you too will see what I see if you look at the paper under this light. In sense 3 (subjectivity as distortion) my judgment *may be* faulty, subjective; perhaps what I take to be uneven spacing is really my astigmatism. In terms of the subjective meaning of my criticizing my secretary (sense 4—subjectivity of ends), it is relevant to know that I am submitting the paper for publication to a fussy editor; I am judging the typing in light of this end. So, since it is from the point of view of my particular motive, my evaluation is subjective. On the other hand, I claim that if you wanted to get published in that journal, you too would notice the typos. Thus the poor typing is objective in sense 5 (objectivity of means suiting ends). I claim to have no axes to grind; I do not dislike my secretary, and insofar as I don't, my judgment is objective in sense 6 (objectivity as unbiased). I am dispassionate at the moment, not overcome, so we shall let sense 7 be (subjectivity of emotion). And as neither the paper nor the quality of typing are sensations (sensations are not perceptions, not about things in the world), sense 8 (Cartesian subjectivity) is, as usual, irrelevant. Although the paper isn't subjective, the sensations I have as I look at the paper are. But then all sensations are, so this makes my evaluations no more subjective than it makes all of my descriptions.

The senses of subjective, at least for the evaluation of a poorly typed paper, do not line up. Rather the same evaluation is both subjective and objective in several different senses.

The senses in which this evaluation is not objective have to do with the absence of an attainable objectivity (subjective as distortion or bias) or they call attention to a condition of all descriptions or evaluations (subjectivity and objectivity of points of view, and the subjectivity of goals and the objectivity of means suiting ends).

Our taxonomy leads us to say that evaluations are objective in some senses and subjective in others. Further the ways in which evaluations are subjective pose no threat to the legitimacy of making them, since these ways of being subjective are shared by descriptions. Still, we have a residual feeling that evaluations are *really* subjective—in a way that does threaten their legitimacy. We shall diagnose this feeling by comparing a disagreement over the description "the rock is hard" with a disagreement over the evaluation "that is a poor chess move." This will also allow us to exercise our senses of subjectivity and see if they can be put to good use. We start by examining what we might say and do if we found ourselves in disagreement with someone about an obvious description. Then we shall compare and contrast this with the course of a disagreement over an obvious evaluation.

Imagine we meet a visitor from, say, the Trobriand Islands who claims that a particular rock is not hard. Perhaps he doesn't understand the use of the word hard. But let's imagine that he is fluent in English, Oxford trained, and, by and large, calls the things we call hard "hard," and he doesn't call the things we don't call hard "hard." Despite this, he insists that this particular rock is not hard. So, to make sure, we bang on the rock and note the pain in our hand; we notice that eggs shatter and windows break on impact with this "not hard" rock. But he still insists the rock isn't hard. What are we to do? What are we to say? There are limits to what we can do to convince him, and in the end we just have to say that he has missed something important about the rock.

Suppose someone said, "From his point of view the rock isn't hard," or, "The rock may be hard to you, but clearly it isn't to him" (attempting to use sense 1 of subjectivity). The usual case of talking about things from other points of view, the case in which such talk explains differences between people, uses the linked senses 1 and 2 (the subjectivity and objectivity of points of view). To see how this talk works, consider the following case.

A golfer gets off a very bad tee shot into the rough onto a low hill. His second shot is equally errant, missing the green. We might explain the failure of his second shot by saying that from his point of view he couldn't see the green, and that's why the second shot was so misguided. Why is this a sensible account? Because we take it for granted that people can't see through trees and hills and that people aim less well when they can't see what they are aiming at. How does this compare with the "not hard rock"? The claim that the "rock isn't hard from his point of view'' isn't helpful. Although we can understand, from what we know about humans, that golf balls aimed from behind obscuring trees and hills miss their mark, we cannot understand, from what we know about humans, how someone who bangs his hand on a rock can fail to notice that it is hard. Unless the point of view the person is said to have can, because of its concrete, relevant details, explain why an ordinary person equipped with sense and concepts gets the understanding wrong, then pointing to a point of view is otiose.

Now in contrast to the hard rock disagreement, let's consider an argument over whether a chess move is good or bad—an evaluation. Suppose someone makes a move allowing her opponent to capture her queen and force a mate, and we call that a bad move. Is this claim objective in the same way(s) that our claim the rock is hard is? Let's bring our Trobriander back. Suppose he denies the ''badness'' of the move. This time we would be considerably less surprised, since they have rocks but not chess in the Trobriand Islands. So we teach him chess (someone had to teach him ''hard''). Once we know he has mastered it—he's even occasionally mated us—then would we be any less mystified by his not acknowledging the ''badness'' of the move than we would be by his failure to acknowledge the ''hardness'' of the rock?

A good move ''from her point of view'' makes more sense than in our rock example. One's view of a green can be obscured by trees; one's view of a particular move can be distorted by concentration on a particular strategic line—the player with the captured queen may have had her eye on the mischief she was planning for her opponent's rook. Saying that she blundered into the loss of her queen because it ''looked like a good move from her point of view'' works if it articulates why her move was a blunder with why it looked good to her; if it doesn't, then it doesn't have explanatory force. So saying it was, or better, it looked like a good move from her point of view doesn't deny it was a bad move; rather, it shows how the error came about while conceding the ''bad move'' evaluation.

We have so far shown how statements about hard rocks and evaluations are similar, but then why do we still feel that the evaluation and not the description is *really* subjective? Recall our hard rock and our Trobriander. It is imaginable that, as Oxford found him, he lacked the English word "hard." And we can even imagine that his native tongue had no translation for it. Still, we would be astonished if he didn't consistently respond to the hardness of some objects and the softness of others. He might have no concept to capture this way in which some objects are similar and others different, but, presumably, he would show us he recognized this feature by the ways he handled hard and soft objects. Recognizing bad chess moves is quite different. We would find it miraculous if someone who grew up in a culture that plays no chess recognized the chess move as bad, or if he in some way responded to good and bad chess moves differently without tutoring in the game. Hardness is the sort of thing anyone sentient in any culture would have to bump into; recognizing the badness of a chess move requires sapience and a certain sort of experience.

The urge to call evaluations subjective may have its source in our understanding that while all people distinguish hard from soft, only some people, those having learned the rules of chess, can tell good from bad moves. Still, in sense 5 (the objectivity of means suiting ends), given that a purpose one has in playing chess is the point of chess—winning—claims about the badness of a move are objective, i.e., corrigible, the sort of thing anyone who knows chess could be led to see. Once the move has been made, if someone is to evaluate it, he has no more choice about which evaluation to give it than he has to say whether a rock is hard or soft. He can, of course, choose to talk nonsense, but nonsense is a defect of descriptions as well as evaluations (see Searle, 1969, on institutional and brute facts).

The hardness of rocks and the badness of chess moves, then, are quite different. But one way they are not different is that commonsense actors treat them (when they are being serious, pragmatic, rather than theoretical) as properties of the external, objective world, rather than like pains, as something about which they have privileged perspective—an "internal matter."

We want to extend our chess story in two directions to see what problems confront us in applying objective and subjective to other human affairs. We shall consider more slippery human actions: does the objectivity of the characterization of a chess move tell us about chess or action more broadly? Once we address this we will be in a position to consider in what sense moral judgments are objective. First to action. In our chess story, the fact that losing one's queen is a move any chess player would find infelicitous is important. But notoriously, different observers of the same act can be expected to give differing evaluations of it, and even different descriptions (see the film *Roshomon*). This lack of consensus seems to challenge the objectivity of all reports about action, seems to allow free reign to the notion that an act was an *a* to Y, or from Y's point of view, while it was a *b* to Z, or from Z's point of view. It would seem that noticing hardness is a matter of *recognition,* while perceiving what someone did is just a matter of *interpretation.* What exactly does the indisputable fact that people often give different accounts (interpretations) show?

First, we may have different accounts of the same act that are not inconsistent. The accounts of a play given by a set designer, the producer, a critic, a member of the audience, or a follower of the leading man may differ—as we would expect them to given their different purposes and interests (subjectivity of ends). Yet each, once he understands the interests and standards of the other, can assess the various accounts. So this kind of difference just reminds us of the subjectivity of ends and the need to have some common standards and commonly understood ends.

Second, disagreement may just show that people are sometimes, or often, wrong. But this is hardly a problem peculiar to discussions of actions. Let's imagine disagreement about something "physical," like the presence of TB, and see whether a belief in the subjectivity of diagnosis follows from this. One hundred radiologists are asked to examine a chest film for TB; fifty say there is TB, and fifty say there isn't. Wouldn't everyone agree that there is nothing subjective about the matter, but that half are wrong? But perhaps this is because of a particular feature of TB: the criterion for deciding whether a person has TB is the presence of the appropriate bacillus. So, not only can we say that half are wrong, but we even know how to tell which half.

No doubt it is more difficult to find criteria for most human acts than for TB, and often there may not even be criteria. But nothing about an irreducible subjectivity of human action follows. Sometimes we can't appeal to criteria in physical cases either: let's say that fifty people call a wall green and fifty call it red. What criteria could we use to settle this issue? Yet even without seeing the wall aren't we all convinced that one group is right and the other wrong? *So are they.* So objectivity doesn't depend on criteria. Indeed, the fact that people do disagree with each other shows they treat the focus of their disagreement as objective.

Then why is there this tug to take disagreement as implying subjectivity? Perhaps it is this: the senses of subjectivity we have examined all involve personal differences, e.g., between what two people see (given their positions) or between what two people want (given their values). "Subjective" is invoked to emphasize differences. But the use of subjective in these ways *does not imply disagreement:* the shared belief that if one claim is correct, the other is wrong. We cannot understand how two claims, one that a person has TB or that a wall is green, the other that a person doesn't have TB or a wall is red, can both be true. The inability to imagine reconciliation shows that we don't have claims from different points of view, subjective claims, but disagreements about the nature of the object. Occasionally we are shown how a disagreement we thought irreconcilable can be reconciled; here we would invoke "point of view" and say that the two positions were not really in disagreement. (Consider quantum mechanics and the light-as-particle/light-as-wave controversy.) So, although subjectivity arises from differences, not all differences imply subjectivity.[5]

AMBIGUITY

Another source of our inclination to say that human action is subjective is a fact about many actions: they are ambiguous.

5. Agreement doesn't imply objectivity either, at least agreement in the sense of having the same response as others. A colleague asked subjects to judge the *saltiness* of Rorschach cards! The judgments were, rumor has it, consistent, both over time and between subjects. But does this show that these willing (even heroic) subjects took it for granted that other people would (or should) judge the stimuli as they did? Or did they take their own responses to be akin to, "I like chocolate ice cream?"—a matter of taste and a matter of coincidence if people's tastes coincide. They weren't asked.

Presumably, none of the subjects would know how to show that any of their judgments was biased or distorted. Nor do senses 1 and 4 of subjectivity apply: what could count as a "point of view"? This particular "judgment," and the semantic differential which it models, is neither objective nor subjective; it is meaningless. Of course one could baptize another sense—subjective as meaningless—but what work would it have?

Ambiguity leads to a failure of consensus, to differences. And differences pull us into subjectivity. So, though ambiguity presents its separate problems (which we can't adequately cover here), we shall highlight a few features of ambiguity and how these features relate to subjectivity.

First, to say that something is ambiguous is often just to say that given the facts at hand, one is unable to commit oneself to a judgment. For instance, our radiologist might have said, after looking at the chest X-ray, that it was ambiguous whether the patient had TB. He would not be denying as a matter of fact that the person either had or didn't have TB, rather he would mean that the evidence is inconclusive. Future lab tests might well allow a decision. And (Schrödinger's cat aside) we would not say that the patient caught or escaped TB at the moment the decisive test was done. This sense of ambiguity relates to the first sense of subjective; we would call cases ambiguous just when we recognize that our point of view does not allow a decisive claim *about the object.* Yet *this* claim is objective in sense 2 (the objectivity of points of view), since it claims that anyone looking from this point of view would also see the indeterminacy. Contrast this with a first-year medical student's claim about the same X-ray: "I don't know whether it shows TB." The medical student might mean that the X-ray was ambiguous, that no one could tell, or just that she lacked the experience to tell.

It is just when the objective facts are uncompelling or ambiguous that wants and beliefs can most easily introduce bias. So objective ambiguity invites subjectivity in the senses of bias (senses 3 and 6). Nonetheless, they are distinct.

Renée Richards displays another kind of ambiguity. The issue of whether Renée Richards should have been allowed to play in the Women's U.S. Open Tennis Championship arose because Renée had been born a male, but had a sex change operation. People found the issue difficult to decide. Why? Were they missing any facts? No. They found it ambiguous because our concepts of man and woman were not set up to cope with such a case.

The concepts were once clear; you could tell a man from a woman on many grounds—which sort of external genitalia the person had, which sort he or she had at birth, whether the person was a mother or father, and lately, which chromosome pattern the person had. Because the features never contradicted one another, there was no pressure to develop a convention about which feature(s) was criterial and which was just a symptom. But technology creates new instances (Austin's cat has delivered a philippic). In the Renée Richards case, the officials had to decide one way or another. Creating a third category wouldn't work—with whom would she play, herself?

Even if we could not resolve Renée's sex, still, we would see how the features we pointed to are relevant, and we also know that other facts about this person were irrelevant to whether Renée is a man or a woman, e.g., the city in which she was born or her skin color. The problem is that, although which features are relevant is objective, which one of them is preemptive is not clear. But still our shared understanding of which features are relevant structures our thinking about the case; objectivity plays a role even here. Indeed, the objective relevance of genitalia and chromosomes creates the ambiguity. Whatever else it is, it isn't a matter of anyone's taste.

Just where a forehead ends and a head begins is also ambiguous, though not in the way Renée's sex is. Border points are ambiguous; we can't say to which side they belong. Even the most precise and careful observations could not settle the issue; nor, in contrast to the TB case, could further information of any sort help. What is needed is not observation but legislation. If it matters, some community could adopt a convention, sign a treaty, or create a rule of language to decide the matter, but until it does, border cases remain border cases. Still, all of this scarcely denies that the concepts forehead and head are objective or that there are points which are clearly one or the other.

Many human actions are ambiguous; imagine that someone tells us after a talk we have given how much they have enjoyed it. Now, we all know that such comments are a part of academic courtesy, so it may not be clear what to make of it. The issue is not, as it might seem, one of sincerity, but of what the actor was doing: we may have been the recipient of sincere compliments or sincere politeness. Of course, if the congratulations go on for a day and a half then it's clear which they are. At the other extreme, a muttered, "Nice talk," offered in the rush from the room is clear. But there are cases in between where neither the recipient nor, perhaps, the host can say. Such cases just are ambiguous.

Perhaps most, or even all, human actions are ambiguous. First, we are not often in a position to know everything that could be relevant to a judgment about a particular act, even our own—and we know it. Second, it may often pay to act ambiguously. Consider flirting. Flirting depends on acting in a way that might be a sexual overture, but also might not—I might just be putting my hand on your shoulder to steady myself. In order to flirt, one must keep one's intentions ambiguous (see ch. 6 for more on flirtation and ambiguity). Further, there is no reason to assume that an actor's intentions need be more articulate than his actions. Ambiguous acts may mask clear intentions or reveal ambiguous ones.

Now suppose it were so that *all* human action is ambiguous. Then why make the claim that human action is objective? Because even if it were so that we never have all the relevant information, still we know how to separate relevant from irrelevant in context. The objectivity of human action rests not on certainty about real cases, but on our shared understanding of what matters and how it matters. And, even if no information could resolve these actions, they are all on the borders of foreheads, still not every *conceivable* action would be ambiguous were it to happen. If it turns out that people can be shown to purposely construct ambiguity, then, presumably we would account for their doing so in terms of their understanding of what wouldn't be ambiguous.[6]

MORALITY

Having assembled our taxonomy, examined an evaluation or two, and considered some ambiguities of human action, we are prepared to think about the subjectivity and objectivity of moral matters. We shall consider separately two different kinds of

6. Suppose there were a culture in which people were taught what the vices are by being told stories of flagrant actions of villains in the past. Further, imagine that these are just stories; such villains never really existed. So the people in this culture learn what greed is—it's what undid the evil elf. All the people in this culture are virtuous; they never repeat the sin of the evil elf. But they're not all that virtuous; all come as close as they can to the elf's sin without committing it. They are so good at walking the line that we would say their actions are ambiguously greedy. The elf's story is just what allows them to act in the way they do to get what they get and not be clearly greedy.

moral claims. An example of the first is "Jim is an adulterer," which is a moral claim just because 'adulterer' is a piece of moral talk. (If the reader doesn't believe that adultery is a moral charge in this culture at this time, we ask her to imagine Ohio in 1953 and to imagine our discussion to be about that culture.) An example of the second is "Adultery is wrong," which explicitly addresses the moral status of adultery. These claims raise different issues with regard to subjectivity and objectivity; yet arguments about the subjectivity of one often intrude into arguments about the subjectivity of the other. We shall try to keep them separate and touch on why they are so easily conflated.[7]

For this discussion, the most relevant sense of subjective is our sense 4, the subjectivity of ends—subjective meaning. It is relevant in the sense that someone might say, "For me, that wasn't adultery." How might we take this? Well, he might mean that he wasn't trying to commit adultery; it wasn't his goal; rather, he was trying to impress a female client to win a new account. But wouldn't we say, "So what; it's adultery anyway!" Indeed, people rarely have adultery, per se, as their goal.[8] Since committing adultery doesn't depend on the meaning of the act for the participant, the claim isn't subjective in this sense. Some moral charges are not independent of the meaning of the act for the actor; but adultery is, and it is not unique. Lying is another. If you lied to an armed maniac to thwart his plan to bomb Hoboken, in praising you we would not deny that you had lied, but point to how your lie had saved a city.

'Murderer' is not like this; it takes account of the subjective meaning of the act for the actor—the actor's point of view—at least to a degree. Killing someone in self-defense is not murder.

7. We stress the distinction between these two sorts of claims in part because Berger and Luckmann have argued that the first sort of claim arises as an issue in every culture, whereas the second sort arises only in special circumstances in specific cultures. In their view, dealing with the first sort of claim is essential to the regulation of a culture; fretting about the second is a frill.

8. It would be misleading, ordinarily, to say that a person's goal was adultery: as these things usually go, the person's goal is having sex. If the person about to perform the act were to discover, at that moment, that his marriage wasn't actually a marriage (imagine that his wife was already married at the time of their wedding unbeknownst to him), he would find that he couldn't (logically) commit adultery. But, presumably, this would not frustrate his immediate purpose, keep him from his goal. Someone might have adultery as a goal, say, to get back at a spouse or to set up the grounds of divorce.

But still, 'murderer' doesn't specify the actor's intentions, either. A murderer need not intend to kill (someone willing to accept the death of some bank guards regrettably near the vault that one must blow up to steal the bonds is still a murderer). So 'murderer' takes account of the subjective meaning of an act to a person, at least to a degree, but only the objective (sense 5) subjective (sense 4) meaning of the act to the person (see Kovesi, 1967, for an illuminating discussion on this issue).

If someone wishes to convince us that their "murder" is really self-defense, they had better be prepared to show: (1) that it was self-defense that was the goal, and (2) that the act was suitable to bring about self-defense, that it was called for. Just thinking your goal is self-defense is not sufficient. One might hallucinate a threat, be sincerely afraid for one's life, and kill a blameless other in fancied defense and not be a murderer. But this would not be because one acted in self-defense, but because one is insane. So, even when the moral assessment depends on the meaning for the actor, and the offense is in this sense subjective, still that meaning must be sensibly related to the objective situation.[9] Just as we found for the evaluations we considered, we find moral claims (of this sort) are not deficient in objectivity because they are in some senses subjective. But now we turn to a second sort of claim in the moral domain, e.g., adultery is wrong.

In what sense could this be subjective: what would convince us that someone was treating it as a subjective matter? First, what would it mean if I said, "It's wrong from my point of view"? One thing it could mean is that in our sense 4 (in relation to my goals) it would be wrong for me: it would make me feel bad or interfere with things I am trying to achieve. But here, "wrong" is being used in a pragmatic, not moral, sense. Also, the claim is objective in sense 5: I am asserting that as a matter of fact I will feel bad or run into trouble. Or someone might mean by it, to change examples, that since he is a policeman it is wrong for him to ignore your speeding. He means that it would be okay for a civilian to ignore the speeding, but

9. Although "Jim is an adulterer" isn't subjective in sense 4, the subjectivity of ends, the claim that Jim is an adulterer could be subjective in a trivial way: imagining an adulterous affair behind the most casual flirtation of one's enemy, Jim, is subjective in our sixth sense (biased).

his role creates an obligation. And in sense 5, this is an objective obligation. In sense 6, it is an objective, unbiased assessment. Or someone might mean, to return to adultery, "My wife is hopelessly insane, and therefore I have a special exemption from the marriage vows." But insofar as the person offering this reason believes it to be a reason, he is acknowledging that adultery is wrong; otherwise, why would he need an exemption? And his claiming an exemption rests on the implicit argument that anyone who had such a wife would be entitled to the dispensation. So in claiming exemption he announces his belief that adultery is objectively wrong.

Another possible use of "X is wrong is a subjective matter" trades on ambiguity. Consider abortion. Everyone agrees that at some point after conception, say, twenty years after, destroying the upshot of the conception is wrong. But, because specifying any point as *the point* at which destroying the upshot is murder seems arbitrary, the issue of the moral status of abortion is objectively ambiguous. Yet some people must act regardless of the ambiguity. So someone who did not have an abortion for moral reasons might say, "Having an abortion is wrong for me," meaning that she recognizes the arbitrariness of *her* boundary drawing, and she recognizes that others might morally draw the line at a different point. But just as the ambiguity of border points does not call into question the objectivity of the concepts forehead and head, so the ambiguity of some questions of right and wrong does not call into question the objectivity, or even clarity, of all decisions about right and wrong.

A famous example of Sartre's leads some to say that morality is subjective. In his example, during the Nazi occupation of France someone is torn between joining the resistance and taking care of his mother. In Sartre's example (1948), one cannot say which is right for him; whichever decision he reaches, he would realize, could not be "universalized," i.e., he (or we) could not say that everyone else ought decide as he decided if they were in his place. He must make a decision about what is right, and yet he knows it isn't an objective one (sense 2 or 5). But this does not show that morality is not objective in general. It is another case of ambiguity, where the ambiguity itself is objective; it is ambiguous in a way similar to the way in which

Renée Richards's sex is ambiguous. In both cases we can see reasons for either decision. In both cases, we can all understand that, although there are reasons on both sides, a decision must be made one way or the other and that the reasons do not compel either way. But taking Sartre's example to show that all moral decisions are subjective, or better, ambiguous, would be akin to taking the Renée Richards case to show that whether every person is a man or a woman is subjective or ambiguous. So, Sartre's case doesn't threaten the objectivity of decisions of right and wrong; it merely highlights the ambiguity of some decisions.

Another possible reason for saying "the issue of whether adultery is wrong is subjective" is the fact of cross-cultural differences in the conceptions of what is right and what is wrong. Right and wrong are not like the hardness of a rock, which is transcultural, physical. But neither is the right or wrong of adultery like the goodness or badness of a chess move—bad moves are derived from the "point" of chess. Perhaps, Aristotle and Aquinas notwithstanding, there is no "point of life" from which to derive right and wrong, and therefore, good moves are not deducible. What instrument to use to get rice to mouth is probably not deducible from a set of first principles either—some would say it is an arbitrary convention. Yet this too is objective, something every member of a culture knows and expects others to know. So even if the rightness or wrongness of adultery turns out to be an arbitrary convention, crosscultural variation gives us no reason to call its wrongness subjective, personal, or a matter of individual taste (sense 4). The rightness or wrongness of adultery is, at least, a cultural fact. Of course, the wrongness of adultery can change. Perhaps in 1953 adultery was wrong; perhaps in 1995 it will clearly be right. And perhaps at the moment it is ambiguous, but none of this shows it is subjective either. Even fashion has its objectivity.[10]

10. A Victorian might find himself drawn toward the subjectivity of morality by a quick reading of Malinowski. What is he to say about Trobriand sexual practices? First, he might say, "That's adultery." But he would have to recognize something wrong in that. After all, they didn't know there was anything wrong in what they were doing, and it's even hard to see how they ought to have known it was wrong—news of God's revelation hadn't reached them yet. And calling someone an adulterer is a moral charge; moral charges are only fair when the target knew better, or ought to have known better, than to do what he did. Still, that fellow was embracing his neighbor's wife. In light of all this, our Victorian might try to use 'adultery' with its descriptive, but not its moral, force. But this will sound

Perhaps what people might mean by saying that the rightness or wrongness of adultery is subjective is that right and wrong come down to feelings. There are at least three ways to take "feelings." One way is to take them to be sensations, i.e., my feeling the wrongness of adultery is akin to my having sensations of redness when I look at a red patch. In this sense, the subjectivity of morality would be just like the subjectivity of the redness of a patch, the size of a square, and everything else, since there are sensations involved when I perceive anything. (Cartesian privacy, if it is a threat, is a threat to everything, not to morality in particular.)

But a second sense of feeling has to do with feeling angry, grateful, proud, and so on. And, as has been argued extensively (see Meldon, 1961; Kenny, 1963; Bedford, 1964), while this sense of feeling includes some sensational element, it also includes something else, something objective. For example, to know that one is angry one must know what anger is—what an angry reaction is, what a provocative act is, etc. (see chs. 2 & 9). If the rightness or wrongness of adultery were a matter of feeling in this sense, then deciding whether something feels right or wrong would depend on knowing right from wrong as an objective matter so that the feeling could be identified. So even if the claim were correct that the wrongness of adultery depends on "emotional feelings," on subjective facts (in the emotional sense), it would not deny that the rightness or wrongness of adultery is objective in the fifth sense (corrigible).

Of course, there is yet another sense of feeling: "I feel that the oil crisis is a hoax." But here "feel" is used, roughly, as a substitute for 'believe', and the claim is objective in sense 5. And in this sense, an anesthetic person could feel the wrongness of adultery or the chicanery of the oil companies.

In any of these senses of feeling, the objectivity of right or

---

odd (if it can be said at all). Perhaps he can get a referendum passed to remove 'adultery's' moral force, but then he'll need a new word like the old 'adultery' to describe his neighbor's sport. And even if this works, there will be an awkward period during which no one knows quite what they mean. All of this might lead our Victorian to say, "Well, adultery is all right for him, but not Anglicans." And furthermore, "Morality is subjective, personal, up to the individual." But notice the "him" refers not to one particular Trobriander, but to anyone in that culture. And the "adultery" refers either to the old word—in which case the problem hasn't been solved—or the new word in which case the "for him" is unnecessary, since the new word is innocent of moral force. So there still is no room for "right for him" with either 'adultery'. Our language and its use evolved to fit our "forms of life," our "moral standards," our "objective evaluations"; they won't fit another culture's.

wrong is left standing against claims that morality depends on feelings.

There is one sense left in which someone might say "Adultery is wrong" is subjective. Perhaps this is meant to deny that the claim is objective in senses 2 or 5 (corrigible). Putting sensations aside, could any claim be subjective in this way? How about, "I dreamt I was king of France." This seems to be a claim. But unless it implies you believe that, "If you were in my position (or had my goals, beliefs, values), you also would have dreamt you were king of France," such a claim is subjective, lacks objectivity in senses 2 or 5. But even this claim depends on our understanding what it would be to be king of France in the world. If we are to understand morality as being subjective in this way, then we must understand what it would be for adultery to be right or wrong as an objective matter. Only then could we understand what it would be for adultery to be right or wrong in this subjective, dream sense.

CONCLUSION

Working from a simple example of a person looking at a tree, and exploring how the language of point of view or subjectivity does its job in the example, we find no reason to say that morality is fundamentally subjective. We do see reason to say that it is a cultural matter, and sometimes an ambiguous matter, but not a fundamentally subjective one. Yet the urge to say it remains. But if it does, it is not supported by the senses we have found. As we suggested when we started the senses of subjective taken one at a time pose no threat to morality. The urge to call morality subjective is, we suggest, a response to the confusion produced when the various senses are allowed to swarm.

CHAPTER ELEVEN

Objectivity on Sand

Imagine yourself in a museum, staring for the first time at a quattrocento painting, say, a Tondo. Now imagine that the person you're with asks you "what you think of it"—to give your evaluation of it. Suppose you "don't know much about art," but you do know that people make a big deal about Italian art, especially Italian art in museums. And you don't know your companion that well—maybe she's a devotee, so you don't want to risk looking silly. This *Adoration* makes you feel gay, and your eyes are captured by the brilliant reds and aquamarines. So how might you answer? "Well, I don't know anything about art, but I do know what I like. And this painting makes me feel happy; the colors really do something to me."

Now imagine that when you return home from the museum, your eighteen-year-old daughter joyously announces she's brought her boyfriend home from college for you to meet. He'll stay over for the weekend—in her room. Suppose you don't share her delight. Indeed, you feel your stomach tighten, your face flush, and an urge to say chilling things. But you know she has her own mind, and this is the way college students think these days, and it would be terrible to have a scene in front of her boyfriend, and it won't do any good to bawl her out—you can't control what she'll do on campus anyway. Besides, you cannot think of a convincing reason why she shouldn't sleep with him—she's careful. Stymied by all this, you swallow your reproach and reflect on your anger: "Why do I feel that what they are doing is wrong?" You can't confront her until you understand your feelings. "But why do I have these feelings? Maybe I'm being unfair, maybe I'm just envious—she's so young and pretty. When I was her age we couldn't get away with things like that. But I don't mind her having fun—it's not that. It's just that I was brought up to believe it's wrong, just wrong." Later you find you can't sleep with her sleeping in the same room with him. So the next morning you have a little talk with her: "Look, you can't sleep with him in my house. It really makes me uncomfortable, and that's just the way I feel. That's the way I was brought up, and that's it." Reason and argument exhausted, you make different sleeping arrangements.

Let's reflect on these stories. In the first case, an evaluation was called for, an aesthetic one. But knowing you don't know anything about art, you substitute something for the evaluation, a report of your reactions: you like it, the colors do something to you, it makes you feel happy. Your friend treats this as an answer to her question, and it saves you from embarrassment or an argument.

In the second story your impulse is to offer a different sort of evaluation, a moral one. But your impulse is checked: you recognize that your daughter won't care, she won't change her behavior, at least when she's out of your sight. Further, you know you can't give her a reason why she shouldn't sleep with him. But you are dead sure of your reaction to her behavior; so you offer her that to keep her from sleeping with him in your house. The substitution avoids a pointless argument, lets you get some sleep, and allows you to get on with your relationship with your daughter.

In both stories, evaluations are called for, but instead reactions are offered. Further, in both stories you do more than give your reactions, you explain them, you supply their causes. In the first it was the Tondo's colors and theme; in the second it was your strict parents.

In a reflective moment these troublesome examples might set you thinking about the nature of moral and aesthetic judgments in general. If your reflection took these as models, you would conclude that *all* moral and aesthetic judgments are really reports of reactions. (After all, we've all been dragged into museums, and many mothers have had trouble with their daughters.) And insofar as people can reason about aesthetics and ethics, you might conclude, all they do is find the causes of their reactions. For example, what's the difference between a good movie review and one that is worthless? Isn't it that a good review captures the reactions of the people who see the movie, while a bad review gives just the critic's reaction, not what people think? Reviews that differ from what everyone else thinks must be personal, idiosyncratic, biased, subjective; good reviews are objective. Your reflection takes you further: you realize that other evaluations are not that different from moral and aesthetic ones. The problem with the judgments of the painting and your daughter's behavior derives from their being evaluations rather than descriptions. Perhaps all evaluations are just reports of reactions; what separates a worthwhile from a worthless evaluation is whether it is consensual and consistent.

Some psychologists, too, see evaluations as reactions (Jones & Nisbett, 1972; cf. contra Sabini & Silver, 1980), quite different from description. They claim that the description of a rock as hard and the evaluation of a boss as hard are different in kind. They go on to claim that the former is objective, a matter of fact, and the latter is subjective, a matter of personal reaction. Not only do they make these claims, but they hold them to be obvious to adults, at least intellectually, as well as to scientists (Jones & Nisbett, 1972, p. 86).

We think this reasoning is neither obvious nor right. Yet it has roots in commonsense reflection on stories like those with which we began. We suspect it is a widespread belief, or perhaps suspicion, or even fear.

To see whether people treat evaluations as simply reports of reactions, let us consider two conversations. One is a disagreement about an evaluation, the other is a discussion of differing reactions.

A: Tommy Ryle is really a great ballplayer. He hit 30 home runs last year, had 106 RBI's, and a 980 fielding percentage.

B: He is like hell! Yeah, he hit 30 home runs, but playing in that band box he plays in, 30 home runs aren't a lot. As for the RBI's, the guys who bat before him are on base

> so often, of course he gets a lot of RBI's, but how many times did he strike out with the winning run on third base? Sure he's got a great fielding percentage, but that's because he's got such a small range he never gets to anything.

Now, in contrast, let's examine a discussion of unmatched reactions:

> *A:* You know, I had the worst reaction to that hot sauce on the shrimp last night. I couldn't get to sleep with heartburn; it just drove me crazy.
>
> *B:* Gee, I didn't have that reaction at all, in fact I slept particularly well last night; the hot sauce seemed to settle my stomach.

In this discussion each participant is describing his personal, subjective reaction to the hot sauce; each is explicitly treating what the hot sauce did to him as a reaction. Neither is disagreeing; neither is attempting to convince the other. Each accepts that the other had the reaction that he said he had. If one person did not, he could only be accusing the other of *lying*, not error. How could someone be mistaken about whether he had heartburn? The Tommy Ryle case is different. In this argument, each treats the other's position as wrong, and wrong about Tommy Ryle. They might say as a summary of their discussion of hot sauce, "Well, you had one reaction; I had another." And we and they can see this summary as fair. Would it be a fair summary of the argument about baseball to say, "Well, you had one reaction and I had another"? In the baseball case, this is an evasion, not a summary. In the hot sauce case there is nothing to evade or resolve; in the baseball case there is—who is wrong about Tommy Ryle.

Similarly, is the claim that a student's paper is disorganized and off its topic a reaction? How about the evaluation that it was poorly typed? If they are all subjective, personal reactions, how could we fairly grade students? Or pick typists? For an evaluation to be fair, the one thing it must overcome is its nature as a personal reaction.

Let's look at the examples more closely, using Schutz's (1973) concept of objectivity (see also ch. 10).

In the Tommy Ryle case, both actors are making claims they take to be objective in the sense that they take them to be about something outside of themselves, in the world—Tommy Ryle's ability and achievement—independent of their internal states, wishes, moods. In fact, they take them to be what any fully informed, straight-thinking member of the culture schooled in the facts of Tommy Ryle's career and the game of baseball would see, or at least come to see. Further, as members of a common culture, indeed subculture, each person expects the other to see the relevance of the evidence he advances with regard to whether Tommy is a great player. Each knows, and expects the other to know, that some facts are irrelevant to the issue of Tommy's greatness, e.g., whether Tommy has brown shoes—even though he may react negatively to brown shoes. In the hot sauce case, on the other hand, both would understand that whether one had heartburn or not is *subjective,* a matter of internal state, a topic for *report* not argument. Both would understand that there are no relevant or irrelevant facts or arguments that could convince us that *A* did *not* have a painful night, unless they were facts bearing on *A*'s candor. Both actors understand that whether *A* was in pain the night before is a matter for him to report, not an issue to debate or discuss.

Our Tommy Ryle example illustrates important aspects of the way people treat evaluations. Actors are sometimes concerned with whether evaluations are correct. They discuss them, argue about them, find support for them, or try to refute them. How can these facts have a place in a view of evaluations as just reactions *since reactions can't be true or false or much else except caused?* When would we be concerned with the *cause* of the evaluation of a ballplayer?

Let's assume that Tommy *is* a great ballplayer; the other fellow has it wrong: Tommy plays in a very big ballpark, not a band box; the people who bat before him actually get on base less often than most; and videotape shows he has more than average range for a third baseman. Would the question "Why did the fellow who got the evaluation *right* get it right?" come up? Wouldn't this seem an odd thing to ask? Here the question "How did he get it wrong?" makes a good deal more sense than "How did he get it right?" since the former focuses our attention on the particular way he went wrong, while the latter is baffling. Still, we might answer the baffling question with "Because he knows baseball!" But this doesn't specify a cause; it provides a warrant.

Imagine that Tommy's supporter became convinced that not only is his opponent wrong, but he is so wrong, or wrong in such a way, that there is no longer a point in arguing. Then Tommy's fan might turn to diagnosing the cause of the ailment of which the mistake is a symptom. To be specific, if Tommy were black and his detractor a Klansman, then Tommy's booster might well conclude that the cynical view of Tommy's worth is due to racism and not baseball. Note that finding that the critic is a Klansman doesn't settle whether his evaluation is right or wrong—that issue can only be decided by Tommy's playing. Once the evaluation has been decided, then racism diagnoses the cause of the error.

Our reflective commonsense theorist might not be satisfied with this banishing of reactions from fair judgments. She might remind us that one can distinguish, say, valuable from worthless movie reviews, while treating the reviews as reactions: is it what everyone thinks? How consistently do they think it? How impervious are they to changes in the size of the screen or the ritziness of the theater? Kelley (1967) has formalized these ideas as a model of how people think about behavior including evaluations. Kelley's model converts the *distinction between truth and falsity* into a *distinction between types of causes*. His solution is to take true evaluations as those having a certain sort of external cause, while false evaluations have internal causes. For instance, for someone to realize that her evaluation of a movie was incorrect or biased would be to realize that although she had thought her distress after seeing the movie had been caused by the movie, an external cause, it was in fact the result of an internal cause, the flu. According to Kelley's view, this is still not sufficient to determine if the evaluation is biased; the best assessment of bias does not depend on the locus of causality of *her* reaction, whether gastric or aesthetic, but that of many. For instance, when we react to a movie with laughter and then claim that the movie is funny, we are, according to Kelley, *really* claiming that the movie is an *external cause* of laughter. This means that we are *predicting* that not only we, but all others (without gastritis) will always react by laughing, no matter how often it is presented, no matter in what medium: stating that the movie is funny is really a shorthand way of making a prediction of the popularity of "funniness reactions" over people, time, and modes of presentation.

Indeed, Kelley assures us he uses this procedure to evaluate his child's homework answers.

> If the answer to a homework problem my child shows me is not different from that to other problems and not reproducible by different methods, by different persons, and on repeated occasions, I am highly doubtful of its validity.
>
> (1967, p. 199)

But this seems a rather odd and cumbersome way to go about deciding whether "7 goes into 50 33 times." Suppose "33 times" is consistent over time (i.e., his child only and always answers "33" to this particular problem) and is consistent across modality (i.e., his child gets the same answer whether he or she hears the problem or reads it). How do these considerations enter? Imagine that the child says, "42÷6=7," but only says it today; yesterday it was "42÷6=9." Does that make the child wrong today? Does Kelley doubt the answer is valid? Suppose, because of a hearing defect, the child only gets it right when reading it; does that make it wrong? Or let's imagine that his child also gives the answer "7" to: 3+4, 5+2, 6+1, 9−2, 4+5−2, 2×2×2−1, 49÷7, or the ninth root of 40,353,607. Are these answers wrong because they are not unique? We hope Kelley does not apply *these* criteria.

So, we are left with consensus. Kelley apparently calls his child's homework correct if and only if he believes that everyone else will give the same answer. Perhaps Kelley means that when he hears the child say "42÷6=7," he makes a mental prediction about what everyone else would say; and since he predicts they would say "7," he calls his child correct or at least doesn't doubt the validity of the answer.

Does he mean that the validity of the answer rests on consensus? Consensus as an account of what makes answers correct is terribly oversimplified. Suppose that Kelley's child were offered this problem in mathematics: "Is Euclid's fifth postulate independent of the others?" and the child answered, "No." Now, if we may take a liberty, let's assume that Kelley and his child lived in the early nineteenth century. When he checked with his neighbors about the answer, most, of course, would not have the foggiest notion about whether it was right or wrong; but we will not quibble about Kelley's claim that the same answer must be given by *all* observers. Obviously, he means all observers who we have reason to believe are competent about such matters. When he did find those neighbors who fit this sensible specification, however, they would have agreed unanimously that the child was correct. But does this make the answer correct? If so, then what are we to say about Lobachevsky and Bolyai, who discovered that it *is* independent? How does the fact that for approximately two thousand years all mathematicians agreed affect the fact that, using the logic implicit in geometry, these descendants of Euclid were able to show Kelley's child wrong? Would it have mattered that it might have taken them ten or fifteen years to convince even fellow mathematicians? It appears that even in mathematics consensus is neither necessary nor sufficient to the truth of a particular claim. Perhaps Kelley just means that on the face of it in *simple* matters of arithmetic, line judging, or color naming, people assume that if everybody believes something to be true, then it is. With this claim we can hardly disagree. But sometimes, especially over more complex matters, people do disagree. And when they do face disagreement, they often know how to decide who is right and who is wrong.

But social matters are different from mathematical problems, and Kelley's theory is about social matters. Isn't it correct in the social domain that to say something is true *is* to predict that everyone will see it that way? Or to put it in its more usual sociological form following Thomas, doesn't everyone's believing something is so make it so? Goffman has put this well:

> When all parties to an action agree as to its cause, they can, in terms of their own culture's selection practices, be wrong. Believing something is true only makes it true (W. I. Thomas notwithstanding) if this belief so fits with other practices for assessing fact in the society that no contrary evidence would be possible in that society.
>
> (1971, p. 99)

So even if Tommy's fan were alone in maintaining Tommy is a great player, by knowing what it is to be a great player he can, if he is willing and persistent, substantiate his belief about Tommy. Consensus doesn't show him wrong in the face of Tommy's accomplishments. So consensus is no better a guarantor of truth in "social matters" than in mathematics.

Kelley's model, then, isn't an adequate account of what it means for an evaluation to be true or false. It's more like a rule of thumb for simple cases. But a rule of thumb can't show that when people *seem* to be assessing truth they are *really* locating causes. And convincing us that assessing an evaluation is really finding its cause is what he and like theorists must do if they are to succeed in convincing us that evaluations, *tout court*, are reactions. And they can't.

But what about the examples with which we began? Even if it is so that *some* evaluations are not just reports of reactions, and some reasoning about reactions is not just a search for causes or consensus, weren't reactions and causes the striking features of the stories about the museum and the sleeping arrangements? Can a model of evaluations based on the Tommy Ryle case cover these cases as well without glossing over their distinctive features? We shall start with our Tommy Ryle evaluation and see what we have to change to get it to look like first the museum and then the bedroom examples.

In the museum you were called upon to give an evaluation, but you "didn't know anything about art" so you offered reactions instead. Well, newcomers to baseball can't evaluate games the way aficionados do either. But they do have reactions, and know which games they like and which they don't. The games neophytes like often differ from those aficionados prefer: people who aren't devotees typically like high-scoring games with lots of excitement. Sloppily fielded games with poor pitching are like that. There will be much to catch the eye and ear—players running, balls flying, the crowd screaming. (People at their first game often find it a shame if the home team doesn't win, too.) But real fans often prefer a different sort of game—a low-scoring game that is well pitched and well fielded. To newcomers, a game like that is dull; there is little to excite their reactions. But as experience grows, so does understanding and with it a change in evaluations. Originally the neophyte used the crowd's consensus to make sure she recognized a good play; now she has something better.

Part of understanding is an appreciation of subtlety; the unrelieved dullness of players making outs is replaced by an appreciation of the skill that produces those outs. Part of the development of appreciation is sensory training to discern the differences between slightly different pitches, part of the education is learning a language to communicate these nice distinctions, and part is seeing this game in the context of the pennant race and, sometimes, of baseball history. So the aficionado's evaluations differ from the newcomer's.

Fan and beginner, then, may reach a different evaluation of the same game. The fan's evaluations will be phrased in the language of baseball and will be expressed in terms of the quality of play rather than in terms of reactions she feels (not to say, of course, that she doesn't react). At this point, the student's evaluation will be less, not more, likely to tally with the reactions of most of the other people in the park, who like the high-scoring, dramatically fielded game. But lack of consensus won't bother the student anymore; she has criteria to evaluate the game and training in applying them. Consensus will now be less important, especially since she can tell the competence of those who disagree. Of course, home runs, with their drama, will still be exciting. Even people who appreciate the art of baseball are taken by what the neophyte noticed, but the place of these features in an evaluation has shifted, become less prominent.

In the same way that the Tommy Ryle conversation was turned into a discussion with someone who "doesn't know much about baseball," we can reproduce the central features of the conversation in the museum: the substitution of reactions for evaluations, the unwillingness, indeed inability, to argue about the merits of the piece, and a reliance on trading reactions. In both cases, the process of being socialized into the "subculture of devotees" enhances understanding, shifts features that are appreciated, provides a language of discourse, substitutes criteria for reactions, and makes the person less dependent on others for certainty about her own evaluations. Still, if baseball, or art, didn't produce reactions in the first place, it wouldn't be likely to attract devotees; if it didn't move newcomers, why would anyone stay with it long enough to become an expert? Further, the dramatic and easily appreciated—home runs and brilliant colors—always have a place in the appreciation of the game even for the expert, but the place changes. A newcomer to art is taken by brilliant colors regardless of how they fit; an aficionado is likely to be more concerned with how they are integrated into the overall work, e.g., Renoir's undeniably striking backgrounds are also overheated. Similarly, newcomers to baseball are taken by a player who hits home runs in eleven to two ballgames; aficionados are more concerned with what he does when it's three to two.

If you alter the Tommy Ryle case by making one discussant a neophyte, you have a conversation about baseball that's like the museum conversation. The museum conversation no more shows that art evaluations are a matter of reactions than a newcomer's conversation about baseball shows that baseball evaluations are just reactions.

But what about the visiting daughter story? The mother, too, finally offered a reaction in place of an evaluation, and the closest she could come to supporting her evaluation was a causal explanation: "That's just the way I was brought up." Can we fit our baseball story to this case, too?

Imagine this discussion: "Marv was a terrible player. He had a lifetime batting average of 212, was just as likely to throw the ball to the wrong base as the right one (if by some miracle he caught it), hit into double plays 73 percent of the time he came up with men on base, and complained every time he was removed for a pinch hitter." Suppose the person you said this to, someone you had trained to understand baseball, said, "I don't care, he was still a great player." And you said, "Do you think he had a better batting average or did better with men on base?" and your trainee said, "No, I don't disagree about the facts; I just disagree about the evaluation." What could you say? You are likely to be mystified. You might wonder, "How can she not see she's wrong?" Suppose she pressed you to tell her why hitting into double plays made him a terrible player. You'd have to just tell her, as Searle (1964) would, "That's what it is to be a lousy ballplayer." It is obvious at this point that further talk about ballplayers is fruitless. You can say no more than you've already said; you don't share a common language. Suppose you wanted to be polite, and also wanted to avoid further futile talk. You might say, "Look, there's no point in our arguing. To me he was a terrible player. When I learned the game,

I learned to feel that players with the kind of record Marv had are terrible players. But look, let's just not talk baseball in the house."

Suppose we substitute "loose woman" for "terrible ballplayer," and "sleeping with him" for "hitting into double plays." The anxious mother in our story knows full well why she thinks her daughter is loose—the sleeping arrangements. Her problem isn't like the problem of the newcomer to the art museum. She has no trouble in reaching an evaluation and no trouble in supplying a reason for it. Her problem is that her daughter does not accept "the obvious": that the "being loose" follows from the fact of her behavior. Her daughter claims that while her mother obviously has a reason for her evaluation—bringing Fred home—that reason isn't really a reason. The daughter is asking not for a reason for the evaluation, but why the reason is a reason. Mother and daughter can't talk because they don't share a moral language. The best the sleepless mother can do to provide an account of why she believes sleeping with Fred makes her daughter loose is to give a causal account of her own upbringing rather than a further reason. This is like the discussion of Marv's ball playing. You can't give a reason for why having his record is a reason to say he was a terrible player either. At the end of both stories, out of politeness and to preserve your relationship, all everyone can do is leave the issue of the evaluation unsettled and compromise behavior instead. When moral (or other) evaluations are deadlocked, pragmatic solutions allowing people to get by with each other must be found *outside* the framework of evaluative discussion. For example, the college girl can refrain from sleeping with her beau, at least at Mom's, *without* conceding she really shouldn't; she can treat her acquiescence not as an admission that sleeping with him is wrong, but as a courtesy to her mother, a considerate way to avoid provoking unpleasant reactions. The dilemma of this example, then, shouldn't convince us that moral evaluations are unreasoned reactions, though it does call attention to some important features of evaluations.

First, a train of reasons, as Wittgenstein (1958) pointed out, must end somewhere. You may have a reason for your evaluation, and you might even have a reason for that reason's being a reason. But you will eventually be forced to give up offering reasons and have to give a causal account instead—or just stand pat. Second, because people who disagree in this irresolvable way often must live with each other whether they agree or not, some compromise in behavior will have to be reached. And this compromise will have to sidestep the issues. Last, treating reasoned evaluations as mere reactions is a handy way to effect a compromise while saving face. But these lessons can be applied to the baseball example, too. So how is the Tommy Ryle evaluation different from the "loose woman" evaluation?

Baseball is not very important; morality is. One can always agree to disagree about baseball; morality doesn't always allow that solution.

Imagine your daughter was not as careful or lucky as you or she thought. She becomes pregnant, and then she announces her upcoming abortion. Now imagine you've been brought up to believe that abortion is a wrong, specifically, murder. And imagine that you have the ability to stop her. Then again, you can stop talking about the matter. But how will that help?

You can't compromise—how can you about murder? You have reasons: you believe the conceptus is a human life and killing it is, therefore, murder. She has reasons, too: she has a right to choose what will happen to her own body, and she believes a fetus is tissue, not a person. And you understand all this, but you are convinced it's murder no matter what she thinks.

These positions are difficult to compromise. There are three things you can do: you might let her have the abortion while still believing it's murder. This route will show you what morality is worth to you, that it is just a matter of reactions—like heartburn, something that should be ignored if paying attention to it is inconvenient. Or you might let her have the abortion while you discover a congeries of reasons why abortion isn't really murder. This will be more comfortable for you; bad faith serves nothing if not comfort. At least you can retain the form of moral reasoning. Or you might stop her. Not because that's what makes you feel good, not because stopping her is your immediate reaction, but just because you are convinced it is the right thing to do. This particular moral action based on an evaluation will not be a treatment for heartburn. On reflection, you will find your position very uncomfortable. Suppose your daughter—just before she refuses to speak to you ever again—asks you, "But why is abortion murder?" And you answer, "Because the child is a human from the moment of conception on." And she says, "Why do you say that?" That will take you aback. What compelling answer can you give? You might say you are Catholic, but you gave that up years ago. Genetic uniqueness? Is it okay to kill an identical twin? Potential to be human? But she could ask, is it murder to kill a sperm? What must you do to live up to *that?*

So now you realize you have a reason to stop her: it's murder. But you have no reason to back up *that* reason. This may be as important an act as you have ever done, yet you cannot give it a finally justifiable chain of reasoning. Still, you must act—either in letting her have it or in stopping her—*while knowing you have no final grounds for acting*. Your position is absurd, as Sartre would note. What can you possibly do: you might appreciate the irony.

CHAPTER TWELVE

Reflections

We suggested in our introduction that our stand-in for a theory was the model, or notion, that people act intentionally and that each chapter was, in some way or another, an attempt to develop that model. We owe an account of how the model fared.

THE INTENTIONAL MODEL

Envy is an emotion, of course, but it is also a sin. The other deadly sins, lust for example, have an obvious pleasure, and, therefore, fit intentionality well. But envy doesn't seem to—why would a rational actor want to pursue it? Chapter 2 tried to resolve this mystery and found self-worth the hidden guest.

In chapters 3 and 4 we addressed this problem: some evils in the world arise, no doubt, from corrupted intentions, desires for the perverse. Others arise through an understandable ignorance of the right course or a problem in following it. And others arise because the evil leads to an obvious good—fame, money, power, etc. These evils are easily encompassed by an intentional model, but some evils, we argued, are more mysterious. Using the behavior of subjects in the Milgram (1974), Zimbardo (1973), and Latanè and Darley (1970) experiments as prototypes, we tried to work out how a person can come to perform patently evil actions without being driven by a corrupted will or being the victim of an understandable ignorance.

Difficulties with intentionality entered our treatment of gossip (ch. 5) in two ways. First, in order to act morally, a person must have knowledge of right and wrong in a concrete situation. Without divine intervention or genetic programming (limited resources both), an actor must come upon this knowledge somehow; we found a place for gossip in this education. Second, although gossip is a form of moral education, that isn't why people do it; rather, moral enlightenment is an unintended consequence of people's trying to do other things. We touched on the playoff between the intended and the accidental in gossip.

A crude intentional model would assume that intentions give birth to actions; in chapter 6 on flirtation we found actions giving birth to intentions. A crude model would also see intentions as necessarily clear, even if their expression were ambiguous. In flirtation, we explored some ways people have to experience, as well as express, ambiguous intents. Also, we treated intentions people do have (or don't but might have) as a resource to be managed. Last of all, we attempted to solve the problem of whether sex has a place in flirtation.

Likewise, procrastination infects our intentions. Hamlet is mysteriously unable to do what he wants to do, ought to do, and knows he has the means to do. It is experienced as a thwarting of the will. Procrastination, as we developed in chapter 7, strains our vocabulary of intention. We showed some of its relations to and estrangements from our thinking about action, desire, and self-knowledge.

In chapter 8 we articulated our vocabulary for assessing character—trait language—with the notion that people act intentionally, or ought to. The psychologist's notion of traits was reshaped by being placed in this new setting.

In traditional treatment anger is taken to be a drive, something distant from our intentions. In our treatment in chapter 9 following Aristotle, to be angry is to be seen, among other things, as having certain goals—something tolerably close to an intention.

In chapters 10 and 11 we dealt with the objectivity of the social world—the field of intentional actions. Much of the bad odor that notions like "intention" had during the flourishing of behaviorism, we suspect, was picked up from the obvious fact that intentions are subjective. But this subjectivity of such concepts is, we argued, no threat to their respectability so long as one keeps careful track of the *senses* in which things are subjective and the *senses* in which they are objective. In these chapters we tried to show that in the sense important to science many of the notions, including intention, which were on the behaviorist's suspect list can be rehabilitated.

So in each of these essays, one or more of the problematics of the intentional model is addressed. Although our focus is on the moral nature of social phenomena, we are also concerned with developing the conceptual scheme implied in commonsense thinking: we do at least sometimes act intentionally.

SOCIAL PSYCHOLOGY: SOME DEBTS

Although our approach differs from traditional social psychology's, it shares, and is developed from, some work in that discipline. Some studies have greatly influenced us.

If any experiment in social psychology is classic, the Asch experiment is (see ch. 3, p. 47 for a description). His experiment stimulated hundreds of research reports about the "causal factors" increasing or decreasing rates of conformity. This was, in our view, largely unrewarding although Asch's own variations were illuminating (1956). What seems to have been lost in this causal search was an important point of the demonstration, that it is very upsetting to find others unaccountably in disagreement about an objective matter, one that ought to be patent and beyond dispute. Similarly, the classic Latanè and Darley experiments started the literature on the causes of "helping," but "helping" appears to have numerous causes (see ch. 3). Our interest in these experiments is different. We are not concerned with stimulating (or even suppressing) helpfulness, but with the fact that in these experiments subjects are, as in the Asch experiments, profoundly influenced by what they take other people's perceptions of the nature of the situation to be; people are inhibited when they are unsure that their view of the objective nature of the situation is correct. In our view, these experiments have fundamentally to do with the taken-for-granted assumption that we live in a shared, objective world and with the fragility that results from this assumption.

In chapters 3 and 4 on moral reproach and the Holocaust, we showed some extension of this assumption into the moral domain. In chapters 10 and 11 we showed how moral matters are objective, although not objective in the way the hardness of a rock is, and how this objectivity figures into our moral reasoning. Milgram's (1974) experiments on obedience to authority (see ch. 4 for a description) are the most dramatic, perhaps the most controversial, and in our view, the most brilliant in the history of social psychology. In these chapters we attempted to develop the insights from his experiments in an analysis of "the evil good people do" and in particular how the bureaucratic organization of evil distorts our everyday moral thinking—sometimes making drudges into monsters.

Schachter and Singer (1962) introduced to social psychology the notion that emotions are not, or are not simply, internal happenings, but are intrinsically involved with the external, public world. In this way the social, moral order is more than just a trigger for emotion. In chapters 2 on envy and 9 on anger we took this point of view to find the external, public aspects of envy and anger. In our urge to rescue emotion and personality from their deep pocket of privacy, we are close to the traditional intent (if not practice) of behaviorists (closer still to Ryle, 1949, than Hull, 1943, to be sure).

We have talked about our differences with the field in general, and our debts in particular. Perhaps it will pay to look at some differences more closely, differences between our work and some of the most active areas of social psychology: attribution theory, Kohlberg's moral theory, and nonverbal communication.

ATTRIBUTION THEORY: SOME DIFFERENCES

Heider (1958) was one of the first contemporary social psychologists to take the understanding of the commonsense actor as the starting point of analysis, an intent we obviously share. Unfortunately, attribution theory, a development of his position, has become alienated from common sense. Because we share attribution theory's concern with commonsense thought, but do not use its findings, we shall develop some of our differences with its assumptions.

Attribution theory arose, in part, in reaction to the stimulus-response (S-R) position, which claims that human behavior is to be understood as a function of immediate stimuli. This sort of theory, for good and bad reasons, bothers people. And it makes them want to say: people don't blindly, passively respond to the stimulus; they respond to its *meaning*.

But this reaction has its own troubles—circularity. Unless we can tell what a meaning is, how can we tell if behavior represents it? So Heider suggested that what we *sometimes* do to "interpret" a stimulus is discover its cause. We are, for example, likely to react to a brick on our desk which we think got there because the wall is collapsing in one way; but we will, presumably, react in a different way to the same brick if we think it was thrown through our window by an irate critic. Kelley (1967) formalized this insight by further explaining causal analysis. He claimed we all do intuitively what John Stuart Mill said we ought to do explicitly when trying to figure out what causes what. Thus, Mill's canons of scientific method became in Kelley's hands a description of intuitive causal analysis and ipso facto an explanation of how people interpret stimuli. Meaning is saved from circularity. Besides, since social psychologists and other scientists understand things by finding their causes, why shouldn't commonsense actors? (See Kelly, 1955, for a model of man the scientist.)

An enormous amount of social psychological research has been encouraged by this theory. And therefore the details have changed (see Kelley & Michela, 1980, for a recent review). Through the thick of it, Kelley has stayed loyal to the view that interpretations *can only be* causal analyses (see Weary & Harvey, 1981; and Sabini & Silver, 1981c, for arguments about this). Indeed, the notion of an "attribution," originally an ordinary English term, has become a term of art bent to the needs of this theory. But since "attribution" remains an English term, as well as a technical one, it is easy to confuse the senses. This makes it easy to slide between one position—that people act in accord with their attributions (beliefs)—a truism, and another position—that people act in accord with their attributions (causal analyses)—an unsupported claim.

Our view, in contrast, claims that people make different sorts of attributions—interpretations—some to causes, some of aesthetic worth, some of moral value, some of pragmatic usefulness, and so on. Unfortunately we, unlike Kelley, don't have a general theory of interpretation, of human thinking (supported or smuggled) but then, we don't have high hopes for such work. But lacking a theory, how can we deal with the problem of circularity?

The notion that people respond to the meaning of something is only troubled by circularity if it is offered as a general principle; in any specific case the circle is broken so long as the objective but particular meaning is supplied from the details of the situation. Our approach relies on the shared assumptions of commonsense actors in particular situations instead of Kelley's, or any, general theory. Of course, we don't account for these particular assumptions—because we can't. In chapter 11, in particular, we argue against attribution theory's confusion of evaluating with locating causes.

Jones and Davis (1965), in their version of attribution theory, also take people's thinking to be coextensive with causal analysis, albeit sans J. S. Mill. In their view, although people interpret behavior by finding its causes, they don't use Mill's canons. Rather, they try to trace acts back to stable dispositions of the actor. In Epstein's (1977) argument these stable dispositions are what our ordinary trait words refer to. And, Epstein suggests, these trait terms are used to predict behavior. In chapter 8 we give this claim an airing; we try to show that prediction is *one* use people might make of trait language, but that there are other important uses. If our talking about people in terms of traits is this complex, so too might be our thinking about people using these concepts. And if our thinking with these terms is complex, so are these concepts. In the same chapter, we make some distinctions among kinds of trait terms, such as, capacities, motives, styles, and defects of character. Like Hamilton (1980) we see thinking about character as not just causal analysis. But, then, we would—we don't think causal questions come first.

KOHLBERG'S MORAL THEORY: SOME DIFFERENCES

Kohlberg (1963) is psychology's most influential contemporary moral theorist. His perspective is antithetical to ours, so it may be useful to mention our differences. Kohlberg asks people to resolve stories involving moral conflicts; he attempts to capture the "moral sophistication" (i.e., "stage of moral development") of his subjects by categorizing the reasons they give in defense of their solutions. He is interested in moral understanding, and so are we. How do we differ?—aside from our lack of focus on development and Kohlberg's lack of interest in the concrete. His method taps people's *reasoning about their moral reasoning*, not their moral reasoning. An analogy will help clarify the difference. The goal of a linguist is to provide a set of rules that describes the grammar of the language people speak. There are at least three ways to go about this. First, a linguist might simply observe how people naturally talk and attempt to construct a set of rules from this.

The problem with this approach is that people often talk in ways *they themselves know* to be ungrammatical. It is chastening to hear a tape recording of an actual conversation one has had. As Chomsky (1957) would put it, these data are relevant to a performance theory of how people actually *talk*, but they do not provide the grammatical rules people *have*. Neither we nor Kohlberg are interested in this sort of theory.

A linguist might ask people directly for the grammatical rules of their language. Unfortunately, people follow rules they do not know explicitly; they know their grammar implicitly.

Perhaps the linguist might present people with instances of grammatical sentences and ungrammatical strings, and ask them whether and *why* they are grammatical or ungrammatical. Then the linguist could throw out people's intuitions about whether the strings or sentences are grammatical and construct the grammar from the reasons people offer. This would be akin to Kohlberg's method. Unfortunately, we have no reason to believe that people know *why* sentences are grammatical or strings are ungrammatical. Their own intuitions about whether a set of linguistic objects conforms to the grammar of their language may not conform to their explicit theories; their implicit theories may not correspond to their explicit theories. People learn the implicit rules that shape their grammatical intuitions in an unconscious, implicit, pretheoretical way; they learn the "rules of grammar" much later, in school, as an addition to what they already know. This is why the linguist does not use this technique—it provides subjects' *theories* of their own grammar, not their grammar or even the data on which linguistic theory is based. Analogously, we believe that Kohlberg's method provides us with commonsense actors' *theories* about their moral reasoning; it does not provide us with the implicit rules that constitute that moral reasoning. Kohlberg's method provides a lay version of philosophical reasoning, not the data that theories of moral reasoning must explain.

To take a specific example, in our essay on envy, we attempt to articulate the rules that are implicit in people's judgment that a person is envious. But we know that if we were to ask people to define envy, they would not produce in detail that theory. That's why we did it. There is no reason why people's implicit judgments that a person is envious should correspond to the *definition* of envy that they offer. We are interested in something closer to the way Meno knows the Pythagorean theorem than the way Socrates does.

SEX, ATTRACTION, FLIRTATION, AND NONVERBAL BEHAVIOR: SOME DIFFERENCES

Among the ways we are social is our propensity to reproduce sexually. Social psychology should, presumably, have something to say about what leads up to this. And it has. After considerable research efforts into the causes of attraction it seems clear that for the most part people are attracted to attractive others. We pass over this discovery in our chapter on flirtation to consider one way sexual relationships develop. Perhaps some of the story of human sexual relationships can be told by ethologists (see Wilson, 1975, and Daly & Wilson, 1978), but unlike the stickleback fish, we lack sufficient genetic preprogramming for our mating dance—presumably there is no specific DNA code for singles bars (pace Fodor). There was another reason for our chapter on flirtation.

The study of nonverbal behavior has become an industry in social psychology (see Weitz, 1979, for a review). But it strikes us that much of this literature fails to grasp the peculiar role that nonverbal behavior plays in human social life. Much of this literature concerns itself with what specific nonverbal signs mean without grasping the senses in which nonverbal behaviors "mean." In this chapter, among other things, we try to place nonverbal behavior among the other techniques we have for expressing ourselves.

A LAPSE

The concept this book misses more than any other is embarrassment. Goffman (1959), Modigliani (1968), Gross and Stone (1964) among others have written on it, generally in an illuminating way. But they haven't as yet convinced us we understand why at a formal banquet a person might sensibly be embarrassed to find that, through no fault of his own, a waiter has spilled vichyssoise on his tuxedo.

Bibliography

Adorno, T., Frenkel-Brunswik, E., Levinson, D., & Sanford, N. *The Authoritarian Personality*. New York: Harper, 1950.

Alexander, C. N., Jr., Zucker, L. G., & Brody, C. L. Experimental expectations and autokinetic experiences: Consistency theories and judgmental convergence. *Sociometry*, 1970, 33, 108–22.

Alexander, L. The molding of personality under dictatorship. *Journal of Criminal Law and Criminology of Northwestern University*, May–June 1949, *40*.

Alston, W. P. Wants, actions, and causal explanation. In H. N. Castaneda (ed.), *Intentionality, Minds, and Perception*. Detroit: Wayne State University Press, 1967.

Alston, W. P. Traits, consistency, and conceptual alternatives for personality theory. In R. Harré (ed.), *Personality*. Totowa, N.J.: Rowman & Littlefield, 1976.

Alston, W. P. Self-intervention and the structure of motivation. In T. Mischel (ed.), *The Self*. Totowa, N.J.: Rowman & Littlefield, 1977.

Arendt, H. *The Human Condition*. University of Chicago Press, 1958.

Arendt, H. *Eichmann in Jerusalem*, 2nd ed. New York: Viking Press, 1965.

Aristotle. *The Basic Works of Aristotle*, ed. R. McKeon. New York: Random House, 1941.

Asch, S. E. *Social Psychology*. Englewood Cliffs, N.J.: Prentice-Hall, 1952, ch. 16.

Asch, S. E. Studies of independence and conformity: A minority of one against a unanimous majority. *Psychological Monographs*, 1956, 70(9), 177–90.

Austin, J. *The Province of Jurisprudence Determined*. London: Oxford University Press, 1954. (First published 1832.)

Austin, J. L. A plea for excuses. In *Philosophical Papers*, 2nd ed. London: Oxford University Press, 1970a.

Austin, J. L. *Philosophical Papers*. Oxford: Oxford University Press, 1970b.

Averill, J. R. Anger. *Nebraska Symposium on Motivation*. Lincoln: University of Nebraska Press, 1978.

Becker, H. *Outsiders: Studies in Deviance*. New York: Free Press, 1963.

Bedford, E. The emotions. In D. Gustafson (ed.), *Essays in Philosophical Psychology*. Garden City, N.Y.: Doubleday-Anchor Books, 1964, pp. 77–79.

Bem, D. J. Self-perception: An alternative interpretation of cognitive dissonance phenomena. *Psychological Review*, 1967, 74, 183–200.

Bem, D. J. & Funder, D. C. Predicting more of the people more of the time: Assessing the personality of situations. *Psychological Review*, 1978, 85, 485–501.

Bennett, J. *Rationality*. London: Routledge & Kegan Paul, 1964.

Berger, P. *An Invitation to Sociology*. New York: Anchor Books, 1963.

Berger, P. & Luckmann, T. *The Social Construction of Reality*. New York: Doubleday, 1966.

Berkowitz, L. *Aggression: A Social Psychological Analysis*. New York: McGraw-Hill, 1962.

Blau, P. *Exchange and Power in Social Life*. New York: Wiley, 1964.

Block, J. Advancing the psychology of personality: Paradigmatic shift or improving the quality of research? In D. Magnusson & N. Endler (eds.), *Personality at the Crossroads*. Hillsdale, N.J.: Lawrence Erlbaum Associates, 1977.

Blumer, H. *Symbolic Interactionism: Perspective and Method*. Englewood Cliffs, N.J.: Prentice-Hall, 1964.

Brown, R. *Social Psychology*. New York: Free Press, 1965.

Buss, A. On the relationship between causes and reasons. *Journal of Personality and Social Psychology*, 1979, 37(9), 1458–61.

Chomsky, N. *Syntactic Structures*. The Hague: Mouton, 1957.

Circourel, A. V. Basic and normative rules in the negotiation of status and role. In H. P. Dreitzel (ed.), *Recent Sociology*, No. 2. New York: Macmillan, 1970.

Cohen, E. *Human Behavior in the Concentration Camp*. New York: Grosset & Dunlap, 1953.

Daly, M. & Wilson, M. *Sex, Evolution, and Behavior*. North Scituate, Mass.: Duxbury Press, 1978.

Daniels, M. The dynamics of morbid envy. *Psychoanalytic Review*, 1964, 51(4), 45–57.

Davis, K. Jealousy and sexual property. *Social Forces*, 1936, 14, 395–405.

Dawidowicz, L. *The War Against the Jews.* New York: Bantam, 1975.

Dennett, D. C. Why you can't make a computer that feels pain. In *Brainstorms.* Montgomery, Vt.: Bradford Books, 1978.

Dentler, R. & Erikson, K. The function of deviance in social groups. *Social Problems,* 1959, 71, 98–107.

Des Pres, T. *The Survivors: An Anatomy of the Death Camps.* New York: Oxford University Press, 1976.

Dollard, J., Doob, L. W., Miller, N. G., Mowrer, O. H., & Sears, R. R. *Frustration and Aggression.* New Haven: Yale University Press, 1939.

Durkheim, E. *The Division of Labor.* New York: Macmillan, 1933. (First published 1893.)

Edwards, T. (ed.). *The New Dictionary of Thoughts,* 1936. New York: Standard Book Co.

Emerson, J. P. Behavior in private places: Sustaining definitions of reality in gynecological examinations. In H. P. Dreitzel (ed.), *Recent Sociology,* No. 2. New York: Macmillan, 1970.

Epstein, S. Traits are alive and well. In D. Magnusson & N. Endler (eds.), *Personality at the Crossroads.* Hillsdale, N.J.: Lawrence Erlbaum Associates, 1977.

Erikson, K. Notes on the sociology of deviance. In H. Becker (ed.), *The Other Side.* New York: Free Press, 1964.

Farber, L. The faces of envy. *Review of Existential Psychology and Psychiatry,* 1961, 6(2), 131–40.

Festinger, L. A theory of social comparison processes. *Human Relations,* 1954, 7, 114–40.

Festinger, L. *A Theory of Cognitive Dissonance.* Stanford: Stanford University Press, 1957.

Freud, S. *A General Introduction to Psychoanalysis.* New York: Washington Square Press, 1935.

Garfinkel, H. Conditions of successful degradation ceremonies. *American Journal of Sociology,* 1956, 61.

Garfinkel, H. Studies of the routine grounds of everyday activity. *Social Problems,* winter 1964, 11(3), 225–50.

Garfinkel, H. *Studies in Ethnomethodology.* Englewood Cliffs, N.J.: Prentice-Hall, 1967.

Gelfand, D., Hartman, D., Walde, P., & Page, B. Who reports shoplifters? A field experimental study. *Journal of Personality and Social Psychology,* 1973, 25(2), 276–85.

Geller, D., Goodstein, L., Silver, M., & Sternberg, W. On being ignored: The effects of the violation of implicit rules of social interaction. *Sociometry,* 1974, 37(4), 541–56.

Gergen, K. J. Social psychology as history. *Journal of Personality and Social Psychology,* 1973, 26, 309–20.

Gerth, G. & Mills, C. W. *From Max Weber: Essays in Sociology*. New York: Oxford University Press, 1958.

Ginsburg, G. P. *Emerging Strategies in Social Psychological Research*. Chichester: Wiley, 1979.

Gluckman, M. Gossip and scandal. *Current Anthropology*, 1963, 4, 307–16.

Goffman, E. *The Presentation of Self in Everyday Life*. New York: Doubleday-Anchor Books, 1959.

Goffman, E. *Asylums*. Garden City, N.Y.: Anchor, 1961.

Goffman, E. *Stigma*. Englewood Cliffs, N.J.: Prentice-Hall, 1963a.

Goffman, E. *Behavior in Public Places*. New York: Free Press, 1963b.

Goffman, E. *Interaction Ritual*. New York: Anchor Books, 1967.

Goffman, E. *Relations in Public*. New York: Harper & Row, 1971.

Gordon, R. Emotion labelling and cognition. *Journal for the Theory of Social Behaviour*, 1978, 2, 125–37.

Grice, H. P. Utterers' meaning and intention. *Philosophical Review*, 1969, 78, 144–77.

Gross, G. & Stone, G. Embarrassment and the analysis of role requirements. *American Journal of Sociology*, 1964, 60, 1–15.

Hamilton, V. L. Intuitive psychologist or intuitive lawyer? Alternative models of the attribution process. *Journal of Personality and Social Psychology*, 1980, 39(5), 767–72.

Harré, R. *Social Being*. Totowa, N.J.: Littlefield, Adams, 1980.

Harré, R. & Secord, P. *The Explanation of Social Behavior*. Oxford: Basil & Blackwell, 1972.

Hart, H. A. L. *The Concept of Law*. Oxford: Oxford University Press, 1961.

Heider, F. *The Psychology of Interpersonal Relations*. New York: Wiley, 1958.

Hilberg, R. *The Destruction of the European Jews*. Chicago: Quadrangle Books, 1961.

Hull, C. L. *Principles of Behavior*. New York: Appleton-Century-Crofts, 1943.

Irwin, F. W. *Intentional Behavior and Motivation*. Philadelphia: Lippincott, 1971.

Jacobs, R. & Campbell, D. The perpetuation of an arbitrary tradition through several generations of a laboratory micro-culture. *Journal of Abnormal and Social Psychology*, 1961, 62, 649–58.

Jones, E. E. & Davis, K. E. From acts to dispositions: The attribution process in person perception. In L. Berkowitz (ed.), *Advances in Experimental Social Psychology*, Vol. 2. New York: Academic Press, 1965, pp. 219–66.

Jones, E. & Nisbett, R. *The Actor and Observer: Divergent Perceptions of the Causes of Behavior*. New York: General Learning Press, 1972.

Karst, G. *The Beasts of the Earth.* New York: Unger, 1942.

Kelley, H. Attribution theory in social psychology. In D. Levine (ed.), *The Nebraska Symposium on Motivation.* Lincoln: University of Nebraska Press, 1967.

Kelley, H. & Michela, J. L. *Attribution Theory and Research.* In M. Rosensweig & L. Porter (eds.), *Annual Review of Psychology,* Vol. 31. Palo Alto, Calif.: Annual Reviews Inc., 1980.

Kelly, G. A. *A Theory of Personality: The Psychology of Personal Constructs.* New York: Norton, 1955.

Kenny, A. *Action, Emotion and Will.* New York: Humanities Press, 1963.

Kinkade, K. *Twin Oaks.* New York: William Morrow, 1973.

Kline, M. *Mathematics: The Loss of Certainty.* New York: Oxford University Press, 1980.

Kogon, E. *The Theory and Practice of Hell: The Concentration Camps and the System Behind Them.* London: Secker & Warburg, 1950.

Kohlberg, L. Moral development and identification. In H. Stevenson (ed.), *Child Psychology* (62nd Yearbook of the National Society for the Study of Education). University of Chicago Press, 1963.

Kovesi, J. *Moral Notions.* London: Routledge, Kegan, Paul, 1967.

Latanè, B. & Darley, J. Determinants of bystander intervention. In E. Macauley & L. Berkowitz (eds.), *Altruism and Helping Behavior.* New York: Academic Press, 1970.

McGuire, W. J. The nature of attitudes and attitude change. In G. Lindzey (ed.), *Handbook of Social Psychology,* 2nd ed., vol. 3. Reading, Mass.: Addison-Wesley, 1969, pp. 136–314.

MacNeil, M. K. & Sherif, M. Norm change over subject generations as a function of arbitrariness of prescribed norms. *Journal of Personality and Social Psychology,* 1976, 34(5), 762–73.

Magnusson, D. & Endler, N. Interactional psychology: Present status and future prospects. In D. Magnusson & N. Endler (eds.), *Personality at the Crossroads.* Hillsdale, N.J.: Lawrence Erlbaum Associates, 1977.

Mann, L. Queue culture: The waiting line as a social system. *American Journal of Sociology,* 1969, 75(3), 340–54.

Matza, D. The nature of delinquent commitment. In E. Rubington & M. Weinberg (eds.), *Deviance: The Interactionist Perspective.* London: Macmillan, 1968.

Melden, A. I. *Free Action.* London: Routledge & Kegan Paul, 1961.

Merton, R. *Social Theory and Social Structure.* New York: Free Press, 1949.

Middlebrook, P. N. *Social Psychology and Modern Life,* 2nd ed. New York: Knopf, 1980.

Milgram, S. Behavioral study of obedience. *Journal of Abnormal and Social Psychology,* 1963, 67, 371–78.

Milgram, S. Group pressure and action against a person. *Journal of Abnormal and Social Psychology*, 1964, 69, 137–43.

Milgram, S. Obedience. (A filmed report). New York: New York University Film Library, 1965a.

Milgram, S. Some conditions of obedience and disobedience to authority. *Human Relations*, 1965b, 18, 57–76.

Milgram, S. *Obedience to Authority*. New York: Harper & Row, 1974.

Milgram, S. & Toch, H. Collective behavior: Crowds and social movements. In G. Lindzey & E. Aronson (eds.), *Handbook of Social Psychology*, 2nd ed., Vol. 4. Reading, Mass.: Addison-Wesley, 1969, pp. 507–610.

Miller, G. A., Falanter, E., & Pribram, K. H. *Plans and the Structure of Behavior*. New York: Holt, Rinehart & Winston, 1960.

Mischel, W. *Personality and Assessment*. New York: Wiley, 1968.

Modigliani, A. Embarrassment and embarrassability. *Sociometry*, 1968, 31(3), 313–26.

Moriarty, T. Crime, commitment and the responsive bystander: Two field experiments. *Journal of Personality and Social Psychology*, 1975, 31(2), 370–76.

Musmanno, M. *The Eichmann Kommandos*. Philadelphia: Macrae Smith, 1961.

Nagel, T. *Moral Questions*. New York: Cambridge University Press, 1979.

Paine, R. What is gossip about? An alternative hypothesis. *Man* (N.S.), 1967, 2, 278–85.

Pastore, N. The role of arbitrariness in the frustration-aggression hypothesis. *Journal of Abnormal and Social Psychology*, 1952, 47, 728–31.

Pepitone, A. Toward a normative and comparative biocultural social psychology. *Journal of Personality and Social Psychology*, 1976, 34, 641–53.

Peters, R. S. *The Concept of Motivation*. Oxford: Routledge & Kegan Paul, 1958.

Peters, R. S. Emotions, passivity and the place of Freud's theory in psychology. In B. Wolman & E. Wagel (eds.), *Scientific Psychology*. New York: Basic Books, 1965.

Peters, R. S. The education of the emotions. In R. F. Dearden, P. H. Hirst, & R. S. Peters (eds.), *Education and the Development of Reason*. London: Routledge & Kegan Paul, 1972, pp. 466–83.

Powers, J. *Do Black Patent Leather Shoes Reflect Up?* New York: Popular Library, 1975, p. 95.

Ranulf, R. *The Jealousy of the Gods and Criminal Law at Athens*. New York: Arno Press, 1974.

Rosnow, R. & Fine, G. *Rumor and Gossip*. New York: Elsevier, 1976.

Ryle, G. *The Concept of Mind*. London: Hutchinson, 1949.

Sabini, J. *Moral Reproach: A Conceptual and Experimental Analysis.* Unpublished Ph.D. dissertation, 1976. City University of New York.

Sabini, J. & Silver, M. Objectifiability and calling rights into play. *Human Relations,* 1978, 31(9), 791–807.

Sabini, J. & Silver, M. Baseball and hot sauce: A critique of some attributional treatments of evaluation. *Journal for the Theory of Social Behaviour,* 1980, 10(2), 83–95.

Sabini, J. & Silver, M. Internal-external: Dimension or congeries? Unpublished manuscript, 1981a. University of Pennsylvania.

Sabini, J. & Silver, M. Introspection and causal accounts. *Journal of Personality and Social Psychology,* 1981b, 40(1) 171–79.

Sabini, J. & Silver, M. Evaluations in commonsense thought: A reply to Weary and Harvey. *Journal for the Theory of Social Behaviour,* 1981c, 11, 1.

Sartre, J.-P. *Existentialism and Humanism.* London, 1948.

Schachter, S. & Burdick, H. A field experiment on rumor transmission and distortion. *Journal of Abnormal and Social Psychology,* 1955, 50, 363–71.

Schachter, S. & Singer, J. Cognitive, social, and physiological determinants of emotional state. *Psychological Review,* 1962, 69, 379–99.

Scheler, M. *Ressentiment* (trans. W. Holdheim). New York: Free Press, 1961. (Originally published 1910.)

Schoeck, H. *Envy: A Theory of Social Behavior.* New York: Harcourt, Brace & World, 1969.

Schur, E. *Labeling Deviant Behavior.* New York: Harper & Row, 1971.

Schutz, A. *Collected Papers,* vols. 1 & 2. The Hague: Martinus Nijhoff, 1973.

Searle, J. How to derive "ought" from "is." *The Philosophical Review,* 1964, 73.

Searle, J. *Speech Acts.* Cambridge University Press, 1969.

Searle, J. *Expression and Meaning.* Cambridge University Press, 1979.

Secord, P. Making oneself behave. In T. Mischel (ed.), *The Self.* Totowa, N.J.: Rowman & Littlefield, 1977.

Sherif, M. A study of some social factors in perception. *Archives of Psychology,* 1935, 27, 1–60.

Sherif, M. Group influences upon the formation of norms and attitudes. In Newcomb et al. (eds.), *Readings in Social Psychology.* New York: Holt, Rinehart & Winston, 1958.

Silver, M. Procrastination and stress. *Centerpoint,* 1974, 1, 49–55.

Simmel, G. *The Sociology of Georg Simmel* (ed. K. H. Wolff). Glencoe, Ill.: Free Press, 1950.

Simmel, G. *Conflict and the Web of Group Affiliations.* New York: Free Press, 1955/original 1899.

Skinner, B. F. *The Behavior of Organisms.* New York: Appleton-Century-Crofts, 1938.

Solzhenitsyn, A. *One Day in the Life of Ivan Denisovitch.* New York: Dutton, 1963.

Solzhenitsyn, A. *The First Circle.* New York: Harper & Row, 1968.

Solzhenitsyn, A. *The Gulag Archipelago.* New York: Harper & Row, 1973.

Sondheim, S. Officer Krupke. In S. Sondheim (ed.), *West Side Story,* 1957.

Speer, A. *Inside the Third Reich.* New York: Macmillan, 1970.

Steiner, J. *Treblinka.* New York: Simon & Schuster, 1967.

Sutcliffe, J. & Hoberman, M. Factors affecting choice in role conflict situations. *American Sociological Review,* 1956, 21, 695–703.

Tedeschi, J. T. (ed.). *Social Influence Processes.* Chicago: Aldine Press, 1972.

Tillion, G. *Ravensbruck.* Garden City: Anchor Books, 1975.

Tolman, E. C. *Purposive Behavior in Animals and Men.* New York: Century, 1932.

Tuddenham, R. & Mac Bride, P. The yielding experiment from the point of view of the subject. *Journal of Personality,* 1959, 27, 258–71.

Weary, G. & Harvey, J. Evaluation in attribution processes. *Journal for the Theory of Social Behaviour,* 1981, 11, 1.

Weitz, S. *Nonverbal Communication.* New York: Oxford University Press, 1979.

Wells, L. *The Death Brigade.* New York: Holocaust Library, 1978.

White, A. R. (ed.). *The Philosophy of Action.* Oxford: Oxford University Press, 1968.

Whyte, W. F. A slum sex code. *American Journal of Sociology,* 1943, 49, 24–31.

Wilson, E. Edmund Wilson's letters: To and about F. Scott Fitzgerald. Reprinted in *The New York Review of Books,* February 17, 1977.

Wilson, E. O. *Sociobiology.* Cambridge, Mass.: Harvard University Press, 1975.

Wittgenstein, L. *Philosophical Investigations.* Oxford: Oxford University Press, 1953.

Wittgenstein, L. *The Blue and Brown Books.* Oxford: Oxford University Press, 1958.

Zimbardo, P. The Stanford prison experiment: A simulation study of the psychology of imprisonment. Script of slideshow, 1971.

Zimbardo, P. The mind is a formidable jailer: A pirandellian prisoner. *The New York Times Magazine,* April 8, 1973.